Mobilities and Complexities

The new 'mobilities turn' has become a powerful perspective in social theory. John Urry's oeuvre has been very influential in the emergence of this new field and has had lasting impacts on many scholars. This collection presents originally commissioned essays from leading scholars in the field who reflect on how Urry's writing influenced the course of their research and theorizing.

The volume gathers contributions in relation to John Urry's path-breaking work. The new 'mobilities turn' made a strong imprint in European social theory and is beginning to make an impact in the Americas and Asia as well. It challenges mainstream theoretical and empirical approaches that were grounded in a sedentary and bounded view of states. It propels innovative thinking about social and media ecologies, complex systems and social change. It bridges many disciplines and methodologies, leading to new approaches to existing problems while also resonating with questions about both history and the future. Mobilities research marks the rise of academic and intellectual cooperation and collaboration 'beyond societies', as nations around the world face the ecological limits of contemporary mobility and energy systems.

The contributors represent several national contexts, including England, Germany, Denmark, Finland, Taiwan, Brazil, Canada, Australia and the USA. The book collects personal essays and gives insight into a vivid network of scientists who have connections of various degrees to the late John Urry as an academic figure, an author and a person.

Ole B. Jensen is Professor of Urban Theory. He has a cross-disciplinary background in political science, sociology and planning. He studies how sociality is reconfigured by complex mobilities in the designed environs and infrastructural landscapes of the contemporary city.

Sven Kesselring is a sociologist and Research Professor in Sustainable Mobilities at Nuertingen-Geislingen University, Germany. His research focuses on mobilities theory, socio-technological change and labour mobilities. His recent publications are *Exploring Networked Urban Mobilities* (2018, with Malene Freudendal-Pedersen); *New Mobilities Regimes* (2013, with Susanne Witzgall and Gerlinde Vogl); and *Aeromobilities* (2009, with John Urry and Saolo Cwerner).

Mimi Sheller is Professor of Sociology and Founding Director of the Center for Mobilities Research and Policy at Drexel University, Philadelphia. She is a founding co-editor of the journal *Mobilities* and past president of the International Association for the History of Transport, Traffic and Mobility. She is the author or co-editor of ten books, the most recent being *Mobility Justice: The Politics of Movement in an Age of Extremes* (2018).

Mobilities and Complexities

Edited by
Ole B. Jensen, Sven Kesselring and
Mimi Sheller

Routledge
Taylor & Francis Group

LONDON AND NEW YORK

First published 2019
by Routledge
2 Park Square, Milton Park, Abingdon, Oxon OX14 4RN

and by Routledge
711 Third Avenue, New York, NY 10017

Routledge is an imprint of the Taylor & Francis Group, an informa business

British Library Cataloguing-in-Publication Data
A catalogue record for this book is available from the British Library

Library of Congress Cataloging-in-Publication Data
Names: Jensen, Ole B., editor. | Kesselring, Sven, 1966- editor. |
Sheller, Mimi, editor.
Title: Mobilities and complexities / edited by Ole B. Jensen, Sven Kesselring and Mimi Sheller.
Description: 1st Edition. | New York : Routledge, 2018. | Includes bibliographical references and index.
Identifiers: LCCN 2018027091| ISBN 9781138601420 (hardback) |
 ISBN 9781138601437 (pbk.) | ISBN 9780429470097 (ebook)
Subjects: LCSH: Spatial behavior. | Movement, Psychology of. |
Sociology--Philosophy. | Urry, John.
Classification: LCC BF469 .M625 2018 | DDC 301.01--dc23
LC record available at https://lccn.loc.gov/2018027091

ISBN: 978-1-138-60142-0 (hbk)
ISBN: 978-1-138-60143-7 (pbk)
ISBN: 978-0-429-47009-7 (ebk)

Typeset in Bembo
by Taylor & Francis Books

Contents

PART II
Travel, senses, natures 39

PART III
Tourism, mobilities, temporalities 87

Contributors

Peter Adey is Professor of Human Geography at Royal Holloway University of London. Peter specialises in the relationship between mobility and security, particularly at the intersections of the political and the cultural. Among other works he is author of *Mobility* (2009, Routledge, 2nd ed. 2017), *Aerial Life: Mobilities, Spaces, Affects* (2010, Wiley-Blackwell) and co-editor of *The Routledge Handbook of Mobilities* (2014) and *From Above* (2014). He is co-editor of the journal *Mobilities* and of the Berghahn book series, *Changing Mobilities*.

Jørgen Ole Bærenholdt is Professor of Human Geography, Department of People and Technology, Roskilde University, teaching in geography and in spatial designs and society programmes. He is currently doing research on tourist place design and social mobilisation for tourism in the peripheries of Denmark while also engaging in innovation projects. He has been associated with the University of Tromsø doing research in the North Atlantic region including the UNESCO MOST Circumpolar Coping Processes Project. His research interests are in tourism, cultural heritage, spatial designs, design processes, mobility, regional development and the circular economy. Books in English include *The Reflexive North* (2001, with Nils Aarsæhter), *Performing Tourist Places* (2004, with Michael Haldrup, Jonas Larsen and John Urry), *Space Odysseys* (2004, with K. Simonsen), *Coping with Distances* (2007), *Mobility and Place* (2008, with Brynhild Granås) and *Design Research* (2010, with J. Simonsen, M. Büscher and J. Scheuer 2010).

Thomas Birtchnell is Senior Lecturer in the School of Geography and Sustainable Communities at the University of Wollongong. Before this, he was a research associate at Lancaster University in a project funded by the Economic and Social Research Council (ESRC) and led by distinguished professor John Urry. The research project (ES/J007455/1) examined the past and future impacts of 3D printing on transport and society. His latest book is *A New Industrial Future? 3D Printing and the Reconfiguring of Production, Distribution, and Consumption* (2016). His research interests lie in the mobilities of people, knowledge and materials globally. His books include *Indovation:*

Innovation and a Global Knowledge Economy in India (2013) and *3D Printing for Development in the Global South: The 3D4D Challenge* (2014, co-authored with William Hoyle). His co-edited books include *Elite Mobilities* (2013, with Javier Caletrio) and *Cargomobilities: Moving Materials in a Global Age* (2015, with Satya Savitzky and John Urry).

David Bissell is Associate Professor and Australian Research Council Future Fellow in the School of Geography at the University of Melbourne. He combines qualitative research on embodied practices with social theory to explore the social, political and ethical consequences of mobile lives. His current projects are exploring the impact of commuting on cities; how mobile working practices are reshaping the home; and how new forms of on-demand digital work are transforming cities. He is author of *Transit Life: How Commuting Is Transforming Our Cities* (2018) and co-editor of *Stillness in a Mobile World* (2011) and *The Routledge Handbook of Mobilities* (2014). He sits on the editorial boards of *Mobilities, Social and Cultural Geography, Transfers: Interdisciplinary Journal of Mobility Studies* and *Australian Humanities Review*.

Monika Büscher is Professor of Sociology, Director of the Centre for Mobilities Research and Associate Director for the Institute for Social Futures at Lancaster University. She co-edits the book series *Changing Mobilities*. She currently leads research on disaster mobilities and ethical, legal and social issues of IT innovation in the EU FP7 SecInCore project. She is co-editor of *Mobile Methods* (Routledge, with John Urry and K. Witchger); of the special issue of *Mobilities* 11 (4) on *Mobility Intersections: Social Research, Social Futures* (2016, with Mimi Sheller and David Tyfield); and of the special issue on ELSI in IT Innovation for Disaster Risk Management, in the *Journal of Contingencies and Crisis Management*.

Tim Cresswell is Dean of the Faculty and Vice President for Academic Affairs at Trinity College in Hartford, Connecticut, having previously served as Associate Dean for Faculty Affairs at Northeastern University, where he was Professor of History and International Affairs. The author of 11 books, Cresswell is an internationally recognised geographer who is intrigued by issues of place and mobility. Some of his most noted books are *On the Move: Mobility in the Modern Western World* (2006), *Place: A Short Introduction* (2004), *The Tramp in America* (2001) and the co-edited volume *Geographies of Mobilities: Practices, Spaces, Subjects* (2011). His most recent work focuses on Maxwell Street Market in Chicago and on its evolution over 130 years. In addition, he is a poet who explores similar themes about space and place in his two collections: *Soil* (2013) and *Fence* (2015).

Monica Degen is Reader in Cultural Sociology at Brunel University London. Her PhD, awarded in 2001 by Lancaster University, was published with the title 'Sensing Cities: Regenerating Public Life in Barcelona and Manchester' (2008). Since then she has published on a diversity of topics such as the sociology of the senses, urban cultures and the politics of time and space, especially in relation to urban planning and architecture. She was awarded a British Academy Mid-Career Fellowship in 2017 to research 'Timescapes of Urban Change' and has worked on several ESRC and AHRC research grants, see www.sensorycities.com and www.sensorysmithfield.com. She has published widely in these areas in journals such as *Space and Culture; Environment and Planning A; International Journal of Urban and Regional Research; Environment and Planning D; Sociological Review.*

Kingsley Dennis is a sociologist, researcher and writer. He previously worked in the sociology department at Lancaster University. Kingsley is the author of numerous articles on social futures; technology and new media communications; global affairs; and popular culture. He is the author of several critically acclaimed books including *The Sacred Revival* (2017), *The Phoenix Generation* (2014); *Dawn of the Akashic Age* (2013, with Ervin Laszlo), *New Revolutions for a Small Planet* (2012) and *After the Car* (2009, with John Urry). He is the co-author of the study 'New Media for a New Future: The Emerging Digital Landscape for a Planetary Society', produced as part of the Fuji Declaration for the Goi Peace Foundation, in collaboration with the renowned global think tank *The Club of Budapest*. He currently serves as Director of Publications for the Laszlo Institute of New Paradigm Research.

Bülent Diken teaches social and cultural theory at Lancaster University, Department of Sociology, and Kadir Has University, Department of Radio-TV and Cinema. He did his PhD at Aarhus School of Architecture from 1994 to 1997. He spent the academic year of 1995–96 as a visiting PhD student at Lancaster University, Department of Sociology, where his project was supervised by John Urry. Diken's research fields are social theory, political philosophy, urbanism, cinema and terrorism. His books include *Strangers, Ambivalence and Social Theory* (1998), *The Culture of Exception* (2005, co-authored with Carsten B Laustsen), *Sociology through the Projector* (2007, co-authored with Carsten B Laustsen), *Nihilism* (2009), *Revolt, Revolution, Critique: Paradox of Society* (2012) and *God, Politics, Economy: Paradoxes of Religion* (2015).

Tim Edensor teaches cultural geography at Manchester Metropolitan University and is currently a visiting scholar at Melbourne University. He is the author of *Tourists at the Taj* (1998), *National Identity, Popular Culture and Everyday Life* (2002), *Industrial Ruins: Space, Aesthetics and Materiality* (2005) and *From Light to Dark: Daylight, Illumination and Gloom* (2017), as well as the editor of *Geographies of Rhythm* (2010) and co-editor of *From the Lighthouse: Interdisciplinary Reflections on Light* (2018). Tim has written extensively on national identity, tourism, ruins, mobilities and landscapes of illumination and darkness. He is currently working on a project about urban materiality: 'Living with Stone in Melbourne'.

Anthony Elliott is Dean of External Engagement at the University of South Australia, where he is Research Professor of Sociology and Executive Director of the Hawke EU Centre. He is also Super-Global Professor of Sociology (Visiting) at Keio University, Japan, and Fellow of the Academy of Social Sciences in Australia. He is the co-author of *Mobile Lives* (2010, with John Urry). He is the author and editor of some 40 books translated into 17 languages, including most recently *Reinvention* (2013) and *Identity Troubles* (2016). His current research addresses global digital transformations, especially artificial intelligence and robotics, and is supported by grants from the European Commission, Toyota Foundation and Australian Research Council. His forthcoming book, *The Culture of AI*, will be published by Routledge.

Bianca Freire Medeiros is Sociology Professor at the University of São Paulo and Coordinator of the UrbanData-Brazil databank. She is one of the main references for those interested in the so-called poverty-tourism field in Brazil and abroad. Her book *Touring Poverty* (2013, 2015), as well as the documentary film based on her research project, *A Place to Take Away* (2012), have been highly praised both in and outside academia. Her work has been published in several languages and she was a visiting researcher at Princeton University, El Colegio de Mexico and Lancaster University, and a Tinker Visiting Professor at the University of Texas at Austin. She has recently organised, with Julia O'Donnell, an edited book titled *Urban Latin America: Images, Words, Flows and the Built Environment* (2018).

Malene Freudendal-Pedersen is Professor in the Department of People and Technology, Roskilde University. She is the co-manager of the international Cosmobilities Network and founder and co-editor of the journal *Applied Mobilities*. Her research focuses on understanding modern everyday life and the transport and mobilities that frame and enable this life. She is the author of *Mobility in Daily Life: Between Freedom and Unfreedom* (2009) and co-editor of *Networked Urban Mobilities* (2018).

Jennie Germann Molz is a sociologist at the College of the Holy Cross in Worcester, Massachusetts where she teaches courses on social theory, travel and tourism, global citizenship and emotion. She is interested in questions of identity, belonging and ethics in the context of mobile togetherness and has conducted research on round-the-world backpackers, travel blogging, food mobilities, network hospitality and the sharing economy, family voluntourism and worldschooling. Her publications include *Travel Connections: Tourism, Technology and Togetherness in a Mobile World* (2012), *Disruptive Tourism and Its Untidy Guests: Alternative Ontologies for Future Hospitalities* (2014) and *Mobilizing Hospitality: The Ethics of Social Relations in a Mobile World* (2007). Since 2011, she has been a co-editor of the journal *Hospitality and Society*. She received her PhD in Sociology from Lancaster University, where she subsequently held an ESRC postdoctoral fellowship in the Centre for Mobilities Research.

Kevin Hannam is a founding co-editor of the journals *Mobilities* and *Applied Mobilities*, co-author of the books *Understanding Tourism* and *Tourism and India* and co-editor of *The Routledge Handbook of Mobilities Research, Moral Encounters in Tourism, Tourism and Leisure Mobilities* and *Event Mobilities*. He has a PhD in geography from the University of Portsmouth.

Juliet Jain is Senior Research Fellow at the Centre for Transport and Society, University of the West of England, Bristol. Jain is a social scientist who applies social theory and methodologies to transport and mobility-related 'problems'. The focus of her research is at the nexus of travel, technology and everyday life. Juliet has made a significant contribution to research examining 'travel time use in the information age' and the journey experience, as well as examining the impact of work-related travel on family life in the digital age.

Ole B. Jensen is Professor of Urban Theory at the Department of Architecture, Design and Media Technology, Aalborg University, Denmark. He holds a BA in political science, an MA in sociology, a PhD in planning and a Dr Techn in mobilities. He has a cross-disciplinary background in political science, sociology and planning. He studies how sociality reconfigures by complex mobilities in the designed environs and infrastructural landscapes of the contemporary city. He is deputy director, co-founder and board member at the Center for Mobilities and Urban Studies and director of the research cluster in Mobility and Tracking Technology. Jensen is a board member at the Center for Strategisk Byforskning, PhD programme coordnator at the media, architecture and design doctoral program and editorial board member of the journal *Applied Mobilities*. His main research interests are within urban mobilities, mobilities design and networked technologies. He is the co-author of *Making European Space: Mobility, Power and Territorial Identity* (2004, with Tim Richardson), and author of *Staging Mobilities* (2013) and *Designing Mobilities* (2014), the editor of the four-volume collection *Mobilities* (2015) and author of *Urban Mobilities Design: Urban Designs for Mobile Situations* (2017, with Ditte Bendix Lanng).

Vincent Kaufmann is Associate Professor of Urban Sociology and Mobility at Ecole Polytechnique Fédérale de Lausanne. Since 2011, he is also scientific director of the Mobile Lives Forum in Paris. After a master's degree in sociology (University of Geneva) he did his PhD at the École Polytechnique Fédérale de Lausanne on rationalities underlying transport modal practices. He has been invited lecturer at Lancaster University (2000–2001), Ecole des Ponts et Chaussées, Paris (2001–2002), Nimegen University (2010), Université de Toulouse Le Mirail (2011) and Université Catholique de Louvain (2004–18). His fields of research are motility, mobility and urban lifestyles, links between social and spatial mobility, public policies of land planning and transportation. He recently published *Mobilité et libre circulation en Europe* (2017, with Ander Audikana).

Sven Kesselring holds a research professorship in Automotive Management: Sustainable Mobilities at Nuertingen-Geislingen University, Germany. He has been a visiting professor at Aalborg University, Denmark since 2011. He is co-editor of Applied Mobilities (2016). He studied sociology, political science and psychology and holds a PhD in sociology from Ludwig-Maximilians-Universität, Munich and a doctoral degree (habilitation) from Technische Universität, Munich. He was a research fellow of Hans Böckler Foundation, Erich Becker Foundation, Fraport, and in 2003 he received a research grant from the German Research Association. He is Director of the International Cosmobilities Network (www.cosmobilities.net). From 1999 to 2006 he was a member of the reflexive modernisation research centre in Munich. His research focuses on mobilities theory, social change and reflexive modernisation, corporate mobilities regimes, urban sociology, auto, aero and digital mobilities and future research.

Claus Lassen is Associate Professor at the Department of Development and Planning, and Director of the Centre of Mobility and Urban Studies, Aalborg University. His research analyses changing social relations in the light of international air travel, and he has published several international articles and book chapters on business travel, aeromobilities and airports. Claus Lassen is a co-founder of the interdisciplinary Center of Mobilities and Urban Studies at Aalborg University.

Chia-Ling Lai is Associate Professor of the Graduate Institute of European Cultures and Tourism, National Taiwan Normal University, Taiwan. Since her thesis Museum in Motion from Lancaster University, she has continued to explore mobility/materiality within museum exhibitions and touring cultures. Her research projects cover global events (world expos, art biennales, museums' travelling exhibitions), mobile technologies and museums and objects in travel. Her publications include articles in *Tourism Mobilities, Journal of Historical Sociology, Route: Journal of Cultural Studies* (in Chinese), *Journalist Studies* (in Chinese), *Cultural Policy of European Union* (in Chinese) and *New Perspectives of Sociology of the Arts* (in Chinese). She currently explores gender and representation, art-engaged social research, critical creative studies and social futures.

Jonas Larsen is Professor in Mobility and Urban Studies at Roskilde University, Denmark. He has a long-standing interest in tourist photography, tourism and mobility more broadly. More recently, he has written extensively about urban cycling and is now also conducting research on running mobilities, urban marathons and sport tourism. His latest books are *Tourist Gaze 3.0* (2011, with John Urry) and *Digital Snaps: The New Face of Snapshot Photography* (2014, with Mette Sandbye).

Phil Macnaghten has worked in the science and society field since the mid-1990s on a series of science and technology controversies, notably GM foods and crops, transgenic animals, nanotechnologies, synthetic biology, geoengineering and fracking. He has developed in-depth qualitative methodologies for researching controversial technologies which, in turn, have informed policy approaches to dialogue and public engagement. More recently, this approach has contributed to the development of the Responsible Innovation framework which is being adopted by UK research councils and implemented across the portfolio of EPSRC-funded research. Currently working at Wageningen University in the Knowledge, Technology and Innovation Group as Personal Professor, he was previously an honorary professor at the University of Campinas, Brazil (2012–15) and Professor of Geography at Durham University (2006–15). His most recent book is *Governing Agricultural Biotechnology: Global Lessons from GM Crops* (2016, co-edited with Susana Carro-Ripaldo). In an earlier life he co-wrote *Contested Natures* (1998, with John Urry).

Peter Merriman is Professor of Human Geography at Aberystwyth University, Wales. His primary research interest is in the geographies and histories of mobility, with a particular focus on the spaces and practices of driving. He also undertakes research on theories of space and spatiality, geographies of affect and theories of nationalism and national identity. He is the author of two books, *Driving Spaces* (2007) and *Mobility, Space and Culture* (2012), and co-editor of a further five volumes, including *Empire and Mobility* (2019), *Mobility and the Humanities* (2018), *The Routledge Handbook of Mobilities* (2014) and *Geographies of Mobilities* (2011).

Lynne Pearce is Professor of Literary and Cultural Theory in the Department of English Literature and Creative Writing at Lancaster University where she has worked since 1990. Her mobilities-related publications date back to a book chapter, 'Driving North/Driving South' (2000) and she has since published widely on the cognitive and affective dimensions of driving, including the book *Drivetime: Literary Excursions in Automotive Consciousness* (2016). She has been delighted to serve as CeMoRe's Director for the Humanities since 2015 and, with Peter Merriman, recently edited a special issue of *Mobilities* on 'Mobility and the Humanities'. With Marian Aguiar and Charlotte Mathieson, she is co-editor of the Palgrave Macmillan (US) book series *Studies in Mobilities, Literature and Culture*, and is currently working on a new book entitled *Mobility, Memory and the Lifecourse* for this series.

Andrew Sayer is Professor of Social Theory and Political Economy at Lancaster University. He has worked on critical realism and the philosophy of social science (*Method in Social Science*, 1992 and *Realism and Social Science*, 2000), political economy (e.g. *Radical Political Economy*, 1985) and on inequality and ethics in everyday life and moral economy, throughout interrelating social scientific and philosophical thought on these topics. His recent books are *The Moral Significance of Class* (2005), *Why Things Matter to People: Social Science, Values and Ethical Life* (2011) and most recently *Why We Can't Afford the Rich* (2014). He is now also working on a different theme: bio-psycho-social relations and their implications for social science.

Mimi Sheller is Professor of Sociology and Founding Director of the Center for Mobilities Research and Policy at Drexel University, Philadelphia. She is founding co-editor of the journal *Mobilities* and past president of the International Association for the History of Transport, Traffic and Mobility. She is author or co-editor of ten books, including most recently *Island Futures: Caribbean Survival in the Anthropocene* (forthcoming), *Mobility Justice: The Politics of Movement in an Age of Extremes* (2018) and *Aluminum Dreams: The Making of Light Modernity* (2014). As co-editor with John Urry of *Tourism Mobilities* (2004) and *Mobile Technologies of the City* (2006), and author of numerous highly cited articles, she helped established the new interdisciplinary field of mobilities research. She was awarded the Doctor Honoris Causa from Roskilde University, Denmark (2015) and in Fall 2016 was Distinguished Visiting Scholar in Global Communication at the Annenberg School of Communication, University of Pennsylvania.

Elisabeth Shove is Professor of Sociology at Lancaster University and was PI of the DEMAND (Dynamics of Energy, Mobility and Demand) research centre from 2013 to 2018 (www.demand.ac.uk). In this role, and before, she has been busy trying to introduce social scientific concepts into other disciplines and debates. She is also known for her work on social theories of practice, especially *The Dynamics of Social Practice* (2012, with Mika Pantzar and Matt Watson) and more recently *The Nexus of Practices* (2017, edited with Allison Hui and Theodore Schatzki). She has previously written about materiality, infrastructures, consumption and everyday life. New projects and interests include concepts of 'flexibility' and the temporal aspects of infrastructures and practices; the history and future of ordinary office technologies and extending theories and concepts of practice in new directions, and into other fields, including the health sector.

Bronislaw Szerszynski is Reader in Sociology at Lancaster University. His research crosses the social and natural sciences, arts and humanities in order to situate the changing relationship between humans, the environment and technology in the longer perspective of human and planetary history. Recent work has focused on the Anthropocene, geoengineering, mobility and planetary evolution. He is author of *Nature, Technology and the Sacred* (2005) and co-editor of *Risk, Environment and Modernity* (1996), *Re-Ordering Nature: Theology, Society and the New Genetics* (2003), *Nature Performed: Environment, Culture and Performance* (2003), *Technofutures: Transdisciplinary*

Perspectives on Nature and the Sacred (2015) and of special double issues of *Ecotheology* on 'Ecotheology and Postmodernity' (2004) and *Theory Culture and Society* on 'Changing Climates' (2010, with John Urry). He was also co-organiser of the public art and science events *Between Nature: Explorations in Ecology and Performance* (Lancaster, 2000), *Experimentality* (Lancaster/ Manchester/London, 2009–10) and *Anthropocene Monument* (Toulouse, 2014–15).

Phillip Vannini is Professor in the School of Communication and Culture at Royal Roads University in Victoria, Canada, as well as Canada Research Chair in Public Ethnography. He is the author/editor of 15 books, including recent texts such as *Doing Public Ethnography* (2018) and *Non-Representational Methodologies* (2015). Vannini's research interests, typically pursued from an ethnographic approach, span the fields of social and cultural geographies, cultural studies and sociology, with research interests in mobilities, everyday life, technology, wilderness, embodiment and the senses. As part of his Canada Research Chair agenda Vannini's research also focuses on ethnographic film as a tool for knowledge mobilisation. His recent films, *Life off Grid, Low and Slow* and *A Time for Making*, have all reached broad global audiences through television broadcasts, video on demand and theatrical screenings.

Soile Veijola is Professor of Cultural Studies and Tourism at the University of Lapland. Her background is in sociology, feminist theories, tourism studies and cultural studies. She has researched gender, embodiment, social formation of knowledge, dynamics and modalities of mixed team sports, tourism work and more recently the tourist dwelling, mobile neighbouring, silence and slowness in tourism, coding society and future tourist initiatives in the undressed places of the global north. She has led research teams on amenity landscapes and tourism as work and facilitated, since the late 1990s, interdisciplinary writing camps around accessible and functional academic writing and thesis design.

Laura Watts is a writer, poet, ethnographer of futures and Senior Lecturer in Energy and Society at the University of Edinburgh. As a science and technology studies scholar her research is concerned with the effect of 'edge' landscapes on how the future is imagined and made, along with an exploration of different writing methods. For the past decade she has been working with people and places around energy futures in the Orkney Islands, Scotland. Her latest book, *Energy at the End of the World: An Orkney Islands Saga*, is due to be published. She is also co-author of *Ebban an' Flowan*, a poetic primer to marine renewable energy, and won the International Cultural Innovation Prize 2017, along with the Reconstrained Design Group, for a community-built energy storage device designed from spare parts. For more on her work see www.sand14.com.

Foreword

Gerhard Boomgaarden

It was a typically grey late winter morning in London, in 2003, when I met John Urry for the first time. I had started at Routledge two months earlier and was still coming to grips with the publishing culture. As these editorial transformations go, there was little information about him or the series, the International Library of Sociology (ILS), which he edited. But I had done enough research to be aware of his standing in the field. I was a little nervous but I should not have been. He charmingly enquired about my past, my experience, and was happy to hear that I had some background in sociology. John was surprisingly easy to get on with but it was a relatively short introduction, as he had to shoot off to a meeting with government advisers. We were to meet many times during the next 14 years.

I got to know him well. He had a special place for Routledge and the ILS. His first two books (*Reference Groups and the Theory of Revolution*, 1973 and *Social Theory as Science*, 1975) were placed with Routledge Kegan Paul, as it was called then.

John was quick and to the point, at least when we sat down to discuss projects, but never without charm. Once we had established our rapport, I became rather fond of his style of communication: expressive and energetic, I would call it. He took email to a new level: 'There is too much of it and it does not require the formal approach of a letter, so you may as well experiment'.

From 2005 onwards, the market for research into immediate paperback editions, then the staple of Routledge's publishing, started to collapse. It meant that previously published books in paperback would now see the light of day in hardback editions with corresponding price tags attached. John hated this. He believed in the wide dissemination of material and that for him at the time was the availability of a cheap paperback edition. Books were of course published electronically but it was a new format back then. Amazon was still one of many and cheap Kindle editions did not exist.

For a few years, our meetings became bargaining/haggling shops to discuss what in the series should go out in hardback and what would still be considered as having sufficiently wide reach to make it out in an immediate paperback edition. He was never a pushover and quickly adapted to the new situation. His more esoteric suggestions started to include a reference to the textbook market. 'Textbook and reading list potential' were the key phrases of the day, used by editors internally at publishing houses the world over to get sign-off for an immediate paperback edition on publication.

I resorted to the supply of 'charts', a list of titles published in the series with comprehensive sales figures and marketing activities attached. I assume now that he thought anything promising should be tried and tested. Sales figures, as the only measure of success, are a poor yardstick indeed. A mutual friend of ours told me some time later of his dislike of the 'charts' and I used them sparingly after. Any editor worth her grit knows when and how to mediate between academic needs and aspirations and the commercial or corporate interests of the publisher. So, we discussed marketing, the author's ability to transcend traditional academic markets, other publishers and the state of the publishing industry. Later on it was climate change, the new classes and probably my and his favourite, 'the new' – just what lies below the horizon?

After a particularly difficult review meeting to loud muzak and poor service (*Gerhard, Thanks for lunch – company if not service!*), we finally settled on 'Ye olde Mitre' near to the old Routledge offices in New Fetter Lane. With its discreet upstairs setting, it was reserved for at least one night every week for the Routledge editorial and marketing crew, where strategy and other things more relevant were discussed. It is still one of the last unpretentious pubs in the area where one can order an ale and bar food with chips. We had some of our most enjoyable and productive meetings in this pub.

John was obviously instrumental in generating and shaping the 'mobilities' paradigm. He managed to get two 'mobilities' books into the ILS but by his third suggestion in a row it was time to start a new dedicated series.

He was very loyal to Lancaster. Every time I came up he would show me around the department and introduce me to people. He loved walking in the Lake District. Pity that I never brought my walking shoes.

When I heard of his death I was shocked. We had just been in touch to talk about a new series and a couple of new projects. Sadly, my last book with John was the 3D printing book he wrote with Thomas Birtchnell. I miss his generosity of spirit, curious intellect and appetite for the new, all clothed in an intensely likeable person.

Foreword for John

Sylvia Walby

Catastrophe was the subject and conclusion of John's last book, *What Is the Future?* (2016). There were caveats; and references to small, bright possibilities of new mobilities such as 3D printing; but, overall, the message was that prospects for the future of humanity are, at best, poor. The planet will burn. Climate change will destroy us.

John's many books were each, and altogether, a theory of society, at multiple levels that included the macro, constituting a theory of societal transformation. This is not the optimism of potential progress found in the early classics of sociology, of modernisation, in Marx, Weber, Durkheim and Simmel; indeed, barely even the double-edged offer of alternative futures. The future is bleak. The art that John sought out to contemplate in his last years was of ruins, apocalypse, catastrophe; his reading of science fiction was concentrated on dystopias.

My catastrophe was different. It was of financial collapse, followed by economic decline and, probably, violence. We discussed which catastrophe would get us first. At best, I would try to joke, 'my' crisis, the financial leading to the cessation of economic growth, would slow down 'John's' crisis, environmental destruction.

John's *Sociology of Catastrophe* is sociology at its best. Drawing on and building sociological theory of society for a purpose. The purpose is to help us think about society, its paths of development and scenarios for its future.

There were earlier moments when John's writing was lighter, more playful. His writing on tourism, *The Tourist Gaze*, turning reflexive thinking about holidays into a sociological reinterpretation of the topic, rethinking and connecting the episodic pleasures of the modern world to theories of society. This was an application of the sociological imagination to what had previously been a practical subject focused on tourism as a trade, turning it into a new field for sociology.

John's creation of a new field of 'mobilities' is probably his best-known legacy. This contained an ambivalence as to modernity: its pleasures and problems. It opened worlds of possibility as well as destroying the environment. It made possible connections that otherwise were absent. Its forms were very varied. As an academic field, 'mobilities' embeds the nuanced appreciation of the spatial and temporal dimensions of society, which runs throughout John's work, in a new conceptual schema, which many others have since deployed. The Centre for Mobilities Research and the journal, *Mobilities*, institutionalised these insights.

Mobilities drew on a longer engagement with the spatial and temporal in John's work. The Lancaster Regionalism Group embedded an analysis of the deindustrialisation of Lancaster in an emerging theory of globalisation (*Restructuring: Place Class and Gender*). John developed this in large-scale comparative analysis of the restructuring, or disorganisation, of traditional forms of capitalism, including in the book *The End of Organised Capitalism* (with Scott Lash).

The sociological engagement with complexity theory is another of John's legacies. Drawing on theories from adjacent sciences, confident that it was possible to borrow and blend ideas from the intellectual apparatus of other fields into sociology, this was an important intervention. My interpretation of complexity theory was different, more rooted in innovations in systems theory. At Lancaster, we developed a plural range of positions on complexity. Our students debated the different interpretations of complexity by Urry and Walby, and developed their own.

The 'book' form of publication facilitated John's publication of big thinking about society. It sidestepped the cautious gatekeepers who review for journals and grants. It offered a more direct route of communication to students, colleagues, researchers and wider publics, to whoever wanted to read the accessible paperback books.

John's way of working, always in discussion with others, in seminars, over coffee, in cafes, called into being the creative intellectual environment in which his work flourished. While John took responsibility for his authorship, he was no lone scholar. This form of intellectual production, mixed with play, was central to his extraordinarily prolific publications. While always willing to coordinate activities (too often today reconfigured as management), he worked regardless of the multiple forms of audit that have been developed and imposed. John fed the intellectual development of others while simultaneously drawing on the innovative thinking of other scholars. This is collegiality (too often today reinvented as mentoring) and cooperation is central to intellectual creativity.

John is missed in so many ways.

Chapter 1

Introduction

Mimi Sheller, Sven Kesselring and Ole B. Jensen

This book is dedicated to John Urry and his path-breaking work as one of the most influential sociologists of his generation. He helped to identify the deep histories, emergent patterns, and key issues that are reshaping the contemporary world. But beyond that he also made many of us more excited about sociology as a vital field of study that could move beyond disciplinary boundaries to engage a more far-reaching social science and humanities perspective. Whether focusing on shifting economies and the consumption of place, human senses and the body, landscape and place-making, mobilities and complex systems, or recent phenomena such as offshoring and climate change, John Urry was a perpetually innovative scholar, blowing away cobwebs and putting things in a new light. He built on the best traditions of social theory while always making it relevant to the concerns of today – as well as urgently necessary for envisioning and making better futures.

At the same time, he was an exemplar of collegiality, conviviality, and friendship, who made pursuing an academic life an inviting prospect for students and colleagues from around the world, many of whom have contributed to this volume. As a teacher, a mentor, an editor, a colleague, a co-author, and even in the (often thankless) jobs of administrator and manager, he always maintained the university as a welcoming place for many who might not otherwise have remained there. His example reminded us of what we valued about the work that we all do, and why we continue to exchange ideas, meet with each other, and develop shared projects. This volume gathers the most important thinkers who have engaged closely with John Urry's work, or who have influenced and/or been influenced by it, and many who are committed to continuing it.

We focus especially on the new mobilities turn, since this is the main focus of the book series *Changing Mobilities*, although contributions also touch on other areas of John Urry's wide-ranging interests. The mobilities turn first became a powerful perspective in European social theory in the first decade of the millennium and has now spread around many other parts of the world, from the Asia-Pacific region to Africa, and from North America to South America, thanks in large part to John's effervescent sociability, world-wide meetings, and practice of making connections between people and ideas. The mobilities turn challenges mainstream theoretical and empirical approaches that were grounded in a sedentary view of states and the bounded societies within them. It propels innovative thinking about social and media ecologies, complex systems, and social change in modern worlds and lives. It bridges many disciplines and methodologies, leading to new approaches to existing problems while also resonating with questions of history and paths toward the future.

Mobilities research also marks the beginning of a new transdisciplinarity and the rise of a new phase in international cooperation and collaboration, especially as societies around the world face the ecological limits of contemporary mobility and energy systems. John's late work moved increasingly toward diagnosis of the social, cultural, political, and economic structures that were preventing appropriate responses to climate change, ranging from the unintended consequences of complex systems to the secret worlds of offshore wealth. While his work on post-carbon futures sometimes seemed pessimistic, it was full of the optimism that we could make a difference by applying our sociological imaginations more fully, more creatively, and more collaboratively. His work instigated many of us to step beyond disciplinary borders and academic protocols, to try to engage our work in the world in new ways.

John Urry's oeuvre has been very influential in the emergence of this new field and has had lasting impacts on many scholars. In this collection we have asked leading scholars to contribute with originally commissioned essays that reflect on how John's teaching, writing, and collaborative work influenced their thinking and the course of their research. The contributors represent a number of national contexts, including Australia, Brazil, Canada, Denmark, England, Finland, Germany, Switzerland, Taiwan, USA, and Wales. The book collects personal essays and gives insight into a vivid network of social scientists who have connections of various degrees to the work of John Urry. Amongst the groups that have formed over the last decade or so in conversation with his work, and many times with his invited participation, are the Cosmobilities Network, the occasional meetings of the Mediterranean Mobilities Network and Pan-American Mobilities Network, the very lively New Zealand/Aotearoa Mobilities Network, the newly launched Australian Mobilities Network, and the just formed Global Mobilities Network. These are in addition to a host of smaller workshops, PhD schools, and symposia that have brought the community together across many locations.

Overall, this book reflects on how John Urry's oeuvre has indexed the emergence of new problems and projects in the social sciences, how it has touched on a disparate yet interconnected number of vital research areas and cross-disciplinary research programmes, and how it has inspired several cohorts of graduate students and international research networks in the undertaking of new endeavours. John was always fond of face-to-face meetings, and this book is both a reflection of those meetings and an imaginary travel of meeting together in his honour once again.

Organization of the book

We have chosen to divide the book into five thematic sections. In Part I the focus is on economies and spatialities, and the contributors reflect on both 'the spatial turn' and 'the cultural turn' in social theory, and especially their impact on British sociology in the 1980s, in conversation with simultaneous developments in human geography. This section includes several colleagues from Lancaster University, and considers how Urry's early work in social theory, regional economies, and the emergence of disorganized capitalism connects to his later work on offshoring, mobilities, critical sociology, and social futures. While many associate the work of Urry with a 'postmodern' perspective, contributors here offer a more complex and nuanced view of the various strands of social theory that he brought together, and the intersections of a kind of cultural approach with the material production of space.

In Part II, a cohort of Urry's co-authors and colleagues considers the contributions of his work to rethinking the relation between natures, bodies, and the senses, and the emergence of what might be called 'the sensual turn' in sociology and cultural geography. Here, a more phenomenological perspective comes to the fore, considering how bodies and spaces are co-constituted through ongoing practices. Sensations, gazes, affects, intensities, virtual travel, and imaginative mobilities all move to the foreground, showing how absence and presence, proximity and distance are experientially entangled. These reflections show how Urry's perspective helped open new spatial, sensory, and temporal dimensions of empirical research and social analysis, as well as allowing for very creative modes of writing.

In Part III we turn to a host of thinkers who took up Urry's work on tourism and everyday travel to investigate both the histories and contemporary practices of travel, and the emerging topographies of tourist performance. While this work is connected both to the interest in embodiment and in mobilities, it takes the specific context of touristic encounters and day-to-day travel routines to unpack some of the more detailed encounters of the travelling body. Funnily enough, in these postcards from various places we also begin to see the academic as tourist: the travels that took John to Denmark, to Brazil, to New Zealand, and to many other places around the world, even ice-fishing in Finland. So much of our work involves both everyday travel, and more occasional distant travel, as well as a kind of mundane travel-time that is so often used for work; perhaps all this travel instils a kind of sociological reflexivity as we move between different cultural settings.

In Part IV we address in wider perspective the full implications of the mobilities turn, as it has impacted on a trans-disciplinary array of questions. Contributors consider both how it emerged in various international and disciplinary contexts, and how it has impacted on a wide range of research areas, throwing disparate fields into new juxtapositions. This has been an incredibly fruitful and productive terrain, generating many new ideas and methodologies for social research, as well as new kinds of collaborations and innovative practices.

And finally, in Part V the contributors take up the post-humanist themes of complex systems theory and the more speculative strains of social futures thinking and 'affirmative critique' in Urry's most recent work. Here we consider what the future holds for social sciences in an era of global limits and surveillant assemblages, as we try to envision a post-carbon future that may or may not emerge out of the spatial, sensual, and mobile practices that Urry's work has charted. We also see his biting critique of hidden wealth and the dark forces that shape global economies and proliferate dangerous systems that are beyond our control. Yet risk, disaster, and inequality remind us again of the commitment to normative social science and to bringing about social change, including by working in more applied arenas, such as John's contributions to the Intergovernmental Panel on Climate Change or the UK Government's Foresight programme.

We round out the book with a thoughtful Afterword by John's colleague over many years at Lancaster University, Lynne Pearce, who brings it all home. The work with this collection of contributions from a very diverse set of scholars is in itself a testament to the fact that John Urry's work on mobilities is carried on. As we stop to collect all these stories the past is obviously at centre stage, however, one need not read many of the entries to this collection to see and understand that the legacy of John Urry is carried onwards and that the scholars represented in this collection (as well as many, many others) as we write these words are taking on the mobilities perspective, appropriating it, transforming it, and rethinking it in different paths and with different trajectories that we are confident would have pleased John Urry immensely had he been present to witness.

So it is with great sadness of John Urry's passing blended with great enthusiasm for the lively academic field that we invite the reader to embark on a journey through the following chapters. The stories gathered here are as much personal reflections, histories, and anecdotes testifying to a humble academic giant, as they are documentations of new perspectives, innovations, and rethinking of a field that still has much work to do as a critical-creative position within social science and beyond for the future.

Part I

Economies and spatialities

Chapter 2

Encountering John Urry
A fragment of an autobiography in theory

Tim Cresswell

In June 2003 I was sitting on some steps in a public square in Paris. I had just disembarked a Eurostar train in Gare du Nord and was making my way to Paris St Lazare to catch a train to Normandy. I like to walk in cities and the reveries that can induce. This was a particularly fine day. I was ten years into my post-graduate career as an academic and had made my way from Aberystwyth on the west coast of Wales. I was used to being invited to talks but not used to being invited to talks in different countries. I was travelling to Normandy to attend the Centre Culturel International de Cerisy, at an event called Les Sens du Mouvement. The costs were fully covered and at that point in my career this was an unusual and exciting invitation. I was not aware at the time that I would spend a great deal of time in the years to come travelling between countries and continents to speak about, and listen to others speak about, the theme of mobility. So this felt like a big deal – a measure of some kind of success. This was probably the kind of thing I was thinking about as I sat on the steps and watched the world. I was also thinking about the people I was going to meet in Cerisy.

About seven months earlier I had received an email from John Urry inviting me to attend this meeting. I was promised four days in a chateau in Normandy with the company of academics I admired as well as policy wonks, journalists, a film maker and representatives of industry. I think the invitation led me to discover Urry's book, *Sociology beyond Societies*, that had been published a year earlier and laid out a bold vision of a sociology centred not on societies but on mobilities. It was around then that Urry (with Mimi Sheller) founded the Centre for Mobilities Research at Lancaster and it would be another three years before the 'new mobilities paradigm' would be formally announced. When I arrived at Cerisy I was overwhelmed by the space, complete with photographs on the walls of the eminent people who had been there – Sartre, Einstein, Derrida, etc. I certainly felt like a very junior scholar at the meeting, having lunch and drinking cider with Ed Soja, Nigel Thrift and, yes, John Urry. Urry was immediately companionable, sharing his recent conversion to the Atkins Diet following some ominous heart trouble he had had earlier in the year. He was thin and gangly with an unpretentious air about him. He was clearly a font of informed wisdom who seemed to have a list of must-read references for everything. I never felt like the junior scholar when I was in his company, but I was being given frequent reading assignments as we shared cider or walked in the grounds. Urry seemed as interested in me as I was in him. While this was the first time I would meet him, it was only one point in a relationship that went back around 15 years.

I think John Urry's name first entered my consciousness some time in the late 1980s. I was a doctoral student in geography at the University of Wisconsin, Madison and much of the discussion among the grad students in my circle centred on two themes, the increasing attention being paid to space in what we might broadly call 'theory', and the reassessment of 'culture' as an active force in social, political and economic life. Discussion of the role of space in social theory was largely inspired by the work of geographers such as Edward Soja (who would also be at Cerisy), Derek Gregory and David Harvey who, from quite different perspectives, were interpreting the work of Henri Lefebvre, whose book *The Production of Space* would not be translated into English until 1991, and Michel Foucault. At the centre of this conversation was the recognition that space had been largely neglected in grand theoretical approaches to society. Harvey had, for a while, been carefully teasing out the implications for spatial thinking in Marx, Soja was engaging with varying forms of post-structuralism and Gregory with both of these as well as the work of Habermas, Giddens, Foucault and others. All of them were arguing that space should not be thought of as dead afterthought of the seemingly more active realm of time and the temporal on the one hand, or the realm generally described as the 'social' on the other. Wanting to avoid the critique of spatial fetishism, and using the language of structuration theory, the focus was on the 'mutual constitution' of society and space – or, to use a paraphrase of Marx that was popular at the time 'people make their own geography, but not in a geography of their own choosing'.

This was an exciting moment for theoretically inclined human geographers who were looking to cement their own contribution to the understanding of the production, reproduction and (hopefully) transformation of society. Space was, we thought, our realm and thus we had a special and important contribution. This came as a distinct relief from being the discipline that looked at patterns, mapped things such as class and race, and studied the spatial outcomes of more primary forces. Geography was suddenly where the action was.

The larger context for the seemingly sudden interest in space was a wide-ranging and often heated discussion of post-modernism, post-structuralism, feminism and structuration theory alongside Marxism. I cannot think of a time since there were so many hotly contested and debated theoretical approaches competing for attention. Secretive reading groups were formed. We argued over the wisdom or otherwise of taking Jean Baudrillard seriously. Urry was not one of the names that was foremost in our discussions. We did not know Urry's position on Lefebvre – we did know Soja's. Despite this, Urry's name kept popping up in bibliographies and during commentaries on the re-emergence of space in social thought.

I think the first essay of Urry's I read was 'Social Relations, Space and Time' in the book he co-edited with Derek Gregory, *Social Relations and Spatial Structures* (1985). To be honest, I was probably reading the book because Gregory's name was on the cover and he was one of the leading geographers in the engagement with what we were increasingly referring to as just 'theory'. The book was theoretically assertive in a masculine kind of way, included essays by 13 eminent men (Anthony Giddens, Nigel Thrift, David Harvey, Edward Soja, etc.) and one eminent woman (Doreen Massey). It is with sadness and gratitude that I note the recent sudden passing of three of the creative and politically engaged theorists of space, time and society who contributed to this volume. All of them influenced my own thinking in so many ways, and all died within a few short months of each other. The collection addresses the central question of the role of space in the production, reproduction and (potential) transformation of social relations. Urry's essay interrogates the role space (and time) plays in the constitution of social relations. It was, and still is, quite dizzying in its reach. We get discussions of absolute versus relative conceptions of space in Descartes, Newton, Kant and Leibniz, a neat jump from John Berger writing about portraits to notions of surplus value, spatial divisions of labour at different scales and the role of space in civil society. It ends with an apology for not also considering the state! The essay is saturated with references and, in what would become a characteristic Urry move, turns into numbered lists of key points. It is as though the sheer number of points of interest is so overwhelming there is no other way to adequately represent them. Reading this essay, I had no idea that Urry was a sociologist. Given the company Urry kept I probably thought he was a geographer for years after this. And although the essay quite clearly uses the language of philosophical realism, it does not make a plea for that particular theoretical perspective over and above all others. Urry's genuine transgression of disciplinary boundaries and his lack of 'membership' in key theoretical groupings are as clear as his nascent love of lists.

In addition to the reassertion of space in critical social theory, the other emerging field within which I dwelled at the end of the 1980s was the 'new cultural geography' – a field I had the good fortune of being educated in as it was being developed. I had taken courses from Peter Jackson, Jacquie Burgess and Denis Cosgrove as an undergraduate at University College London in the mid-1980s. I read their manifestos as they were published and Jackson's book, *Maps of Meaning*, in manuscript form before it was published in 1989. I was particularly inspired by the interface between geography and the new field of cultural studies associated with Birmingham's Centre for Contemporary Cultural Studies and, particularly, the work of Stuart Hall. While this field was clearly connected to the more abstract space and social theory field, it tended to have a quite different set of key authors – John Berger, Raymond Williams and Susan Sontag alongside Stuart Hall and Angela McRobbie. At the core of the new cultural geography and cultural studies was a realignment of the idea of 'culture' so that it was seen as a central terrain of social contestation and not a sleepy backwater to the more important stuff of economics. In many ways the debate mirrored the debate around society and space. Culture had been thought of as a decorative and trivial superstructure to the economic base – the famous site of Althusser's 'final instance'. Just as geographers and others were busy activating space so cultural theorists were rejecting this essentially passive role for culture. Drawing on the idea of cultural hegemony from Gramsci and the cultural materialism of Raymond Williams, the field of cultural studies began to explore culture as an active realm in which resistance was both present and effective – a realm of contestation and not just reflection. One of the many sources of crossover between the society and space debates and the debates around culture and economy was John Urry. Urry was not a cultural geographer, or a central figure in the emergent field of cultural studies. And yet his name was peppered among the references for this group.

The first monograph with Urry's name on it that I recall encountering is Scott Lash and John Urry's *Economies of Signs and Space* (1994). Strangely, I do not recall thinking the book was about mobility despite the proliferation of mobile objects and subjects within it. There was no mobility turn at that point so it was not easy to read as a text about mobility. What grabbed my attention, I think, was the combination of the key words 'signs' (making me think of semiotics as it occurred in both post-modern social theory books and the new cultural geographies readings) and 'space' (which was, by the mid-1990s, everywhere). The addition of the word 'economies' probably reminded me of the endless discussions of the base-superstructure model following E.P. Thompson, Raymond Williams and Stuart Hall. I remember encountering a lot of discussion of capitalism and whether or not there was a new kind of capitalism. But this was interspersed with sudden discourse on Georg Simmel, the nature of objects or terms such as 'aesthetic reflexivity'. Looking back, it is clear that many of the themes that would work through Urry's published work over the next 20 plus years are there in nascent form in this book – reflexivity, mobilities, tourism and more. It is a kind of road map for what was to come. Central to the book was the claim that contemporary society (in 1994) was (dis)organized around flows. Given everything else I was reading and being inspired by at the time there were certainly elements of Lash and Urry's argument that resonated deeply.

> Thus we have an account of the seemingly endless profusion of 'space odysseys', of subjects and objects travelling at increasingly greater distances and speeds. Objects are emptied out both of meaning (and are post-modern) and of material content (and are thus post-industrial). The subjects in turn are increasingly emptied out, flat, deficient in affect. This is mirrored in recent social theory, of post-structuralism which deconstructs subjects, and rational-choice theory which reduces them to calculating unit

acts with preference schedules, Postmodernism (or hypermodernism) is indeed the cultural logic of late capitalism. (15)

Here, as in much of Urry's work, there is a generous inclusiveness in the references, reading and ideas. While others appeared stuck in a fervent role of advocacy for some theory or theorist, Urry was capacious in his ability to see something of value in a range of approaches. The thrown-togetherness of these readings created sparks that were always suggestive of new directions. It is not surprising, in retrospect, that Urry's career would lead in so many productive tangents.

In the years that followed *Economies of Signs and Space* I began a post-doctoral academic career in Wales. Urry's work on tourism, and particularly *The Tourist Gaze*, began to pepper the material I was reading as well as lectures on geographies of tourism a colleague was teaching. I had finished converting my doctoral thesis into a monograph and had turned my attention to the theme and problem of mobility. Mobility, to me, seemed like a vast unexplored area that was both central to my discipline and yet strangely invisible – taken for granted. It had always been central to my own interests without me spending much time exploring it. There were few places to look for inspiration. My interest in mobility grew out of the two fields of inquiry from my graduate school days that Urry had been a part of – the respective roles of space and culture in the constitution of society. Mobility represented a particular form of spatiality that contrasted with more familiar forms, such as place or territory. Mobility was also clearly a cultural enterprise – freighted with stories and narratives that had a particular resonance in the contemporary world. I did not recall the centrality of mobile subjects and objects in *Economies of Signs and Space* so did not return to Urry's work when thinking this through. His work on tourism, however, did catch my interest.

In November 1999 I brought together a number of scholars around the theme of 'mobilities' at the University of Wales Conference Centre in Gregynog, near Newtown. The conference was directed to address the fascination with all things mobile that was emerging across the social sciences and humanities – embodied in notions of spaces of flow, nomadology, travelling theory and the like. The immediate inspirations for me were figures such as James Clifford, Manuel Castells, Gilles Deleuze, Caren Kaplan and Rosi Braidotti. At the same time the conference addressed the increase in attention being paid to actual empirical cases of mobility – of migrants, tourists, the homeless and the exiled. We wondered if the two were related. Someone from Lancaster University was there, I forget who. John Urry's name came up a lot.

In 2005 Urry was once kind enough to write a review for the manuscript of my book *On the Move*. Among some kind words he reflected on my 'idiosyncratic' approach to things. I had never particularly thought of my work as idiosyncratic but decided I could own that description once I reflected on our conversation. Perhaps that was how he thought of his own work? I became involved in an ultimately doomed attempt to convince the Economic and Social Research Council to fund mobility as a thematic priority. On two occasions Urry agreed to act as an external examiner for PhD students I had supervised. On no occasion did he say no. Over the years between our first meeting in Cerisy and his death in 2016 I met Urry on many occasions as we were both invited to talk at meetings with a focus on mobility. Appropriately enough our time together was spent travelling, either staying briefly some-where at a conference or in airports and on planes. We shared a plane travelling back to London from Limerick, another from Oslo. During one of these flights, I forget which, Urry asked me about my projects and the talk I had just given. We reflected on giving lectures in continental Europe in which we had been asked to align ourselves to some theorist or other. Neither of us were comfortable in that role – as advocates for theory clubs. We shared, by then, a desire to think through themes and problems that seemed both intellectually challenging and emblematic of problems in the world. Our different ways of doing intellectual work frustrated those who wanted to allocate it to a con-venient category. Neither fit with mainstream social science ways of doing. What Urry's early work on society and space and the role of the sign, as well as his work on mobilities, share is a decentring of foundational commitments to 'economy' and 'society' or, indeed, any other foundational commitment. His texts, in their magpie-like attraction to interesting ideas wherever they can be found, do not allow us to settle easily. They have a certain mobility about them and, in this sense, they can be described as post-modern. In more recent years I have read Urry alongside other maverick and anti-foundation scholars such as Zygmunt Bauman with his repeated insistence on the liquid nature of current times (though with far fewer references than Urry) or the cultural theorist Iain Chambers with his arguments for the centrality of migrant sensi-bilities. Urry was a part of an intellectual structure-of-feeling that eschewed membership and embraced heterogeneity in thought. I suspect Urry is very much like that elephant in a darkened room in the Buddhist parable – with each person only grasping a small aspect of Urry's total oeuvre. To many he will always be the author of *The Tourist Gaze* and a leading theorist of tourism in contemporary society. To others he will be remembered as an advocate of complexity theory, open systems and turbulence. To me, and many others, his work on mobilities has been foundational. And even this work on mobility is internally diverse including conceptualizations of the communications–travel nexus, the future of the automobile and the processes of off-shoring to name but three. I have no doubt that Urry's capacious and generous spirit and mind will continue to inform and inspire me in the years to come. I remain grateful that John wrote to me in 2002 so that we could share cider in Cerisy.

Chapter 3

Will there be an Urryism?
The dialectic of a plural thinker in singular times

Thomas Birtchnell

Introduction

In a world long on 'isms' the notion of an Urryism finding favour in the future – that is, a group inspired by John Urry's canon – is problematized by the sheer breadth of his intellectual pursuits and his habitual rejection of monist thinking. While Urry's effort at issuing in a 2010 paper, somewhat tongue-in-cheek presumably, 'ten commandments' on climate change could be interpreted as legacy building, the call to arms on that particular issue fell short in capturing his raison d'être as a scholar in the same fashion as Marx's *Communist Manifesto* forged Marxism. John Urry thrived on pluralizing topics in order to uncover the novelty of the concepts he broached. In this brief appraisal, I consider five examples: society to societies, mobility to mobilities, nature to natures, climate to climates, and ultimately the future to futures. John Urry had many sides to many people; however, he was erudite at also finding many sides to a theory. The depth that could be given to apparently planar subjects stimulated his productivity and will perhaps be his legacy. His signature was to generate theories through the inspiration of others' ideas, rather than to inspire others to adopt his own.

That John Urry's conception of the world was undoubtedly pluralist is demonstrated by his early references to William James, the author of *The Pluralistic Universe*, in the beginning of the published version of his PhD thesis. Similar to John Urry, James was committed to pluralism as an optic. Surely it was a sign of the times that John Urry's book title on that occasion adopted the singular for 'revolution'. Notwithstanding that instance, he was throughout concerned with a plural topic, namely reference groups: the *omnium gatherum* behind social change.

John Urry went on to pluralize many concepts in his career: the notion of society, nature, mobility, the climate, and even the future. His legacy will be the depth he gave to all of these subjects as well as the critical awareness that there are more sides to most stories. The pluralism John Urry wrought throughout his social theories was partly a product of his generation's rejection of modernism and embracement of post-modernism; however, it was also uniquely his way of seeing the world, one that is intractable to generalization and resistant to base rudiments.

In its heyday, in the late 1980s, post-modernism was resonant with many academic thinkers since it unsettled grand narratives and dominating discourses. While John Urry was far from a typical advocate of this movement, his command of post-structuralist philosophy evidently furnished his own brand of social theory as citations to Michel Foucault and other leading figures illustrates. Yet, John Urry belongs in a class of social thinkers who are set apart from post-structuralism and remain so: Ulrich Beck, Zygmunt Bauman, Anthony Giddens are exemplars of this group.

Societies and mobilities

One of the first examples of his pluralist tendencies is in his call for sociology to move beyond societies. The impetus for John Urry's pluralization of the idea of 'society' was the pressure the social sciences felt in the 'rebranding' (read dissolution) in the 1980s of the Social Science Research Council due to Prime Minister Margaret Thatcher's assertion that 'there is no such thing as society' as well as the response from the British sociological community that sought to uphold the idea in a somewhat essentialist way. John Urry foresaw in this monist idea of *a* society both the critical viewpoint of the economistic mantra of the global free market that Thatcher espoused and the later resurgence of nationalism underpinning both the Brexit vote and the rise of Trump in the same year as John Urry's death.

Yet it was far from the case that he agreed with Thatcher that there was no society. For John Urry, the most puissant response to her suggestion was to ruggedize sociology, classically the study of society, and draw it away from either economics and its neoliberal doctrines or idealism about the nation-state. Instead, sociology would address topics that could include a diversity of elements, for instance technologies or resources, alongside citizens and policies. To take sociology *beyond* society through pluralizing the idea would put it in tune with his later ideas about mobilities, particularly automobilities, wherein states become metaphorical gamekeepers, rather than gardeners, able to influence people's choices around oil or car use, but not able to contend with the automobility regime of globally roaming herds of hybrid 'car drivers' and the ways they transform and fragment nations.

In a sleight of hand John Urry artfully reduced Thatcher's aspirations to be a national leader of global relevance in charge of her 'garden' through the dissolution of the idea of society as an entity in itself. She became in his vision a mere gamekeeper taking political pot-shots at wild animals. Instead of simply upstaging Thatcher, John Urry instead proposed a reinvigorated sociology, able to work with policymakers to articulate government policies. Sociology was there for Thatcher if she could have just understood its power.

He was by no means the sole forerunner in the scholarly study of movement. In his pluralization of mobility to mobilities John Urry exercised his *modus operandi* again. However, Urry's innovation, with colleagues Kevin Hannam and Mimi Sheller, was in pluralizing the concept and broadening the range of inquiry to include people but also objects, capital, information, and so on. John Urry was keen to focus on the issues of mobility rather than mobility per se. Mobilities are not simply a range of transport modes (bus, car, train, and so on). Rather, the plural denotes intensities of movement.

Later in his career he would fill this void himself through work with the UK government's Foresight programme and Department for Transport. Moreover, he would hone his ideas about global automobilities through tracing the issue to its source, namely, oil. For societies so utterly compelled to automobilities the problem of dependency on an energy-dense, storable, mobile, and non-renewable resource that is crucially limited in supply was of great concern, yet oddly absent from political debate. The resource-blindness of scholars signified a pressing lacuna in sociology and the social sciences more broadly and awareness of the core place of oil in societies would require the critical exploration of 'social futures'.

Natures and climates

'In this book we seek to show there is no singular "nature" as such, only a diversity of contested natures' (Macnaghten and Urry 1998: 11). John's collaboration with Phil Macnaghten in 1998 was a precursor to much of the recent work on the Anthropocene, a term denoting the present epoch where humans are impacting upon climatic forces through greenhouse gas emissions, and a planet that has experienced many episodes of volatility.

By rejecting the notion of a single 'mother earth' – that is, Nature with a capital N – they elected to bring to the fore how different people experience the environment, often in contradictory ways. Think for instance of the rolling moorlands of the designated Area of Natural Beauty the Forest of Bowland overlooking Lancaster University that undoubtedly inspired Macnaghten and Urry's thinking. To some it is an oasis of calm and grandly timeless vistas; to others it is a 'sheep-wrecked' deforested landscape long cleared of biodiversity. The role human agency plays in environmental change is often problematized by how natures are perceived to be free from human agency.

John Urry returned to the topic of nature in his book on climate change, interestingly electing to adopt the singular in the title for 'society' presumably to signify the global response needed to tackle catastrophic (to humans) global warming. 'Climate change should not be understood as a single "cause" or a single set of "effects"' (Urry 2011: 6). Here the pluralization is applied to climates instead to orient the debate towards the inherent instability, and indeed inhospitability, in the earth's environment. The world has sustained numerous climate changes and the present epoch within which human societies have arisen is startling for its remarkably stable climate on average. The message John Urry evinced in *Climate Change and Society* was that humans take the current climate for granted and that it should not be assumed that an adequate response will be made to this issue. Humans should prepare for, and adapt to, impending catastrophes which at the moment are difficult to gauge.

Futures

'Futures are now everywhere' (Urry 2016: 1). The future was on John Urry's mind a great deal throughout his career and his contractual work for the UK government's Foresight programme inspired him to reflect on sociology's long relationship with futurology, futurists, and the more recent field of futures studies. As a side note, one of the key founders of the popular integral futures method, Richard Slaughter, was a PhD student of John Urry's in the 1980s. In typical Urry fashion the methodology of 'social futures' involves the conception of multiple scenarios paying attention to social movements, groups, culture, and other social things and rejecting technological determinism or the assumption that the future is simply derived from the ways the present is unfolding.

John Urry indeed experimented with creating social futures in his later publications inspired by his work with the Futures Company, in particular Andrew Curry, and the UK government's Office for Science and Technology Foresight programme. The exercise laid the foundations for the creative scenarios he adapted in many of his books.

The futures that originally inspired John Urry were composed from a 2 x 2 matrix built on two axes of uncertainty: acceptance of/resistance to intelligent infrastructure and high-/low-impact transport. The method creates extremes that correspond well with John Urry's pluralistic viewpoint and have a lineage in sociology going back to Alvin Toffler and Daniel Bell. Advocating for a pluralistic method for understanding futures meant that John Urry was able to privilege a nuanced and critical perspective in tune with his oeuvre.

Conclusion: on ists and isms

Thomas Carlyle, in the preface to Ralph Waldo Emerson's *Essays*, reflected on the social thinker: 'If he prove a devout-minded, veritable, original man, this for the present will suffice. *Ists* and *Isms* are rather growing a weariness. Such a man does not readily range himself under *Isms*' (1841: x). Raymond Williams, similarly musing on 'isms' in his *Keywords* noted that 'they are still used, wittily or contemptuously (often with a sense of rapturous originality) but usually from orthodox and conservative positions' (1983: 174). In this appraisal of John Urry's unique worldview I do not wish to foreclose the possibility of a disciplinary field oriented around his work, whether it is to be termed 'Urryism' or otherwise. But similar to Emerson, John Urry was not prone to scholarly lineages and it would be expected that those in his networks (I refrain from using the terms disciples or followers!) would also exercise their own identities sufficiently in their work and make their own intellectual spaces. And similar to Williams, critical awareness and humility pervade Urry's writing as does an unorthodox take on the world.

It would not be fitting to finish an appraisal of John Urry's oeuvre without a list. Listing was one of his hallmarks and a practice he fell back on numerous times in his publications. First, Urry's penchant for plurality did not come at the expense of clarity. Despite being a complexity thinker by trade since the mid-1990s at least a true talent of his was the capacity to draw out meaningful themes and order them into programmes of theory in a straightforward way. While never perhaps reaching the airport bookshop shelves, a goal he had quipped to aspire to on more than one occasion, his ability to speed read and his distaste for verbosity both stemmed from his impulse towards effortless, succinct prose. Rarely prolix, John Urry's commitment to clarity was a theoretical and instrumental commitment.

Second, despite his voluminous contributions to social theory John Urry was an empiricist. Neither qualitative nor quantitative methods particularly bounded his intellectual endeavours; however, his respect for empirical rigor informed the various strands of his research. In recent times, forays into Social Network Analysis and mobile methods demonstrated a passion for progressive methods. A book on the latter method co-authored with Monika Büscher and Katian Witchger expounds a programme for this approach and its significance continues to be felt beyond the mobilities paradigm.

Third, John Urry's research finds a natural bedfellow with spatial research and has an affinity with the discipline of human geography despite his adamance that sociology was his intellectual home. While regularly attending the British Sociological Association's annual conference, rather than the Royal Geographical Society's, ideas from human geography were mainstays in his own thinking. Writing by John Urry on tourism, nature, mobilities, and cities finds its way into human geographers' bibliographies on a routine basis still. Doubtless, Doreen Massey was an influence, as John Urry reminisced on 16 March 2016 in a reply to the posting of her obituary in the journal *Environment and Planning D: Society and Space*: 'really sad loss of such an innovative thinker – she made us sociologists think space!'. Indeed, John had published a paper, 'Some Social and Spatial Aspects of Services' in Volume 5 of this key geographical journal back in 1987.

I certainly do not wish to seem to be dabbling with irreverence in this appraisal. I simply wished to point out that the dialectic that guided John Urry's corpus was neither contrarian nor polemical; I proposed to advance that it is the humanism of John Urry's work that will be remembered most as time goes on. A recurring thread in his publications is the necessity to adhere to scientific consensus and measured reason without neglecting emotion, empathy, altruism, and care for others. At its core his oeuvre stayed true to his deep concern for social justice, equality, non-violent protest, and respect for the environment. If

I have learnt anything from John it is that there is space in academic life for these concerns to be brought to the fore and championed in order to invoke real change. If he has inspired my own work it is through his generosity towards those who are uneasy with the status quo, yet mindful of the system. Those who reject intellectual conventions without forfeiting reason and humility. Those who are able to balance novelty with critical care and academic gregariousness. Such a legacy is not fossilized in suffixes and neologisms.

References

Emerson, Ralph Waldo. 1841. *Essays*. London: James Fraser.
Macnaghten, Phil and John Urry. 1998. *Contested Natures*. London: SAGE Publications.
Urry, John. 2011. *Climate Change and Society*. Cambridge: Polity Press.
Urry, John. 2016. *What Is the Future?* Cambridge: Polity.
Williams, Raymond. 1983. *Keywords: A Vocabulary of Culture and Society*. Oxford: Oxford University Press.

Chapter 4

Migration, the sociology of mobility, and critical theory

Bülent Diken

Being one of my PhD supervisors, John's influence on my intellectual life has been decisive in many respects. However, his work has inspired me especially in relation to three fields: immigration, the sociology of critique, and the critique of mobility. The following is a reflective account of this. First I focus on immigration in the prism of mobility. Then I turn to the sociology of critique in the framework of mobility. Finally, I revisit the link between critique and immobility, relating this to the sociology of the camp.

Immigration and the economies of signs and space

My acquaintance with John's work dates back to my PhD project *Strangers, Ambivalence and Social Theory*, which had the ambition to articulate the contours of social theory that can deal with ambivalence (rather than trying to extinguish it) as an alternative to the existing research framework in the field of immigration in the 1990s. Empirically I was focusing on Turkish migrants in Denmark. In this prism I made use of Lash and Urry's theory of 'economies of signs and space' to make sense of the systems which set the structural framework of immigration. This move was also a reaction to culturalism, the dominant tendency in the immigration debate which tended to frame the issues of unemployment, exclusion, and discrimination almost exclusively in cultural terms.

The main idea that inspired me in John's work in this respect was that societies are systematically and socially organized differently in different spatial and temporal contexts in the *longue durée*. Along the same lines, different societies also give way to different sorts of ghetto and underclass formation processes. Thus the ghetto and the underclass have much to do with the nature of the society in which they emerge. In other words, to understand the contemporary ghettoes and processes of underclass formation, we have to look at the main features of change in contemporary societies.

To discuss this, I identified three main periods of immigration in Denmark since the late 1960s. My temporalization of the three phases of immigration was grounded in Lash and Urry's work *Disorganized Capitalism* (1987), which analysed major changes in Western societies by a tripartite periodization: firstly, 'liberal capitalism', which roughly characterized the period after the Industrial Revolution up to the late nineteenth century and the early twentieth century; secondly, 'organized capitalism' of the twentieth century; and thirdly, 'disorganized capitalism' since the late 1960s. In their later work, they renamed the last phase 'economies of signs and space'. In my context, organized capitalism constituted the broader context in which the first phase of immigration took place. That is, when immigrants from Turkey, the former Yugoslavia and Pakistan first came in the 1960s, Denmark was an 'organized' capitalist country. The process of 'disorganization' (of the 'organized' capitalism) is the broader context in which the second phase of immigration took place. And the proliferation and consolidation of economies of signs and space is the broader context in which the third phase of immigration took place.

This temporality was reflected in space. Thus, the first period of immigration was predominantly characterized by economic integration and a lack of social integration. The second period was characterized by diminishing integration in the economic subsystem and increasing social integration in the welfare state's ghetto, which was born at the beginning of this second phase. But the character of the ghetto changes in the third phase. In the second phase, the ghetto was similar to what Lash and Urry call the 'classic ghetto', where minorities are forced into particular enclaves in which the central institutions of the wider society are duplicated. But in the third phase, most contemporary ghettoes, according to Lash and Urry, no longer have these characteristics, mainly because governing institutions, that is, economic institutions, markets, and welfare state institutions are increasingly emptying out of the ghetto, and an outflow of population is following, especially the part of the population having a chance of upward mobility. This emptying out, or 'disorganization', of the classic ghetto in contemporary societies is an important dimension regarding any systemic analysis of immigration in a broader context.

What I found interesting was that there seemed to be significant convergences between neo-liberal 'impacted ghettoes' and the Danish ghettoes. But there were some important differences, or divergences, as well, and these mainly concerned family structure and the institutional mix; even if some institutions had already moved out, institutions of governance had not emptied out to the same degree as they had in impacted ghettoes. But this had an important price: to avoid impactedness, Denmark had accepted the formation of an 'overregulated ghetto'.

This overregulation seemed to curtail immigrants' social and cultural mobility. To be sure, migrants move between different geographical settings, cultures, and social spaces. Hence I argued that a theoretical approach in the context of immigration must be as mobile as the research object. It was in this context that I found John's work most inspiring. It helped me to articulate three different frameworks in which mobility is relevant. Firstly, mobility can be taken as an ability to move between social theoretical analyses of systems and life-worlds. Secondly, mobility can be taken as an ingredient of interdisciplinary work, which seeks to communicate with more than one of the established academic disciplines. Thirdly and lastly, it can be taken as a methodological 'oscillation' between coming as close as possible to the object of study by using hermeneutic methods *and* moving away from the issue of immigration by 'deferring' it. It goes without saying that such a mobile social theory of immigration must be particularly aware of the merits of interdisciplinary work: if strangerhood is being both inside and outside, a mobile theory is a stranger in that it crosses borders and territories of institutionalized scientific fields, which necessarily produces hybrids. Just as the passports of strangers are 'juridical fictions', academic territories are ideally 'scientific fictions' for a mobile social theory.

John's early work, or the disorganization thesis in general, was particularly important to me at this stage because it was pointing toward interrelationships and mutual penetrations between different structures and spheres: between the 'social' on the one hand and the economic and the cultural on the other; between the economy (disorganized capitalism) and cultural change (postmodernism); between the economy and political regulation; between the social and the spatial, on the one hand, and the social and the temporal, on the other; between production and consumption (e.g. of places); between industrial production and post-industrial service economies; between production of knowledge and of signs; and so on.

Mobility and justification

In the following years John more explicitly proposed mobility, especially in *Sociology beyond Societies*, as a key concept for the reorientation of social theory in a way that transcends the nation-state-framed concept of 'society'. In this context his work on public space, social networks, and disputes about access to urbanity through collective or individual transportation has influenced me in several ways. I was particularly interested in the ways in which mobility is a contested issue. This is obvious, especially if mobility is thought of in terms of power. After all, mobility seemed to be one of the most important factors of power and stratification. Thus it was necessary to politicize mobility. To frame this politicization it was useful for me to relate John's work on mobility to justification and critique in the sense that Boltanski uses the terms. Power needs legitimation (justification) and legitimation can be delegitimized by critique. My point of departure here was that critique is based on justification. Justifications can only be criticized on the basis of other justifications. In order to understand critique we therefore need to understand how we justify. We need a theory of critique as well as a critical theory of mobility, investigating how different forms of critique (on mobility) are grounded rather than doing a research that grounds a certain form of critique. In other words, I was interested in a 'sociology of criticism' as well as a 'critical sociology' in the context of mobility.

Obviously, mobility can be justified or criticized from within several regimes of justification. For instance, the artistic discourses, or the 'regime of inspiration', perceives mobility as a source of inspiration, spontaneity, originality, creativity, and movement. The 'industrial regime' relates it to efficiency, performance, productivity, and utilitarian functionality. From within the 'market regime' mobility signifies competitiveness, richness, the desire for scarce goods, and a willingness to take risks. In the 'regime of opinion', mobility is what enables one to be able to move in accordance with public opinion, while in the 'regime of domesticity', mobility is persistently thematized as a stumbling block for traditional hierarchies and communal relations. The most interesting regime for me, however, was what Boltanski and Thévenot called the 'civic regime', the grandeur of which is common will and equality. Whereas the arguments against mobility generally favour 'territorialization' within the regime of domesticity, within the civic regime of justification the argument seems to be 'slowing down'. Within this regime, mobility and speed are often seen as the enemies of politics and reflection. Democracy, debate, and civic life require concentration, and in this sense mobility is 'small'. This form of justification/critique is easy to find in the works of social theorists such as Sennett, Bauman, and Virilio. What makes mobility relevant for them is the fact that it tends to transcend democratic politics. And if mobility transcends all critique, criticism must be in favour of slowing down, if not stopping. In this context John's work was helpful for me to articulate the question of mobility in another way, thinking about the ways in which mobility can be justified and criticized on the basis of mobility. Can one speak of mobility itself as a common good? A question which forces us to rethink the relationship between capitalism, critique, and mobility.

As Boltanski and Chiapello showed in *The New Spirit of Capitalism*, capitalism had received mainly two forms of critique until the 1970s: the social critique, from the Marxist camp (based on the concept of 'exploitation'), and the aesthetic critique, from the post-structuralist French philosophy. Since the 1970s, the social critique has been silenced, and capitalism has found new forms of legitimization in the aesthetic critique. Hence the emergence of a nomadic capitalism, which justifies itself and advertises its products with reference to aesthetic inspiration and a new discourse based on metaphors of mobility. Whereas mobility had been a critical concept with which we could criticize the established relations of power, now, with the new capitalism, we seemed to be condemned to mobility as power. What had hitherto been subversive reappeared as its opposite, as a dispositif of power. The decisive question in this context was whether it is possible to reinvent politics, to rearticulate the common good in terms of a relationship between mobility and civic politics. Is politics possible in the network age, when mobility compromises the political and the social? Should critique be based on a 'social critique' (Boltanski), on 'slowing down' the speed of nomads (Bauman), or on imagining 'mobile futures' (Urry)?

What I found in John's work in this period was the possibility of criticizing mobility in mobile terms. Particularly the two books *Offshoring* and *Climate Change and Society* were relevant to me in this respect. What, in my view, proliferated in these two books was a critique of the actual systemic mobilities. At the point at which we thought mobility makes us free, systemic mobilities were exposing our relationship to mobility as a relationship based on domination and captivation. This forced me to think about the relationship between the sociology of critique and radical critique.

Crucially in this respect, the sociology of critique is an empirically orientated approach and focuses on historical (that is, already established), generalized conventions which, it claims, grounds critique. In a certain sense, therefore, the sociology of critique aligns critique to what exists, to existing values, and brings it into line with the governmental idea of 'reform'. Against this background I tried to juxtapose the sociology of critique and radical critique in the context of mobility. After all, the normative pivot of critical theory is the conviction that social life can become a 'problematic', that is, an object of critique and change, only on the condition of imagining a different, better society. Critique is that which enables us to contemplate our present condition in the prism of the possible, without which social life would turn into bare repetition, into an endless, Sisyphean reiteration of the same. Therefore at the most elementary level critique is to experiment with the link between what exists and what is possible. Critique is not reducible to what exists. Central in this respect is the paradoxical relationship between mobility and immobility. Along the same lines, I tried to think of the essence of mobility in terms of immobility.

Immobility, the critique of mobility, and the camp

The best source to understand the role of immobility in relation to mobility is perhaps Benjamin's work. So I revisited his understanding of modernity as mobility and progress, as a mobile hell, the ideal of which is captivation and bare repetition, the eternal recurrence of the same non-events which produce no difference. Thus 'revolution' to Benjamin is the 'emergency break' of history, which makes it possible to arrest the indistinct flow, to break free from the historicist conformism. This idea is present in the later philosophers of mobility such as Deleuze and Guattari. It is well known that theirs is a mobile ontology of becoming, in which everything is in movement. Everything is a mobile and hybrid machine, that is, an assemblage, a process of interaction and connection between heterogeneous elements. What is most significant, however, is that machines or assemblages face two tendencies at once: organization and disorganization. In so far as they constitute the relations that result in stratification, assemblages are part of actual, extensive reality. But on the other side assemblages face something else: what Deleuze and Guattari call the 'body without organs', which causes disorganization and disarticulation to already organized and stratified reality. The body without organs is, like Spinoza's monist 'substance', an all-encompassing flux, a mutable chaos, from which everything emerges and to which everything eternally returns.

Indeed, this concept, the body without organs, takes us to the heart of not only the question of mobility but the paradox of all life, all sociality. Everything, every society, has an actual existence, is stratified and stabilized in one way or another, while at the same time it contains within itself potentialities for change, which links it to the body without organs. The body without organs is, as such, the indicator of the fact that every social relation, all life, can become different, can be reactualized in other ways. Things can change, events can occur, because everything has its body without organs.

If nothing – no 'body', no 'society' – is reducible to its empirical aspects, to actual machines, what matters then is the 'surface' between the machines and the body without organs. This surface is the source of all events, a body's or society's potentialities (its 'body without organs'), which are always in *excess* of its actual, empirical aspects. We do not know, to paraphrase Spinoza, what a body or society can do. In turn, an actual body/society is per definition always *lacking* in terms of its potential possibilities. Therefore, the paradoxical relationship between the machines and the body without organs, one presenting a lack and the other an excess, is always a cause for disequilibrium, and it is this disequilibrium that makes events possible.

Then, what is at play in a mobile ontology is a dialectic of connection and disconnection, mobility and immobility, all at once. Therefore, at the heart of the production of the machines, which create social stratification and organize life, we also find a tendency of anti-production; at the heart of a mobile ontology, we encounter immobility: machines work not only through mobility but also through immobility, by 'breaking down'.

In this prism, the urgency of reconsidering immobilities is grounded in the fundamental relation between power and mobility. It is well established a fact that, due to increasing mobility, today colossal numbers of people and commodities flow across borders. And the control of this flow comes with considerable consequences. Most significantly in this respect, contemporary technologies of mobility constitute a new social topology in which the old geographical/institutional delimitations have become obsolete. We live in an increasingly fragmented society in which distinctions between culture and nature, biology and politics, law and transgression, mobility and immobility, reality and representation, immanence and transcendence, inside and outside … tend to disappear in a 'zone of indistinction'. The camp, in Agamben's sense, is the hidden logic beneath this process that creates a new social topology. No doubt that the camp emerged as the concentration camp, as a space in which the life of the 'citizen' was reduced to 'bare life', stripped of form and value. However, as the inside/outside distinctions disappear, the production of bare life is today extended beyond the walls of the concentration camp. That is, today, the logic of the camp is generalized; the exception is normalized. Consequently, as Agamben claims, it is no longer the city but the camp that is the paradigm of social life. Along the same lines, it is necessary to reconstruct the 'problematique' of mobility on the basis of the paradoxes of the camp.

Social theory has hitherto understood the camp as an anomaly: an exceptional site situated on the margins of the polis to neutralize its 'failed citizens' or 'enemies'. As such, the camp articulates an image of 'society' as if it is dissolved or has disappeared, as if it has imploded into a state of nature. Unlike what sociology conceives of as social relation, these emerging socialities paradoxically promote unbonding as a form of relation. In this way, connecting and disconnecting, mobility and immobility, play equally significant and equally legitimate roles. In other words, contemporary social development has transformed the logic of the camp into a form of sociality.

The camp is no longer a historical anomaly but the *nomos* of the contemporary social space. Our society sees itself today in the light of the camp. What is crucial here, however, is not only the fact that the camp is promoted against the 'city' or 'society'; rather, and more significantly, the inversion signals the emergence of an instability in which it is impossible to distinguish between the camp as exception and exception as the rule. When exception becomes the norm, the norm disappears. But when the norm disappears, exception disappears, too.

Thus, what strikes one immediately in the contemporary global society is a strange bipolarity. Ours is a world characterized by false distinctions between apparent enemies that feed upon each other; a hyper-mobile, 'trans-political' order in which the only distinction imaginable is one between the Right (Macron) and the extreme Right (Le Pen), between old establishments and neo-despotisms, between terror and the war against terror, and so on. A world of reversals and emptying out, a simulacrum, in which McDonalds can engage in anti-obesity campaigns, fascists accuse their adversaries of being fascists, private companies take on public responsibility … with the unavoidable result of a revamped, self-referential Orwellian language – 'peace is war' and 'war is peace'.

It is on the basis of this obscenity that Baudrillard, already in the 1980s, was asking: 'Why does the World Trade Center have *two* towers?' The twin towers of the World Trade Center were perfect parallelepipeds whose smooth surfaces merely mirrored each other, confirming the irrelevance of distinction and opposition in the 'end' of history. Cancelling out difference, upon which politics is based, the World Trade Center was a symbol of trans-politics: an obscene system in which differences and dialectical polarities no longer exist, a simulacrum, where acts disappear without consequences in indifferent signs and images.

I hope mobile sociologies, in which John invested much intellectual energy, do not become accommodated by this mobile hell one day.

Chapter 5

Post-disciplinary encounters between Lancaster and the rest of the world

Andrew Sayer

While wary of the hype, collective amnesia and self-enchantment of enthusiasts that characterise 'turns' in social science, they do usually include elements of more lasting value. In this piece I shall reflect on John's part in the coming together of interests in critical realism, space and social theory, uneven development and radical political economy, and the way in which his work helped to liberate social research from the constraints of disciplines, canonical fideism and arbitrary spatial containers. Examining how these interests were developed both theoretically and empirically, and at both local and global levels, I shall suggest what some of the lessons are from these themes in John's work.

I first came across John Urry's work in the mid-1970s, when our interests in critical realism, political economy and social theory and space overlapped. I want here to discuss these early themes and some of the ways in which they developed in his later work. But first I want to say a few words about him as a person. John Urry contributed to social science not just by publishing, but through example, by his way of being an academic. He showed that to be an effective researcher or teacher, you didn't need to try to dominate, or to cultivate a 'formidable' persona, or an abstruse writing style. What was most important was curiosity and a love of learning. He was more interested in constructing than demolishing, and he obviously enjoyed working with others, particularly junior researchers. He was critical without ever being scathing – he could disagree in an agreeable way – and he was always straightforward both in his writing and relations with others. He was totally free of affectation or concern about status. His laid-back, good-humoured manner belied a sharp critical mind, an extraordinary appetite for work and an enthusiasm for exploring new issues. Hearing laughter coming from John's office was a familiar and reassuring part of life in the department. It made you think that whatever the neoliberalisation of universities threw at you, you'd be OK. Throughout his career, John proved to be extraordinarily resilient, able to continue publishing at the same time as getting through a prodigious amount of administrative work and giving talks all around the world, and yet remaining as focused and quietly confident as ever. He could discuss worrying issues like climate change and environmental destruction in a calm and thoughtful manner.

John was not interested in pieties to the founders of the discipline, but was open to whatever ideas illuminated the particular topics that concerned him, regardless of their provenance. He had an eye for social developments that others more tied to mainstream agendas missed – be it tourism, time, mobility, oil or 'offshoring'. For him social theory was to be *used adventurously*, and to be improved by applying it to new topics. And he made a reputation for arriving 'first on the scene' in many cases. While personally, I'm wary – and weary – of the hype, collective amnesia and self-enchantment of enthusiasts that characterise 'turns' in social science, they do usually include elements of more lasting value, and so it has proved to be with the innovations associated with John's research.

The development of the modern academic division of labour from the late 19th century has created walls between disciplines that pay little attention to the rich interconnectedness of the social world. Each discipline, sociology included, tends to be both parochial and imperialistic. As a committed 'post-disciplinarian' (Sayer, 2000), wary of disciplines and their restrictions, and coming from a university that at the time had no departments (the University of Sussex), I appreciated the breadth of vision and willingness to follow connections wherever they led that John and many of his colleagues shared. It was partly this openness that attracted me to move to Lancaster University half-way through my career. However, I do remember John once saying that sociology could become a post-disciplinary subject; in my view that would be just another form of disciplinary imperialism and, like all imperialisms, ignore other ways of seeing in favour of its own. Nevertheless, John's view of the world was broader than most.

John's role in helping to kickstart critical realism is often overlooked. His book *Social Theory as Science*, written with philosopher Russell Keat, was published in 1975 at a time when social science was far more preoccupied with the philosophy of social science than it is now. In fact, in the 1970s into the early 1980s it dominated social theory. Along with Roy Bhaskar's *A Realist Theory of Science*, published in the same year, John and Russell's book launched critical realism as a philosophy for the social sciences (Bhaskar, 1975). Positivism was to be overthrown not only because it failed to address the meaningful character of human action, but also because it couldn't understand causality or structure and agency either. Critical realism made it possible to see that particular causal mechanisms could have different outcomes, depending on context, and particular outcomes could arise from different mechanisms, so the search for explanations based on empirical regularities in events was misguided.

However, there was a tension in some of his subsequent work between realism and strong forms of social constructionism, particularly in his *Contested Natures*, co-authored with Phil Macnaghten and published in 1998. The most basic realist proposition is that the world exists largely independently of a particular observer. Of course, the world includes social constructions and transformations of nature, but these can usually exist independently of a particular observer's construal of them. In its extreme forms, social constructionism conflates interpretations (construals) with substantial constructions. Even shared construals do not necessarily lead to the construction of anything of consequence. I and other like-minded thinkers in Europe have certain critical ways of construing US politics or the extraction of oil from tar sands in Canada, but unfortunately these have failed to make a difference to either. Wishful thinking, even in collective forms, does not necessarily work, because of the otherness and intractability of the physical and discursive materials it attempts to mobilise. Social constructionism – a product of sociological or culturalist imperialism – fails to recognise this otherness, and the consequent fallibility of knowledge, including conceptions of nature. When we changed from a flat earth theory to a round earth theory, the earth itself didn't change shape. Moreover, the fact that nature has been in many respects transformed through social action (e.g. agriculture, reproductive technologies) does not mean that the whole of nature is now a social construction or is wholly cultural. For realists, culture is an emergent property of a subset of nature. Culture, of course, produces real effects, but it changes nature only where it manages to find ways of activating its independently existing properties – that's why it's so difficult to get reproductive technologies to work – or activates them unintentionally; not just any cultural construal will work. Recent climate change is socially produced, no doubt about it, but as social constructionist Bruno Latour had to concede, that does not mean nature has no independent powers and cannot 'bite back'. I assume John's subsequent interest in climate change also made him draw back from strong versions of social constructionism and adopt what Latour called a 'realist attitude' (Latour, 2004). Actually, later, around 2007, I do remember John telling Roy Bhaskar that he still considered himself a realist.

John played a leading role in sociology's dialogue with human geography in the late 1970s and early 1980s. I was one of the many coming from human geography who were seeking ways of engaging with social theory, while John was coming from the opposite direction, making overtures to geography. Human geography was already using social theory and political economy to understand subjects like urban housing and uneven regional development. Both disciplines were heavily involved in the 1970s and early 1980s' revival of Marxism in academia.

Such work led to more abstract reflections on space and society, in which it was concluded that sociological and other social scientific research had necessarily to attend to the spatial form of social processes, since this always made a difference. Nothing happens outside space. Space is socially constructed or transformed, and societies are spatially structured. The 1985 collection called *Social Relations and Spatial Structures*, edited by John and Derek Gregory, and to which I contributed, was an influential marker in this debate. Later books by John such as *Sociology beyond Societies* and *Offshoring* showed that he continued to problematise sociology's spatial frames throughout his career, indeed when the topic of space and society had become less fashionable. The old assumption that societies could be taken as spatially conformable with nation states was shown to be untenable, though of course it persists. Sociology and other social sciences still have some way to go in following connections and relations of dependence wherever they lead. Post-colonial theory was to make a similar point, albeit with added political import, for one of its implications is that for too long, social scientists in industrialised countries have overwhelmingly stayed within their home national frames, overlooking important forms of dependence on the global South.

One of the contributors to the Gregory and Urry collection was Doreen Massey, who died a month before John in 2016. She argued in 2005 that space is the dimension of multiplicity in the sense of 'contemporaneous plurality' and 'coexisting heterogeneity', in which there is much interdependence between different places. Further, space is not a realm of stasis, counter-posed to time as a realm of change, as some assumed, but a realm of a multiplicity of processes of change, of a 'simultaneity of stories so far' (Massey, 2005). So all histories are also geographies, all geographies are also histories. While the idea of con-temporaneous plurality is easy to accept in principle, it is hard to operationalise in substantive research, not least because of the difficulty of tracking what is happening in many places at once, including their interdependencies. Even where this can be achieved, the unavoidable linearity of discourse makes it difficult to write up such research. Usually we can only hope to track a few parts of the simultaneous, interdependent stories. John's focus on forms of mobility, of course, provided a different way of thinking of space in terms of change, and a different way of cutting or travelling through the evolving fabric of space-time, as various other contributors to this volume show.

Abstract theorising about space and society was closely related with concrete empirical research on the theme of unequal urban and regional development, and the Lancaster Regionalism group was one of many teams of researchers looking at localities in the 1970s and 1980s. In line with the rethinking of the relations between space and society, the many research projects that sprang up across the country were in no way parochial; they always linked the local to the global – again, following processes and relations wherever they led. This accorded with the Marxist concept of *combined* and uneven development. Locality studies also allowed social relations to be studied concretely, in the substantial, spatial forms in which they are lived, rather than in terms of national aggregates and their quantitative dimensions. In this way, these studies connected with the emerging theme of globalisation. Incidentally, this shows that there is nothing strange in the fact that John chose to spend his entire career in a provincial town in north-west England, while writing about globa-lisation and mobility, and doing a gruelling amount of travelling himself. It is not only world cities like London that link the local and the global: any place does, in its own way, and each place provides a different window onto a wider world, adding its own illumination.

It was in this period when he was working on space and society that I think I first actually met John. It was at a meeting of the Regionalism group of the

Conference of Socialist Economists (CSE). This might sound surprising now, but in the late 1970s through to the mid-1980s, radical academia in the UK was closely associated with the CSE, then a highly active organisation, encompassing people ranging from fundamentalist Marxists through to socialist feminists and social democrats. With hundreds of members from many disciplines, the CSE organised regular weekend workshops across the country on a wide range of themes, including urban and regional development. It felt like we were not merely engaging with academic issues but participating in a political movement. It was a time of intellectual excitement, when universities were relatively anxiety-free places where academics could research topics for their own sake, and the world of league tables was unimaginable.

Not surprisingly, given the context of the CSE and the beginnings of Thatcherism, the localities research were also connected to overviews of how capitalism as a whole was changing. In the 1980s and 1990s various binary histories became popular in radical social science, in which the new was presented as the opposite of the old. The binary history of Fordism and post-Fordism gained most support, even though the empirical basis for these categorisations was flimsy and the arguments were strangely preoccupied with changes in what was referred to as 'the labour process', singular, as if capitalism could ever have just one kind that mattered, and as if most other things could be read off from it.

While many chose to characterise the new era as 'post-Fordist', I found John and Scott Lash's account of the period in *The End of Organized Capitalism* (1988) more persuasive. True, it was another binary history, and incorporated some of the Fordist/post-Fordist story, but it was much broader and more sophisticated, involving multi-scalar analyses of different levels of organisation and disorganisation. Disorganised capitalism – again – can't be understood apart from its spatial configuration, in terms of growing mismatches between government spheres of action and those of companies, for example. Some of these mismatches came about not by accident but by design, as ways of concentrating power. Later, in *Offshoring*, John was to explore how companies and neoliberal governments were able to collude in constructing mismatches between the spatial reach of companies and governments that benefitted a rising plutocracy. Most importantly, *The End of Organized Capitalism* had a more substantial empirical component than many other such overviews of capitalism, comprising reviews of five leading capitalist countries' recent histories. These included political changes in relations between the state and businesses and trade unions, class de-alignment in political affiliation and cultural pluralism. All of these changes and others were summed up of course in those familiar numbered lists of points that some friends of John teasingly called Urry-lists. In retrospect we can say that they didn't foresee the rise of financialisation, neoliberalism and China, but then many others, me included, missed them too.

Then, in the 1990s there was the cultural turn and postmodernism. While the latter marked a disastrous but thankfully short-lived lurch into idealism and obscurantism, the former was long overdue; for too long reductionist treatments of culture in both traditional and Marxist-influenced research had enabled the importance of culture as a set of forces in its own right to be overlooked. The cultural turn enabled important advances, though in my view our understanding of culture has benefited more from ethnographic work than from speculative and still somewhat grand theorising about signs and reflexivity. Like most so-called 'turns', it was also accompanied by a turn away from what went before, so economic matters were downplayed or dealt with reductively through references to 'post-Fordism' and 'flexibility', and just at the time neoliberalism was taking hold. Even so-called 'cultural political economy' was at first economy-lite, preferring to study how financial traders talked to one another rather than studying what financialisation meant for economies.

Lash and Urry's *Economies of Signs and Spaces* reflected this turn, albeit in selective terms that retained a significant Marxist element. In its attempt to combine and develop a wide range of themes from diverse social theories, it was even more ambitious than *The End of Disorganized Capitalism*. Again, there were interpretations of empirical cases: the UK, the US, Germany and Japan. 'Flexibility', 'mobility', 'flows' and 'reflexivity' were among its key words, and there was a strong influence from Ulrich Beck in terms of claims about a coupling of individualisation with increased reflexivity. There were also chapters on time and memory, migration, culture industries, travel and tourism, services and underclass. They argued that the dominance of social structures was being replaced by the domination of information and communication structures. In light of the information revolution, the latter certainly become more prominent, but they seem to work more in concert with social structures than the authors anticipated at the time. Notwithstanding the empirical cases, the book seemed too much an exercise in the speculative use and display of new concepts for my taste.

In the years that followed *Economies of Signs and Spaces* our work took different paths, but in the last ten years they began to converge again, and we found ourselves following and discussing similar political and economic trends and events, including the return of 'the rich class'. In that time, John published a series of more problem-oriented books that in different ways contributed to thinking about the future, and the unsustainability of existing societies. These were: *Climate Change and Society* (2011), *Societies beyond Oil* (2013) (imagine: a sociologist writing a book on oil!), *Offshoring* (2014) and the posthumously published *What Is the Future?* (2016). They also give more attention to economic matters, taking seriously the rise of neoliberalism, increased inequalities and, above all, our dependence on nature. Again, their topics require consideration of the shifting relations between space and societies. As John Berger said, 'space hides consequences from us' (Berger, 1974). These books highlight the importance of hidden, often long-distance relations between people and between practices: relations between those who produce waste in one place and dispose of it in another, often in a different country; relations between emissions of CO^2 in one place and desertification or floods in another; and relations between where profits are made and where they are declared for tax purposes.

These issues also force a temporal dimension into view that social science has generally ignored: our relation to future generations. In my view, social science just *has* to consider the future – not as yet another academic fashion to get enchanted with for a while, not as a way of indulging fascination with the latest technologies, not as a vehicle for demonstrating cleverness and not as a source of grants – but for the sake of future generations whose quality of life is threatened by our own actions and those of our recent predecessors.

I would suggest the future is as much a normative issue as one of speculation about possibilities. Yet much social science tries to avoid normative thinking. (Actually, I got the impression that, beyond the noting of problems, John didn't see normative reasoning as something social scientists should engage in, but then I guess I'm in a minority in thinking it should be.) In liberal modernity, normative issues of what is good or bad are widely regarded as merely subjective. And in modernity generally, as sociologists have long argued, instrumental reason swamps normative reasoning about our ends or goals. In neoliberalism, competitiveness becomes an end in itself. To borrow an image from Robert and Edward Skidelsky, we are like a crowd of travellers lost in a desert, not knowing where we're going, but caring only that we are not falling behind the others. (Think of university league tables.) But of course we do need to consider where we might be heading; we need to think through possible future scenarios as John did.

Global warming is without doubt the biggest challenge human society faces. Although many well-known social scientists still find it possible to write tomes on the future of capitalism and society with scarcely a mention of global warming, John was one of the first social scientists to recognise the importance of fossil fuels in the development of modernity, and think through the implications of climate change for everyday life. While most of us drive our research forward by looking in the rear view mirror, John also looked ahead. Other worlds – better or worse – are possible, and as he showed, social scientists can and should think through and assess them.

References

Berger, J. (1974) *The Look of Things*, New York: Viking.

Bhaskar, R. (1975) *A Realist Theory of Science*, Leeds: Leeds Books.

Latour, B. (2004) 'Why Has Critique Run Out of Steam? From Matters of Fact to Matters of Concern', *Critical Inquiry*, 30, 225–248.

Massey, D. (2005) *For Space*, London: Sage.

Sayer, A. (2000) 'For Postdisciplinary Studies: Sociology and the Curse of Disciplinary Parochialism/Imperialism', in Eldridge, J., MacInnes, J., Scott, S., Warhurst, C. and Witz, A. (eds), *Sociology: Legacies and Prospects*, Durham, NC: Sociology Press, pp. 85–97.

Chapter 6

Following

Mimi Sheller

I am proud to call myself a follower of John Urry's work, which I have been following one way or another (often in many directions at once!) for about 30 years. Following, however, has been given a bad name. Although its meanings are multifaceted, we often associate the word with "a group of fans or supporters" and in an academic context this may have negative overtones of groupies, fanatics, acolytes. John Urry himself never aligned his thinking as a follower of any particular theoretical school, and despite working with dozens of graduate students, postdoctoral researchers, and colleagues, never cultivated a following as such. A following may define a school of thought, but it may also suggest a mindless mob. Even more negatively, we understand followers as those who "obey or act as ordered by someone." We often hear "Be a leader, not a follower!" and our individualistic societies champion actions like leading, exploring, discovering, or opening up new frontiers, not following like sheep.

Yet there is something to be said for other nuances of following. Following is also a kind of deliberate and mindful movement, perhaps a sympathetic one. To follow can also mean "to go in the same direction as a road or path" and "to have great interest in something or watch something closely." We can imagine following John Urry as a co-mobility, partly following along a path trodden by many others before us, but partly moving together along a new way. This kind of following requires actively sensing a direction, finding the way, attunement to another. This may perhaps happen because we are part of "a group of people who support, admire, or believe in a particular person, group, or idea" – such as the "mobility turn" – but it might also be a form of attention, a kind of living practice, even a mobile practice. To follow is also "to understand something as it is being said or done" or "to read the notes or words of a piece of music at the same time as they are being played or said." Following, in this sense, is performative, live, present, co-operative, improvisational, and moving (whether physically, mentally, imaginatively, or emotionally).

If following in the first sense has a temporal aspect of coming after, then following in the second sense is more synchronous, a live happening. And it is this kind of following that I want to claim and revalue. I believe I first read some of Urry's work on capitalism and postmodernism as an undergraduate at

Harvard, where French poststructuralist theory and postmodernism were the hot topics of the mid-1980s, in my case filtered through feminist critique and an American inflection. But it was in graduate school in the mid-1990s that I read the 1985 co-edited volume *Social Relations and Spatial Structures*. This introduced me to a range of ideas coming out of British Marxist geography in conversation with historical sociology and social theory, that for me at the time seemed very pertinent to understanding the slave plantation complex of the Atlantic world, which I was studying in advance of writing my PhD dissertation. As a historical sociologist, it helped me to think about the geographies of circulation that connected the Atlantic world, as well as the local spatial organization of slave societies, plantations, islands, and the question of the relation between the public sphere, public space, and counterpublics. I remember sketching little maps of the formal spatial structures of the sugar plantation contrasted with the vernacular spaces of the provision grounds, fruit trees, and kitchen gardens that enslaved people grew. I began to understand that space and power, landscape and labor, were interconnected, and contested across a vast global economy.

And soon this global economy would take me across the Atlantic, as I moved to London to conduct my dissertation research on post-emancipation democratization movements. Over the next five years I moved back and forth between London and New York, and John's work became a beacon of a kind of expansive sociology that connected my historical training at the New School's Center for the Study of Social Change in New York, with currents of continental European social theory filtered through a British perspective grounded in political economy. The British interpretation of French poststructuralism, postmodernism, and the "cultural turn" differed significantly from that in the U.S. insofar as it infused it with both Marxist political economy and elements of cultural studies. In the U.S. cultural thinkers and economic thinkers seemed diametrically opposed and incommensurable. So Urry's work offered a window onto other ways of thinking. I saw this as a way forward: a path to follow.

So it was that my interest in John's work led to my first academic position as a lecturer in sociology at Lancaster University, beginning in 1998. Following these ideas to Lancaster, I found a sympathetic place where my interests in history, literature, feminist theory, postcolonial theory, economic development, and democracy could all be welcome. People there could "follow" me, in the sense of getting what I was talking about. Yet by following this pathway, I also diverged somewhat from my historical training and my American grounding, moving towards a more British contemporary sociology infused with cultural geography, which shaped the rest of my career. When we follow concepts they can take us in new directions, they can open new pathways, and they can change who we understand ourselves to be following in a temporal sense. We string together our intellectual genealogies retrospectively, reinterpreting our influences, setting our ideas in new contexts, and calling into focus different elements.

I found in Lancaster's Sociology Department an exciting and lively setting in which to follow all kinds of ideas to see where they might take me. There was Sarah Franklin's feminist technoscience; Bob Jessop's work on political economy; Andrew Sayer's critical realism; John Law's actor network theory; Jackie Stacey's feminist cultural studies, and many other colleagues in the department and adjacent departments whose influences I happily imbibed. But above all, I found my conversations with John to take interesting turns, as we followed each other in the sense of an ongoing practice, a co-mobility in which our ideas met up and went in new directions. Our discussions on urban space and automobility, for example, led us to co-write "The City and the Car," which was published in 2000, followed by our article "Mobile Transformations of 'Public' and 'Private' Life" in 2003, which continued a conversation about mobility, urbanism, public space, private space, and social change. At the same time, I was working on my book *Consuming the Caribbean* (2003), which intersected with some of John's ideas on consuming nature, the tourist gaze, and mobilities, but led me to suggest to him and argue for a need to foreground issues of postcoloniality, differential power, and (im)mobilities as a relational concept. When John invited me to publish the book in the Routledge International Library of Sociology I felt that my work could join with a wider set of intellectual travelers who appreciated a kind of heterogeneous thinking that encompassed history, literature, visual imagery, cultural studies, political sociology, and various kinds of theory.

This brings me to think about the mobility of concepts and specifically the conceptual moves enabled by the concept of mobilities. It is an idea that can move across disciplines and fields, turning up new questions and perspectives along the way. This to me is what makes it so significant: not simply that we are studying various kinds of mobility, but that mobilities theory is a kind of flexible thinking that deals with relations, processes, and becomings, moving across time, space, scale, and disciplinary boundaries. This is certainly the case made by John in *Sociology beyond Societies* (2000), with its trenchant critique of sedentary perspectives and national containers. So while I share in the empirical fascination with studying various kinds of mobility, such as driving, passengering, walking, wheeling, or cycling; and studying various kinds of mobile subjects such as air travelers, migrants, refugees, tourists, pedestrians, etc.; and studying the infrastructures that unevenly shape such mobilities, I understand these topics as just one dimension of mobilities research. Equally, if not more important, are the ways in which it might enable me to think across (following John) not only cars and cities, but also tourism and global cultural events, financial flows and offshoring, climate change and oil economies, complexity science and futures. Indeed, this is where our conversations began, this is where we together followed lines of thought that began in nineteenth-century transatlantic histories and took us to the twenty-first-century crises of the Anthropocene.

When these lines of thought came together around "mobilities" we took the opportunity to create the Centre for Mobilities Research in 2003, to co-edit a volume on *Tourism Mobilities: Places to Play, Places in Play* (2004), to hold the Alternative Mobility Futures conference in January 2004, to accompany it with a Mobile Communications workshop, and out of those dual events to co-edit a special issue of *Environment and Planning A* on "Materialities and Mobilities" (2006), in which we first declared "The New Mobilities Paradigm," as well as a Routledge volume on *Mobile Technologies of the City* (2006). While I certainly understand the irk felt by many who distrust such imperialistic claims of novelty and new paradigms, I think at the time it was just the sense of excitement of a gathering who were following a path, finding a way of moving together in a new direction. It was a community of practice and shared discourse, and we sought to follow it by naming it. And we did so in part by co-founding, with Kevin Hannam, the journal *Mobilities* as a place to gather this community of discourse. At no point did John express himself as "leading" this "turn" (though others may have) – rather, its naming was the articulation of an act of following in which we were all trying "to understand something as it is being said or done," in other words, to see where playing this music might lead us.

With that said, let me turn to where I see the field going. My own journey took me back to the United States, and to an effort to bring the mobilities perspective into an American context where it was not well known. Given the divergences in the cultural histories of academic disciplines in the U.S. versus the U.K., not to mention the many other places where the mobilities paradigm has been taken up, this was no easy task. American sociology is extremely nationally focused, empiricist, positivist, self-reproducing, and at times utilitarian (certainly research funding applications have to hit all these notes in justifying the expenditure of tax payer money). So I found myself maintaining all of my connections with the mobilities research community around the world – meeting up and exchanging ideas with colleagues not only in the U.K., but in Denmark, Norway, Sweden, Germany, France, Italy, and soon extending to Australia, New Zealand, Canada, South Africa, and eventually Latin America. It was a self-constituting community of "followers" of mobilities, some who had studied with John, or visited Lancaster, or met us at conferences, or contributed to a book or journal we co-edited. I have been incredibly thankful for this group of "groupies" around an idea, not a person, who enable me to escape the isolationism of the United States, to stay connected with and through mobilities, and to keep following it in new directions, even in John's absence – for the following continues, even without his direct presence.

In March 2016 John and I published "Mobilising the New Mobilities Paradigm" in the first issue of *Applied Mobilities*. We wanted to reflect on the ten years that had passed since our first article on that idea, with no inkling that John would not be there for the next ten years. In retrospect, it was fortuitous, and felicitous, and fitting that we seized this last opportunity to follow mobilities together. We reflected on the relation of mobilities-centered theoretical approaches to complexity theory, transition theory, and social practice theory. Each calls attention in different ways to dynamic processes of emergence, social change, and social futures – the topic that John was writing about in his final book. We also reviewed the many activities connecting together the diverse sites in the field of mobilities research – the events, the people, the networks, the publications, the centers. John felt quite optimistic about its continuing significance, while recognizing some of the institutional and disciplinary limitations on funding research and training in such a diffuse field. Nevertheless, we saw a turn towards applied research as quite promising, with mobilities research potentially playing a crucial part in post-petroleum, low-carbon transitions. We argued that the mobilities paradigm offers some of the missing theoretical and methodological approaches for crossing micro and macro scales of bodily, urban, transnational, and planetary mobilities that are at the heart of mitigating climate change and advancing post-carbon energy transitions.

Now one year later I am more convinced than ever that we were following the right path. The reactionary backlash of fossil-fuel-funded politics in the United States, the continuing offshoring of vast amounts of wealth, the escape of elites from taxation and regulation, the ongoing privatization of water and forests across the world, the tragically absurd denial of climate change and refusal of the need to reduce energy demand in the United States, and, of course, the ongoing disaster of the Trump administration's incompetence, obstruction, and dismantling of the state and all of its protections: all of these are outcomes of the structured and relational (im)mobilities of people, capital, commodities, information, and energy in the world today. I strongly believe that the best way to achieve a transformation of these global tragedies is through a campaign for mobility justice. Mobility justice appears to me as a way to simultaneously attack all of these interconnected crises by following new paths forward, as I argue in my book *Mobility Justice* (Sheller 2018) which is of course dedicated to John. I hope mobility justice can become the basis for assembling a following, in the best sense of the term.

References

Sheller, M. *Mobility Justice: The Politics of Movement in an Age of Extremes* (London: Verso, 2018).

Sheller, M. and Urry, J. "The City and the Car," *International Journal of Urban and Regional Research*, 24(4) (2000): 737–757.

Sheller, M. and Urry, J. "Mobile Transformations of 'Public' and 'Private' Life," *Theory, Culture and Society*, 20(3) (2003): 107–125.

Sheller, M. and Urry, J. (eds). *Tourism Mobilities: Places to Play, Places in Play* (London: Routledge, 2004).

Sheller, M. and Urry, J. (eds). *Mobile Technologies of the City* (London: Routledge, 2006).

Sheller, M. and Urry, J. "The New Mobilities Paradigm," *Environment and Planning A*, 38 (2006): 207–226.

Sheller, M. and Urry, J. "Mobilising the New Mobilities Paradigm," *Applied Mobilities* 1(1) (2016): 10–25.

Part II

Travel, senses, natures

Chapter 7

Proximity from a distance

Virtual and imaginative mobility through the intimacies of life on screen

David Bissell

'Places are chosen to be gazed upon because there is anticipation, especially through daydreaming and fantasy, of intense pleasures,' wrote John Urry (1990, 3) in the introduction to *The Tourist Gaze*. This book took the intensities of pleasure seriously. So seriously that Urry warned readers early on that the book's topic might seem trivial to an academic world apparently possessed by weightier issues. Yet in this landmark text, Urry opened our eyes to a brand-new field of study. Fascinated by how places are fashioned, he helped us to reflect on why it is that we might be lured into travelling; why people 'might leave their normal place of work and residence' (1) for new sights; and why people might seek out experiences that touch them anew.

Developing his interest in the evolution of economic power that resonated with his earlier works, Urry was particularly interested in charting the rise of commodified tourist experiences, and how whole industries were increasingly being set up to create specific sorts of extra-ordinary experience. But he was also careful to situate these experiences historically. He detailed how the rise of the solitary 'romantic gazer', for instance, was an 'invented pleasure' (1990, 44) that emerged at a specific historical moment. Further denaturalising tourists' desire, Urry deftly showed how the tourist gaze is also culturally and technologically mediated, especially through visualisation technologies such as photography which he argued serves to reproduce specific ways of seeing.

As processes of globalisation intensified, Urry's ideas about mobility developed in tandem with a revolution in digital communications. The rise of the internet and mobile phones during the latter part of the 1990s was to change the way that people sensed places, changing the contours of distance and proximity, thereby reconfiguring the tourist gaze. These themes were centre-stage in *Sociology beyond Societies*, where Urry clarified that communications are not just about connecting people, as other scholars had previously implied, but crucially, they are about moving people. Through the term 'virtual mobility', Urry captured the way that technological developments mean that we do not necessarily have to leave our places of work and residence to travel. As he describes, 'it becomes possible to sense the other, almost dwell with the other, without physically moving either oneself or without moving physical objects' (2000, 70).

But what might it be to dwell with the other, without physically moving oneself? At this moment in his writing, Urry's analysis focused on how novel methods of communication at a distance, especially through the rise of virtual online communities, gave rise to new forms of spatial inequality. However, this chapter responds to the question by considering how virtual and imaginative forms of mobility can transform our sense of proximity, drawing on some of Urry's key writings on this concept. It is punctuated by four personal sketches which are intended to resonate with the themes of the essay.

His gaze follows the lines that form the shape of a scene that is firmly grooved into his everyday habits. The pleasing sweep of two sets of railway tracks mirrored above by the delicate mesh of suspended overhead wires. These sets of lines travel and then join at a point in the background, and become the outline of the mountain that rises behind where gnarled rock faces are crowned by snow. This distant webcam is a window onto the mountain and a wormhole to another world. The image is still, but you can click to refresh the scene if you want. It's a minute-by-minute, real-time, slow-motion film, where differences between the scenes creates the action. The train is there. Then it isn't. A woman in sunglasses is sitting on the bench. Then she is gone. In summer, the dark green umbrellas and red and white chequered tablecloths are there. The alpine meadows are a blaze of green and shadows are short. In winter, the rows of wooden benches are there. The snow softens the distinctions between platform and meadow; meadow and mountain. The time-difference between the location of the webcam and where he is means that during the day, mostly he sees two red lights that pierce the darkness, until the flat silhouette of the mountain is offset by the pastel tones of dawn.

'Both the virtual and changing forms of physical travel will transform the very nature and need for co-presence,' wrote Urry, a few years later (2002, 266). As the revolution in communications through internet and mobile telephony continued apace, Urry was increasingly preoccupied with the question of why, exactly, travel still happens. He sought to understand the curious situation of why physical travel was continuing to rise in parallel with the rise of virtual travel. His response was people's need for proximity. Urry explained that people need to be in proximity to each other to develop 'tight social worlds' (261). Given the importance of 'co-present interaction' to social life, Urry explained that 'virtual travel will not significantly replace physical travel' (259).

Accordingly, in writing at this time, he was increasingly interested in the phenomenon of meetings. Here he drew on Simmel's work to emphasise the importance of eye contact in face-to-face interaction. His point was that 'eye contact enables the establishment of intimacy and trust' (2002, 259), because it is the most direct form of reciprocity. Expanding his object of analysis away from just the mobility of tourists, here he became particularly interested in mobilities associated with work. But even with this shift of field, focusing on something ostensibly hard-nosed and utilitarian, he continued to emphasise the rich, 'multi-functional' nature of these encounters. Meetings might involve 'reinforcing friendship as well as distance, judging commitment, having an enjoyable time and so on' (259). For him, this was evidence that mobility was crucial to the formation of social capital. Although he was adamant that travel is never an end in itself, we can see how the pleasures of proximity continued to play an important role in his analysis of increasingly mobile worlds.

Yet proximity was also being transformed by the imaginative mobilities of screens. 'Distant events, personalities and happenings are mundanely brought into the living room and transform everyday life' (2000, 69). For him, images on screen give rise to what he calls 'imaginative' mobilities. Necessarily making his observations before the rise of online video streaming, where virtual mobilities in Urry's analysis are mainly about technologies of communication such as phones and computers, it is images on television screens that are the primary conduits of imaginative mobility.

Against a sociology focused mainly on propinquity, Urry showed that there are many forms of 'imagined presence'. Screens loop us into distant places. Through images on screens we are at those places. As Urry pointed out, 'these events are part of our lives' (2000, 67), as we are 'thrown into the public world' (68). This voyeurism blurs the public and the private spheres to create a kind of 'para-social interaction' (69) which creates striking new and crumpled topologies. It is this para-social interaction that creates a distinctive sense of community. As Urry explained, as a consequence of images on screens, 'we imagine ourselves sharing events, experiences and personalities with many others, with whom we constitute certain kinds of community' (69).

Imagination for Urry is about a sense of being affected by the others, and the various ways that the other takes hold of us and grooves into our being. It is the imaginative capacity of images that move us, sparking all kinds of backward-tracing connections, daydreams and fantasies. Imagination is therefore not a discrete form of mobility, but about being transported elsewhere by images and people. In this sense, imagination is an integral dynamic of the experience of mobility. As he put it, 'the relations of co-presence always involve nearness *and* farness, proximity *and* distance, solidity *and* imagination' (2002, 266).

Have you seen this? He remembers his father emailing him over ten years ago with the webcam hyperlink. His father would often share hyperlinks with him. Short messages with things that had piqued his interest at this moment; mostly links to music and webcams. They used to come to this place in summer on family holidays, camping trips to the town in the valley, the four of them together. These were halcyon days where time has smoothed the more jagged edges from their collective memories. Picnics of Emmentaler and ham in kaiser rolls with chewy Landjägers, all cut with a Swiss army knife. On the last visit, he remembers that they had talked about Stravinsky's Petrushka for a college project, humming lines together. These lines wove a path to the mountain station in the webcam. Since then, phone talk often seems to drift back to this scene. Sometimes, difficult conversations about things that have cut them up become lightened by something that one of them has noticed. Once, a low chain fence got put up along the side of the railway track. Have you seen what they've done? I can't believe it! You must look!

'A body's corporeal location is less relevant in these networks of person–person communication, communication that will be increasingly visual and hence may foster a kind of virtual "telepresence"' (2002, 267), wrote Urry. Given the role of mobility to social capital and preventing social exclusion, Urry was interested in whether virtual mobility could bring about at least some of the characteristics of co-presence. His answer was that virtual mobility made the concept of proximity much more complex, especially in light of new technologies at the time such as videoconferencing that enabled people to actually see each other at a distance. As ever, Urry's reflections on these nascent video-based technologies were prescient, given the current prevalence of camera-based mobile technologies that allow people to see each other whilst talking. He explained that 'virtual travel produces a kind of strange and uncanny life on the screen, a life that is near and far, present and absent, live and dead' (267). This is significant because the kinds of 'presencing involved will change the character and experience of "co-presence", since people can feel proximate while still distant' (267).

It is this complex folding of absence and presence that Urry found particularly fascinating about how mobility was changing the nature of social connections. His thinking on the matter was influenced by his interest in complexity theories as a way of understanding distanced relationships. Where complexity theories led to his interest in networks and fluids as apt metaphors for describing globalised processes, complexity theories also appreciated how multiple diverse elements could be held together in tension rather than be analytically resolved one way or the other. As such, rather than analysing relationships through more traditional social science dichotomies, such as absence or presence, Urry understood that all relationships are better grasped through their diversity of connections. As Urry pointed out, 'social relationships always involve diverse "connections", which are more or less at a distance, more or less intense, and more or less mobile' (2004, 28).

Strange new qualities of co-presence might happen in certain situations. Urry described this sense of connection with striking acuity. He said:

> It may be that there will be other contexts where temporal coordination is achieved between two or more people who are not in 'embodied presence', contexts where the screen provides a co-presence that temporally links people engaged in the same event and enables a kind of conversation, between them but not without bodily co-presence. (33)

These are nothing less than new spaces, 'new social topologies', as he put it, 'with people both here and there, present and absent' (2004, 34). For him, this is fire-like; a strange '"flickering" combination of presence and absence … both here and there, both inside and outside, rather like a Möbius strip' (34). Magical, almost.

> Look at the webcam now! He remembers his father texting him, a year or so after they'd discovered it. Striking out on a new path, his father had driven on his own one summer to stay at the town in the valley. At home, he remembers turning the computer on, waiting for the dial-up connection, and opening the webcam page. The image filled the top left part of the screen. There he was! A little grainy, but it was definitely him, in a green polo shirt and dark red shorts, standing the other side of the railway tracks. The way he stood was instantly recognisable. He texted his father back. Can you stand a little closer to the overhead mast? He waited and refreshed the page. His figure jumped a few metres to the right, head down with phone in his hands. He waited and refreshed the page again, this time he was looking at him. His hand was raised, waving. Even though he knew that his father couldn't see, he raised his hand and waved back. He refreshed the page again, he had jumped to the left again, standing facing the mountain. His head was down this time. He refreshed the page again. This time he was gone.

'To live a mobile life is, to be sure, a mixed blessing,' wrote Urry with Anthony Elliott in *Mobile Lives* (2010). Two decades after the publication of *The Tourist Gaze*, Urry's thinking on mobility developed an even greater sensitivity to the complex qualities of the embodied experiences of mobility. A revised third version of *The Tourist Gaze* with Jonas Larsen sought to remedy some of the criticisms that had been levelled at previous versions that suggested that the idea of the 'gaze' was too occularcentric and came at the expense of other modes of bodily experience. Accordingly, and reflecting growing social science interest in the complexities of bodily experience, the new version was much more concerned with the embodied, performative nature of mobility.

Where the updated version of *The Tourist Gaze* sought to address the complexity of embodied experiences of leisure travellers, *Mobile Lives* explored the complexity of personal intimacy at a distance from the perspective of families where one family member is working 'away' from home, often for long periods of time. This collaboration provided Urry's perhaps most intimate and emotionally complex account of mobility. Here, the more abstract systems and network analysis that had become such a hallmark of his thinking after *Sociology beyond Societies* was supplemented by a much more intimate style of analysis which explored how close personal relationships are stretched by distance. The premise here was that emotional dimensions are often overlooked in social theories that have focused on analysing the shape of networks or connections, rather than the intensities of emotional experience.

Elliott and Urry explored the possibilities for intimacy at a distance, or 'mobile intimacies' (2010, 85), as they put it. Echoing Urry's previous writing on the complexities of connections, here together they showed how the emotional dimensions of being together apart involve a curious torsion of absence and presence. Zooming in on the mundane everyday practices of people who live together apart allowed them to explore the kinds of practices that people separated by distance develop to connect with each other. Crucially, this might not be just about conventional modes of connecting, such as through talk or text. Instead they described how 'mobile intimacy revolves around diverse contingencies and coincidences' (101). They explained how people living together engage in all kinds of experiments to sense each other's presence, finding new ways of being close to someone. This way, 'people can be near, in touch and together, even when great distances tear them physically apart' (100).

> Together apart, they still visit the mountain. Separated by over ten thousand miles, they rarely see each other in person. A few snatched precious days where the thrill of being together is both intensified and threatened by imminent departure. He is there and then he is gone. Back home, weeks, even months go by without looking at the webcam, but then he

Figure 7.1 Bahnhof Kleine Scheidegg Webcam, 11:30 CET, Wednesday, 10 January 2018.
Source: reproduced with kind permission from Jungfraubahnen Management AG

remembers it, and is drawn back to it. He sometimes saves an image on a day where the scene touches him in an unexpected way. Lives lived in a meantime of hurt and loss; of sparkle and euphoria. Amidst the tumult that endlessly weaves personal melodrama with worldly tragedy, this place endures. As he looks, every scene is contained virtually in this present one. This density of memory inflates the richness and depth of this scene as it is felt now. Each scene resonates together. His father's figure of years ago still stands waving by the overhead mast. Their eyes follow the lines that form the shape of a scene. They visit this place, apart together.

References

Elliott, A. and Urry, J. (2010) *Mobile Lives*. London: Routledge.

Urry, J. (1990) *The Tourist Gaze*. London: Sage.

Urry, J. (2000) *Sociology beyond Societies: Mobilities for the Twenty-First Century*. London: Routledge.

Urry, J. (2002) 'Mobility and Proximity', *Sociology*, 36(2), 255–274.

Urry, J. (2004) 'Connections', *Environment and Planning D: Society and Space*, 22(1), 27–37.

Chapter 8

Postcards from a city

Monica Degen

I have always divided my time between cities, most recently travelling between my adopted home in London and Barcelona, the town of my birth. In the last few years these visits have increased, as my father gets older and frailer. Switching cities within a two-hour flight, often unexpectedly following a call from hospital, has made me more receptive to the changes in character, or atmospheres, of these two great cities. As I try to make sense of the manifold sensations and experiences that embed me in these places, many of the themes discussed with John Urry during my PhD (1997–2001) come to the fore.

My aim in this short account is to explore some of the key themes that John developed in his work and which helped me figure out my own analysis of cities, namely the link between spatial, sensory and temporal politics. To help me with this endeavour I draw on the precious notebooks I still have from our supervisions. One of John's first tips to help figure out what my PhD was about was to ask: 'If you had to summarise your thesis on a postcard, what would you say?' So what follows are three different postcards from the neighbourhood of El Raval in Barcelona, the place I focused upon during my PhD research and which, since then, I have continued studying to understand the 'extraordinary array of "global" processes which appear to be redrawing the contours of contemporary social experience' (Urry 2000: 12).

El Raval 1997: the physical and symbolic process of urban redevelopment

Dear John,

I have been walking through various neighbourhoods in Barcelona to find a case study for my work. I think I found a place that would allow me to explore how space, politics and aesthetics – which I understand as sensory experiencing – are linked: El Raval. This area is situated in the 'Old City' of Barcelona, the historical city centre, the area most drastically redeveloped through the city's democratic resignification and Olympic renewal.

As I walk across its streets and observe the 'regeneration' of its spatial structure I witness a 'place at war' as some residents describe it, as the dark sound of bulldozers demolishing walls and the high-pitched grinding of cranes resonates across El Raval's narrow streets. The leftover walls indicate the lives that were inside these buildings, turning rooms into homes: the shadows of a bedframe, the bleached white indentations left by picture frames taken away. They are sensory clues to lives in these buildings but also temporal markers of bygone lifestyles and tastes. Watching and experiencing this process of destruction and reconstruction day to day exposes the deeply visceral nature of urban renewal and makes me want to understand in more detail the relevance of sensory experience in the making of urban life.

We are here in a neighbourhood that has been over centuries Barcelona's backstage – its original name signifying 'periphery'. Situated between the city's second and third Roman walls this had been in medieval ages an agricultural neighbourhood. Then, the north of the area started to house hospitals, monasteries and poor houses – providing shelter to those not wanted in the central city. In the 18th century the south of El Raval became, alongside the Poble Nou, one of Barcelona's first industrial neighbourhood. Hence, as factories started to expand, cheaply built working-class housing was constructed next to them to house the waves of internal Spanish migrants coming to work here. The harbour transformed the south of the neighbourhood in the late 18th century to Barcelona's most bohemian area, peopled by erotic sex businesses, theatres, cafes and 24-hour entertainment and led it to be infamously known as the 'Barrio Chino' – Barcelona's 'red light' district. El Raval became one of Europe's most densely inhabited areas. And over its existence, a range of urban planners from Cerda to the GATPAC group, the Catalan equivalent of Le Corbusier, tried to draw up plans to demolish and sanitise it. However, different events such as the Civil War stalled such a process. It is only since the advent of democracy that the neighbourhood has undergone a comprehensive urban renewal programme. Hence, the north is being transformed into a Cultural Quarter hosting Richard Meier's new Museum for Contemporary Art and its cloisters and charity homes are transformed into research centres and museums to resignify the area to create a 'destination' for a new public. The south is witnessing the construction of a major boulevard, the 'Rambla del Raval', which, in classic Hausmannian fashion, is cutting through its toughest and most impoverished streets.

Overall, one can observe a radical, spatial, material and sensory redesign of place which is aimed at giving El Raval a new identity and recoding the negative reputation it has had amongst the bourgeois population of Barcelona. At the moment it is clearly a time of change and transformation, the north now houses a big new square bordered by the pearl white Contemporary Art Museum used as a venue to stage cultural and public- and private-sponsored events such as design fairs and music concerts. The streets leading to the museum, the 'regeneration corridors', have also been redesigned, cleansed and refurbished: smoother, lighter and less oppressive, to attract visitors. New signage creates awareness of the new Cultural Quarter and guides visitors in.

Some of the local shops have put notices up, selling everything half-price and indicating their need to move 'because of the redesign of the neighbourhood'. Local estate agents are speculating with the rise of rents and properties.

It is interesting that the main changes and demolitions are happening in the core of the north and south of the neighbourhood, partly with the council's aim to 'air' the neighbourhood, creating new public spaces and places to meet for a new type of transient public: foreign visitors and the visiting middle classes, as well as investing heavily in the social infrastructures of El Raval. Thus, alongside the physical regeneration, one can observe a social regeneration as new sport centres, old people's homes and children's centres are inaugurated and landlords are being offered subsidies to refurbish their flats. Many of my interviewees, both residents and officials, point out the need for an intervention, due to the extreme degradation El Raval has suffered over the centuries. However, while officials talk about a conscious resignification of place to 'modernise it', 'opening up to the rest of the city' and 'invigorate its public life by bringing light into El Raval', locals feel that their neighbourhood has been consciously neglected by the city council over decades and are not happy with the sudden and quick pace of the regeneration which destabilises their sense of belonging as their immediate physical and social surroundings transform: 'this is not my neighbourhood anymore', one lady told me.

The implementation and experience of an urban regeneration project brings up questions of how the changes in the material environment are exercised through, and affect, everyday sensory experiences in contemporary cities. Thus, it highlights how 'agency is not a question of humans acting independently of objects in terms of their unique capacities to attribute meaning or to follow rules. Rather what are crucial are the ways in which the physical world and artefacts are sensuously experienced by humans' (Urry 2000: 14). Focusing on society as a hybrid construction between humans, materials and artefacts reveals complex and subtler notions of power that are implemented through the redesign of our cities which operate on a spatio-experiential level. Cities are human-made products, hence analysing their 'look and feel' reveals how material structures express and construct socio-political hierarchies and values.

El Raval 2012: 'trendification' and diversity

Dear John,

This year marks the 20-year anniversary since El Raval's regeneration started. Since I first examined this neighbourhood some unexpected changes have occurred that have led the regeneration process to develop to its own rhythms, rather than those predicted by official plans and discourses. Thus, while property speculation has certainly led to a rise of property prices and rents in the neighbourhood, gentrification has not followed the footsteps of the Anglo-Saxon model where middle-class residents replace the working-class ones. The regeneration processes have evolved, been redefined and altered by different types of mobility, diverse sensory constellations and complex spatial politics as 'places are economically, politically, and culturally produced through the multiple mobilities of people, but also of capital objects, signs and information moving at rapid, yet uneven speed across many borders' (Urry 2004: 205). Let me explain.

There is little doubt that spatially and physically the neighbourhood has been radically transformed, however only in parts. The spatial regeneration has radiated concentrically from the heart of the neighbourhood. Thus, the Cultural Quarter is now a buzzing area as universities have opened up next to the new cultural venues attracting a steady flow of students and visitors that mingle with office workers and locals. El Raval is now undeniably a fixed stop on the global tourist map. Its main museums attract healthy numbers of visitors and the neighbourhood receives over 21 million visitors a year. The MACBA and its square with its cream-coloured and smooth surfaces has become one of Europe's skateboarding hotspots featured on international websites and magazines – the rattling sound of rollerblades and its abrupt stop and go becoming a regular soundscape along El Raval's narrow streets. Indeed, one could argue that the strong visual impact that the newly designed places initially had has been engulfed, and somewhat dispersed, by the everyday activities of those using these spaces: 'local communities are places of consumption … part of the experience of many such places is that they are constituted as places which are consumed by various others, whose sights, noises, smells and touch can attract or repel' (Urry 2000: 141). This highlights how the other senses such as sounds, tactile experiences, odours and tastes always frame and mobilise an array of gazes. To be more concrete, the visuality of the MACBA is constantly reconfigured by the social rhythms and activities surrounding it, from organised institutional events such as concerts, to skaters using the ramps of the museum, or locals and tourists alike sitting on the museum's square eating their lunch and consuming the lively atmosphere or homeless people seeking shelter at nighttime in the weather-protected crevices and corners of the museum. However, when one walks away from the Cultural Quarter, and ventures deeper into the neighbourhood away from the 'regeneration corridors', a different, parallel world emerges where much of the still existing poverty becomes tangible. Here, houses can show an extreme level of dilapidation, the smell of urine and damp is persistent and open doors into stair cases and open windows allow an insight into housing facilities that are in need of repair. While the Rambla del Raval has created a new public space in the neighbourhood, it has not had the radiating 'healing' effect hoped for by its planners. And while new social facilities are certainly improving the life of its inhabitants, El Raval still has one of the lowest life expectancies in the city.

Two main forms of mobility have transformed the social set up of the neighbourhood: migration and 'cool' tourism. A diversity of migrant groups have led to an increase of non-Spanish residents, from around 5 per cent in 1996 to 50 per cent in 2012. Different ethnic groups, Filipino, Pakistani,

Moroccan and Algerian, have settled in distinctive parts of the neighbourhood and are replacing El Raval's former vulnerable population for a new one due to its relatively low rents and its possibilities for flat sharing. These newcomers are reconfiguring the public life of the streets with new spatial practices and sensory experiences. Simultaneously, many of the refurbished and expensive flats are let out to Erasmus students or rented through Airbnb to transient visitors. In terms of El Raval's public life, this means that a diversity of experiences can be encountered from one street to the next: halal shops are next to Asian grocery stores, international call centres and Moroccan bakeries: 'places are not fixed and unchanging but depend upon what gets performed within them by the "hosts" and especially by various kinds of "guests"' (Urry 2004: 205). At street level, along the regeneration corridors, one can describe a 'trendification' process, a change of shop ownership has taken place from old neighbourhood shops to a mixture of hipster, trendy shops, from organic cafes and restaurants, art galleries and design shops to a series of tattoo parlours, cocktail bars and skateboarding shops – many of them owned by north European migrants. Yet, overall, as various recent studies show, general poverty levels have not improved, which is evident when one looks up at the houses and sees the state of disrepair of many of the flats. Hence, El Raval is turning into a 'cool youthful place' (Sheller and Urry 2004) where guests and hosts revel in what is considered a more 'authentic experience' of Barcelona, away from mass tourism and the sun, sex and beach stereotypes, as this description from El Raval's Airbnb site attests:

> If the Gothic Quarter is Barcelona's tourist star, El Raval is the slightly shadowy figure on the sidelines. The neighborhood's edgy mix of art, attitude, and street life attracts cosmopolitan crowds. Once famous for its debauched nightlife scene, El Raval is gradually being converted into a cultural hub as its cabaret houses transform into forward-thinking museums. El Raval's character is constantly defined and redefined by the people who call it home, and its locals celebrate their neighbourhood's against-the-grain nature. When you're in El Raval, revel as its inhabitants do. (Airbnb website, accessed 5 May 2017)

One can buy postcards that represent its most emblematic spatial changes such as the MACBA and the new Rambla del Raval, a Hausmannian-style boulevard which cuts through the neighbourhood that different websites brand as a key neighbourhood to visit in Barcelona, often described as an attraction for its fashionable and bohemian character. Simultaneously, graffiti culture has taken over the neighbourhood and many of its walls and doors feature pieces by famous graffiti or urban art artists. Hence, in El Raval a transformed bohemian feel is emerging that attracts new types of 'cool' tourists that consume the new sensory atmospheres of place which have been constituted through a range of mobilities and global processes: 'bodies encounter other bodies, objects and the

physical world multi-sensuously ... Tourism always involves corporeal movement and forms of pleasure and these must be central in any sociology of
diverse tourisms' (Urry 2002: 152).

El Raval 2017: time and urban change

Dear John,

Believe it or not I am back in El Raval, this time to use it for a case study to
think about temporality, senses and the production of space. While I have
written over the years how regeneration is made effective through the organisation of sensory experiences and how the management of urban atmospheres
has become of crucial importance in the branding and consumption of a
regenerated neighbourhood like El Raval, I have forgotten to explore a key
aspect which frames the sensory-spatial politics of place, namely time.

As you point out 'a reconfigured sociology has to place time at its very
centre ... because of the way in which time has come to the academic agenda
criss-crossing disciplinary boundaries and offering opportunities for novel
intellectual developments' (Urry 2000: 105). This is particularly relevant for
processes of urban change which have had a tendency to focus on the spatial
implications rather than temporal ones. Indeed, few studies have actually 'followed' a regeneration project over a long time, and it is precisely such long-
itudinal studies of urban change which offer new insights into spatial politics, as
I will now argue.

Space and time lie at the centre of urban change, as David Harvey (1989)
reminds us. The urban environment solidifies the passing of time, revealing
through its materiality investments trends and political and social interests.
Urban planning can be understood as a deeply temporal activity: it works on
the present in order to manage the future. Following the development of El
Raval over time has allowed me to observe how 'global processes' such as
regeneration projects which tend to follow a similar pattern of design, aesthetics
and planning get digested over time through a range of mobilities (people,
images, trends, etc.) in a variety of ways through the local, as I discussed in my last
postcard. Thus, the linear chrono-logical logic of urban regeneration discourses is
revealed as a much more dynamic and fragile process.

The lens of time also allows us to understand how different technologies
reconfigure places in new ways and how 'new technologies appear to be generating new kinds of time which dramatically transform the opportunities for,
and constraints upon, the mobilities of peoples, information and time' (Urry
2000: 105). Informal chats with skaters, tourists and hipsters in El Raval in
recent years reveal that awareness of the neighbourhood is gained through
social media or word of mouth, thus bypassing traditional media or tourist
outlets. For example, the MACBA is used as a backdrop for photoshoots to be
posted on Instagram or Snapchat or videos that are uploaded onto Facebook.
Thus, when looking up El Raval hashtags on Instagram, particular atmospheres

are displayed that capture specific moments, places and activities, thereby emphasising mostly the temporal contrasts between old and new buildings: traditional forms of urban sociability such as cups of coffee or food; captions of public life frozen against the background of urban art or graffiti. The use of Instagram allows for the reassembling of the neighbourhood as a collage of particular experiences, mostly excluding its less attractive and impoverished parts, and provides new users of the city an already prescribed path of experience, 'a set of personalised, subjective temporalities which are self-generated and involve "life-calendars" focused around non-work or leisure identities' (Urry 1994: 137).

A focus on time further exposes how diverse users of the city such as residents, visitors or tourists create a variety of temporal dynamics. Their daily practices create particular rhythms that might characterise a neighbourhood or provide a sense of place: the opening and closing of shop shutters, the voices of children at school break, the familiar song of the news at 3pm and 9pm indicating lunch and dinner time. Long-term engagements with these rhythms produce a sense of belonging, they are the familiar sensory cycles of a neighbourhood, the street ballet that Jane Jacobs famously described as grounding our sense of place. I mentioned in an earlier postcard that the spatial and temporal changes that urban development can foster have a tendency to disrupt people's sense of self and place attachments. This undoubtedly happened in El Raval. However, more recently there is a further disruption that locals are strongly opposed to: the noise of rolling suitcases when tourists arrive, which has become a dreaded sound in many neighbourhoods in Barcelona such as El Raval.

While Barcelona has successfully repositioned itself as a global tourist destination, attracting 32 million tourists in 2016, an increasing local opposition has developed. While until recently the city council heavily relied on 'the postcard city' and eagerly increased hotels and restaurant and cafe licences, locals felt that 'their city' was being overrun. As the current left-wing mayor Colau has explained, due to tourism, the 'way of life for all Barcelonians is seriously under threat' (2014) and her government is currently imposing a range of measures to 'regulate' tourism in the city. In terms of thinking through tourism as an embodied and temporal experience, it is interesting that many of the contestations between hosts and guests debated in local newspapers were around the clashing of urban practices and sensory experiences (as well as blaming the rapid expansion of tourist flats as the culprits for the high rental prices in Barcelona). Thus, many emblematic public places in the city, from the famous Ramblas to the square of the gothic cathedral or the streets surrounding the Sagrada Familia, have become 'no-go areas for locals' as it is felt that expensive cafes, tourist shops and crowds of tourists are colonising these spaces, transforming them into 'places of excess', overriding local uses and practices: 'corporeal travel has … taken on immense dimensions and compromises the largest ever movement of people across national borders. Because of these liquidities the relations between almost all societies across the globe are mediated by flows of tourists, as place after place is reconfigured as a recipient of such flows' (Urry 2002: 141).

While this is not the last postcard to be written about a place such as El Raval, these three snapshots through the spatial, sensory and temporal dimensions of the regeneration of El Raval show that '[p]laces in advanced societies are never self-contained such that clear and distinct boundaries can be easily and unambiguously drawn. Rather, places should be viewed as social processes whose outcomes are not fixed or given' (Urry 1994: 146).

References

Colau, A. (2014) 'Mass tourism can kill a city – just ask Barcelona's residents', *Guardian*.

Harvey, D. (1989) *The Condition of Postmodernity*, Oxford: Blackwell.

Sheller, M. and J. Urry (2004) *Tourism Mobilities: Places to Play, Places in Play*, London: Routledge.

Urry, J. (1994) 'Time, Leisure and Social Identity', *Time and Society*, 3(2): 131–149.

Urry, J. (2000) *Sociology beyond Societies*, London: Routledge.

Urry, J. (2002) *The Tourist Gaze*, 2nd ed., London: SAGE.

Urry, J. (2004) 'Connections', *Environment and Planning D: Society and Space*, 22(1): 27–37.

Chapter 9

The sensory pleasures of the disoriented tourist

Tim Edensor

John Urry's focus on the tourist gaze (2012) marks a momentous shift away from singular, functionalist and extraordinarily ethnocentric theories about what tourists do, understand and feel. A key suggestion was that contemporary tourists typically anticipate visual encounters with cultural and natural sites upon which they subsequently gaze. This epitomizes a historically distinctive way of seeing, embedded within a particularly ocularcentric culture in which images proliferate.

The most prominent visual practice enacted by tourists, the romantic gaze, is inspired by historical constructions of the picturesque and the sublime. This has promoted the promiscuous photographing of scenes to produce images similar to those consumed beforehand in promotional media, creating what Urry calls a 'hermeneutic circle' (2012) within which similar images continually circulate. The emphasis on visual consumption led Urry to identify other distinctive forms, including the 'collective', 'spectatorial', 'environmental' and 'anthropological' gazes. In addition, other scholars itemized the 'mutual', 'humanitarian' and 'social-mediatized gaze'. A few years after *The Tourist Gaze* was first published in 1990, it was my enormous luck to undertake a PhD study with John, a kindly saviour who offered me the opportunity to work with him at Lancaster University, rescuing me from far less supportive doctoral study elsewhere. John's ideas continue to influence my research and significantly inspired what became my own published monograph, *Tourists at the Taj* (Edensor, 1998), and influenced my coining of two related terms: the 'reverential gaze' that accounted for the intense spiritual scrutiny of Muslim visitors towards the Quranic script carved into the site's stone walls, and the 'pharmacological gaze' that captured the drug-induced visual perceptions of the backpackers who had partaken of a glass of *bhang lassi*, a yoghurt drink laced with cannabis.

Though the visual is indeed integral to many tourist pursuits, along with others, I have come to think that tourism should be more broadly considered as multi-sensual in practice and experience; that the gaze is frequently subjugated by sonic, tactile and olfactory sensations. In the updated *Tourist Gaze 3.0*, Urry and Larsen respond to such critiques by acknowledging that the gaze is entangled with olfactory, sonic and tactile oral experiences. Yet there remains an insistence that the visual is the organizing sense amongst tourists, that by visually apprehending the surroundings in which experiences are to occur, all other sensations are contextualized. In my opinion, it seems misplaced to necessarily privilege the visual in this way, and I have explored a multitude of tourist practices through which highly diverse sensations are sought and experienced, though I continue to pursue Urry's crucial idea that tourism is a cultural arena in which the valuing and experiencing of sensations are fundamental. A quick review of diverse tourist practices underlines that there is no need to privilege the gaze, and that we can immediately identify a wealth of more-than-visual experiences. For instance, the beach holiday solicits experiences ranging from the warmth of the sun on skin to the tactile effects of waves upon the swimming body, and extensive walking and cycling demand muscular exertion, balance and an acceptance of pain and exhaustion. Moreover, I contend that the range and diversity of sensory experiences made available for tourists is expanding.

This increasing variety may partly emerge out of responses to intensifying contemporary efforts to regulate the social and sensory experience of space, maintain smooth mobile flows, declutter spaces and reproduce normative aesthetic order. Perhaps the prevalence of such regulatory strategies has instigated the pursuit of unfamiliar kinetic, aromatic, sonic and visual sensations by those dissatisfied with the sterile 'blandscapes' that eventuate. Yet despite this urge, and although influential accounts characterize tourism as moving from the quotidian towards the extraordinary, authentic or liminal, many common tourist experiences are replete with routine, unreflexive habits performed in serial resorts, themed spaces and enclaves (Edensor and Falconer, 2012). Such realms are sensually regulated to minimize disruption and provide a comfortable homeliness in which the body is cosseted into relaxation. Themed designs remove disturbing sights, incense and aromatic blooms waft through space, harsh sounds are purged and replaced by piped muzak, silken textures and air-conditioning enclose bodies, and smooth floors encourage seamless movement. Such locations satiate desires for reliability, comfort and unselfconscious relaxation, and encourage shared performative conventions of walking, lounging and consuming. While these spaces cater for the suspension of everyday stress and workday routines, they instantiate a new set of habits, reiterations and predictabilities.

However, in addition to these familiar, reliable sensory realms, numerous other tourist practices seem to strive to escape highly ordered space, seeking out visceral, enlivening pursuits in which sensory apprehension is challenged or intensified. The quest for immersive sensation is evident in action sports such as bungee jumping and white water rafting, the white-knuckle thrills sought at amusement parks and the somatically enlivening endeavours of hang-gliding, mountain biking and canoeing. Depicting a more sensorially radical engagement, Stephanie Merchant (2011) reveals how scuba divers learn new sensory skills, notably in developing very different ways of touching and hearing, since the senses that they usually rely upon are unreliable when underwater. Though this may be initially alarming and awkward, such sensations may be thrilling in their alterity. And in illustrating the sheer multi-sensory entanglements of certain tourist occasions, Arun Saldanha (2002) describes a Goan beach rave in which the sounds of music, smells of sweat, kerosene and cannabis combine with the sight of the moon and swaying coconut trees, the tactilities of moving bodies, sand underfoot and humidity. Such intense sensual experiences also provide a sensory alterity that significantly diverges from everyday apprehension.

A more sustained immersion in sensual otherness is also exemplified by forms of space in which backpackers temporarily dwell. Movement through the sensually rich, socially diverse, cluttered materialities of such 'heterogeneous' honeypots solicits encounters with rough textures, undulating pavements and dust. Noises emitted by machines, people and animals, the horrible and delicious smells that emanate from a market, and the disruptive tactilities provoked by dense crowds and uneven surfaces also offer unaccustomed sensory experiences. In seeking sensual otherness, tourists may welcome or recoil from these unfamiliar stimuli. For instance, at the start of their adventures through India and Thailand, many female backpackers did not want to be sheltered from harsh sensations, expecting and accepting repellent smells, dirt and noise. In demonstrating an ability to cope with such sensations, these young travellers developed self-pride and acquired cultural capital. Yet despite this disposition to embrace the sensually repugnant, over a longer period they developed a tendency to modulate sensory experience, moderating physical hardships and sensory onslaughts with visits to comfortable hotels and air-conditioned restaurants that served familiar food (Edensor and Falconer, 2012).

This example demonstrates how many tourists typically manage desires for both sensory familiarity and alterity in a single trip. Both forms of experience are considered to be differently desirable, underlining how the senses, rather than facilitating an unmediated encounter with reality, are mobilized and interpreted according to particular cultural values, a process that is underscored in *The Tourist Gaze* where tourist practices are profoundly shaped by situated cultures of looking. The cultural conventions through which we interpret what we sense veer from the cosmological to the moral, and from the aesthetic to the political, and vary enormously across time and space. Yet it is also vital to acknowledge that these interpretations of sensory experience are invariably entangled with the affordances of the world we encounter. As tourists, we tell stories about what we have encountered *after* an immanent, immersive sensory engagement with the world, even though we may well have arrived furnished with well-worn notions about how to look, touch and listen.

Accordingly, although tourists seek out specific sensorial qualities, movement through even the most regulated realms cannot always preclude the surprising, the contingent and the unexpected. Such irruptions of sensory alterity cannot be anticipated. When they emerge during tourist experiences, they may be frightening and disturbing, but equally, may be welcomed as memorable, and narrated after the event as momentous. In this way, our phenomenological experiences of the sensory world are thoroughly intertwined with the meanings we bestow on our encounter with the currents and energies of a world-in-formation, with the affordances of the sites and spaces we gaze upon, move through, smell, hear and touch. Furthermore, we cannot escape from the ways in which our distinctively human sensorium apprehends how light falls upon landscape, negotiates the undulations on the surface of the ground, receives the sound channelled by buildings and landforms, and smells the scent of leaf mould or perfume. Sensation is thus biologically shaped, culturally conditioned and subject to more-than-human agencies all at the same time.

I now underline the sheer diversity of the sensations offered in the diverse and complex arena of contemporary tourism, by exploring how the desires for sensory comfort and alterity play out during a visit to a distinctive tourist attraction in Queenstown, South Island, New Zealand. This exploration into the more peculiar sensory experiences of tourism can, of course, be traced back to John Urry's original focus on the sense of the visual in *The Tourist Gaze* and is intended to honour the provident insights that emerged from that seminal work. I explore how the sensations experienced at this venue further interrogate the privileging of the gaze and reveal the limits of subsequent attempts to make sense of and transmit stories about what happened. For though this is a highly managed and regulated space, it offers a range of sensations that seem even more unanticipated and indescribable than the sensory thrills delivered by thrill rides and adventure sports.

Queenstown, commonly advertised as the 'adrenaline capital of the world', is a tourist honeypot that attracts large numbers of young people intent on participating in a vast array of adventure sports staged within the scenic environs of mountains, lakes and valleys. The *Fear Factory*, however, is not an adventure tourism site; it is promoted as a haunted house through which visitors follow a labyrinthine route along narrow wooden corridors in complete darkness, guided only by a small, dim red light at ceiling height. I have written elsewhere about the ways in which darkness has been reviled in Christian and Enlightenment discourses (Edensor, 2017), conceived as a condition conducive to devilry, deviance, danger and ignorance, but it has also been actively sought for its positive qualities. I have underlined its ambiguity by foregrounding the potentialities that darkness may offer, focusing on the enhanced conviviality, heightened non-visual sensations, interaction with the landscape and imagination that can be solicited by various encounters with gloom and complete blackness. In offering pleasures for tourists, darkness has been deployed as an integral part of the appeal of diverse attractions. For instance, London's 18th-century pleasure park, Vauxhall Gardens, featured a dark walk where illicit liaisons, convivial encounters, mystery and manifold sensations could unfold. Fairgrounds, later sites of mass leisure, deployed darkness to accentuate carnival thrills, with tunnels of love permitting close physical contact that was otherwise subject to social disapproval, and most closely akin to the *Fear Factory*, ghost trains produced a ride along a dark, twisting track with sporadic encounters with whistles and hooters, air blowers, cobwebs, opening coffins, springing ghouls and optical illusions. Subsequently, more recent dark attractions have focused less on these titillating impulses and sought to encourage sensual pleasures of a walk in a dark-sky park, passage through simulated urban spaces of renown, and theatrical and musical experiences staged in the pitch black. However, chiming with pervasive, persistent fears of darkness that are capitalized on by the ghost train and the horror movie, the *Fear Factory* offers an intense, hilarious and pleasurably managed form of dread.

Visitors walk up the stairs of a rather non-descript building located in the centre of Queenstown, arriving in a gloomy reception area. After paying, our party of three were instructed to wait outside a red door and prepare for the light to turn green so that we could enter. Once this occurred, we entered the door and instantly pressed a button to dim the lights and install complete darkness except for the small red illuminated dot that we followed along the sequence of twisting corridors, gingerly feeling the sides as we went. Advised to hold on to each other as we haltingly made our way along the route, tense hands gripped shoulders or midriffs. Right from the start, as we were plunged into darkness, very loud, sharp explosions frightened us into an attentive wariness. Very soon, the utter blackness was interrupted by the hideous faces of clowns, horned devils and beasts, visages that unexpectedly appeared inches away and which continued to intermittently materialize for the duration of the journey, flashing into view and immediately disappearing. Lamentations from

Figure 9.1

unseen presences, whispers that entered the ear from very close by, along with creaks and clanks constituted a shocking soundscape. These wails and soft entreaties were supplemented by hands touching fingers, grasping at feet and brushing across hair and ears, generating an enhanced tactile awareness that was intensified by suddenly uneven and unstable flooring, strands of wispy hanging material and mild electric shocks that further befuddled the body. The frenzy of shocks that continuously confronted passage through these pitch-black channels fostered a giddy delirium, with infectious laughter and shrieks producing an intensely communal experience. Finally, we blundered through a door, blinking into the light as we arrived back at the point of entry, suffused with relief that the surprises were at an end, and utterly confounded about the length of time and distance, or the number of people who had tormented us in the gloomy corridors. But we had made it to the end, unlike the one in seven visitors who supposedly chicken out and never make it to the finish.

This powerful experience of the *Fear Factory* raises three issues that I now discuss in the light of my focus on tourism and the senses. First, in drawing attention to visual apprehension, the attraction offers a highly distinctive mode of looking, which is wholly divergent from most forms of tourist gaze but nevertheless supplements the diverse forms of looking identified by John Urry and others. For most of the time, we are plunged into complete darkness but do not see nothing, rather, we perceive an enveloping blackness in which we persistently strain to ascertain anything identifiable. The boundaries of the body are indistinguishable from the surroundings and make impossible the archetypally omniscient gaze of the individual tourist detached from the landscape. Yet we cannot but imagine the characteristics of the place that we are in but cannot see, construing mental pictures to cope with the opacity and to make sense of the sonic and tactile sensations. In addition to this imaginative 'seeing', a journey through the *Fear Factory* does foster a particular experience of the visible: very brief flashes of light that illuminate an adjacent scene of monstrosity or, more alarmingly, a grotesque countenance inches from one's face. This cannot be subject to a gaze but is sensed via a *glimpse*. Here we are in a realm where we can only see others momentarily, but these others are able to see us. Indeed, this limited visual perception is integral to the success of the *Fear Factory* in which the actors create instantaneous impressions that provoke shock and surprise but importantly deny critical visual scrutiny.

Second, as with other experiences with deep darkness, the non-visual senses are foregrounded, and are equally integral to the journey. As is evident from the above description, sonic eruptions are overwhelming and acutely sensed in the absence of vision, while electric shocks and the tactile intrusions of unknown others supplement the grips and clutches between companions, and the feel of the smooth wooden corridor walls provide some orientation. Unlike my previous account of another tourist attraction, *Dialogue in the Dark*, where a guide that we had not seen gently steered us through various simulated spaces of Manhattan in the pitch black to minimize disorientation and combat fear, the presence of these other unseen persons was far from reassuring. In fact, discussions about the ways in which light and darkness are sensed and conceived are extremely paltry not only in tourist studies, but across the social sciences. Stimulated by John Urry's focus on the sensing of tourist space, place and landscape, I have explored a range of practices that take place in various degrees of darkness, including dining, concerts, dark sky parks and cycling, and investigated the effects of illumination at light festivals and exhibitions (Edensor, 2017). The experiences solicited during these adventures reveals the sheer multiplicity of sensory effects generated by gloom and light, but also indicates how tourism is an excellent field in which to explore the cultural and phenomenological ways in which proliferating tourist venues and experiences may expand the human sensorium.

Third, as I have emphasized, most meaning-making processes in tourism take place after the event: the sensing of places, scenes, food, people and non-humans precede the articulation and representation of the experience. Following John Urry's identification of the hermeneutic circle, tourists anticipate what they will do and see, capture the experience through photography (or increasingly, travel blogs) and narrate the experience according to discursive and representational conventions. Such travel stories tend to excise most of the immanent experiences that often emerge – the moments of discomfort and social unease, unexpected sights and inexplicable events. In the more immersive, transitory pursuits of adventure sports and thrill rides, the intense sensory excitations, though disorientating at the time, are nevertheless explicable and can be recaptured in the retelling.

What is striking about the experience of the *Fear Factory* is that these usual lineaments are unavailable. We had no idea of what to expect other than that we would be entering a dark space and that actors would attempt to frighten us. Once inside the pitch black, winding corridors, the route could only be followed by focusing upon the dim red light, with no other cues. As such, there was nothing to prepare us for the experiences that were to unfold, instances that seemed completely random and could not be dwelt upon because we were compelled to keep moving towards the end of the passage and because their impact was obliterated by the next intrusion. Because of the sudden immediacy of each engagement – whether with ghoulish face, touch or whisper – it was difficult to focus on what was happening or brace ourselves for the next intervention. In this multi-sensory whirl, the high level of disorientation meant that it was difficult to pin down impressions or even remember them. Following the event, and after the surge of hilarity and relief, the experience was difficult to recapture or relate, and it has been difficult to agree amongst us on what unfolded. Given the darkness and suddenness of the interruptions, there was no possibility of photographically recording the events, although three photographs are made available upon arriving back at the reception desk, taken at points beyond recollection. This is what remains of my experience: photographs of a man adopting increasingly fearful expressions.

This adds to the extraordinary qualities of the experience in generating pleasures that are certainly related to the popular cultural titillations of the horror film and scary ride but also offer a thorough disorienting of the ability to make sense of time and space.

References

Edensor, T. (1998) *Tourists at the Taj*, London: Routledge.

Edensor, T. (2017) *From Light to Dark: Daylight, Illumination and Gloom*, Minneapolis, MN: Minnesota University Press.

Edensor, T. and Falconer, E. (2012) 'The Sensuous Geographies of Tourism', in J. Wilson (ed.), *New Perspectives in Tourism Geographies*, London: Routledge.

Merchant, S. (2011) 'Negotiating Underwater Space: The Sensorium, the Body and the Practice of Scuba-Diving', *Tourist Studies*, 11(3): 215–234.

Saldanha, A. (2002) 'Music Tourism and Factions of Bodies in Goa', *Tourist Studies*, 2(1): 43–62.

Urry, J. and Larsen, J. (2012) *The Tourist Gaze 3.0*, London: SAGE.

Chapter 10

Some personal reflections on the social production of multiple natures

Phil Macnaghten

I first met John Urry at a job interview in 1992. I had just completed a PhD in social psychology at Exeter University and had little idea what to do next. Even though my PhD – loosely a critical discourse analysis of the rhetorical power of multiple constructions of nature carried out in a psychology department – had been both rewarding and productive, by then I was dissatisfied with the impasse that existed between the twin camps of critical/discursive psychology locked in battle with the rigidities of methodologically individualist cognitivist social psychology. To my mind this debate appeared both inward-looking and regressive with little to say about the fundamental societal challenges of the day. As a passionate and politically active environmentalist I was searching for something more engaging to spend my limited time on planet earth. I remember reading the job advert written by John and thinking along the following lines, 'if I knew my mind and was able to write this is exactly what I would say and how I would say it'. The job itself was linked to John's then passion for tourism, a couple of years following his seminal *The Tourist Gaze*, and would have been focused on an ethnographic study of tourists in the Lake District in the north west of England.

Even though I was unsuccessful at the job interview I must have made an impression as I was offered a post at Lancaster University's newly formed Centre for the Study of Environmental Change, working on a project called *Leisure Landscapes* for the environmental non-governmental organization, the Council for the Protection of Rural England (Clark et al. 1994). John and I worked closely on the project for the best part of two years. We worked at the more sociological end, seeking to understand conflicts in the countryside as part of tensions with hyper-/post-modernity. We viewed current conflicts over heritage, the countryside and tourism as part of a complex set of trends in modern society, which John characterized in terms of a visualization of culture, a collapse of stable identity and a compression of time and space. I remember at the time being mesmerized by John's capacity to link empirical research (some of which I was responsible for) with state-of-the-art social theory.

Following *Leisure Landscapes* I was awarded a British Academy postdoctoral fellowship on 'The cultural invention of British environmentalism', a rare and glorious award with three years' funding and the absolute minimum of bureaucratic oversight. By then, as a mentor and friend, John and I took this opportunity to develop a solid writing partnership. Our first major venture was a co-authored article published in the journal *Sociology*, 'Towards a sociology of the environment' (Macnaghten and Urry 1995). John was understandably bored with the debate that was taking place within the burgeoning environmental sociology community between realist and constructivist approaches and wanted to make it more interesting. I concurred. Following John's dictum that everything one writes should be either 'the first', 'the last' or 'the best', we set out a paradigmatic sketch of our vision of a more interesting sociology of the environment. We argue in the paper that sociology thus far had made only a modest contribution to the examination of environmental change (to our minds it had been unduly captured by economists and natural scientists) and set out what a more full-blooded sociological engagement could look like. Characteristically sweeping, John focuses on the pedigree of sociological thought, which had presumed a preoccupation with the domain of society, rendering *ultra vires* a focus on the domain of nature (and the environment) due to a tacit division of labour demarcated between social facts versus natural facts, the latter of which had been given uncritically to the natural scientists. This we term the 'Biology First' model, where the modest role of the social scientist is that of 'addressing the social impacts and implications *of* environmental problems, which had been initially and accurately described by the natural scientist' (Macnaghten and Urry 1995: 204; italics in original). It was this framing that we wished to critique not least because of its hegemonic status, as for instance embedded in major international research programmes on environmental change, and because of its instrumentalist ramifications, in effect reducing the role of the social scientist to that of the social engineer, 'manipulating and "fixing" society to aid in the implementation of a "sustainable" society' (Macnaghten and Urry 1995: 204).

In its place, we claim that there is a whole lot of history in the idea of nature; indeed, following Raymond Williams, we argue that nature is not only perhaps the most complicated word in the English language but also linked to many of the key concepts underpinning Western thought. Following a short historical journey into key transformations in the idea of nature (and naturalness), and of how current versions of environmentalism are a product of these transformations, we then sketch out what we termed 'a tentative agenda for a critical, engaging, and reflexive sociology of the environment' (Macnaghten and Urry 1995: 208). First, we speak of the need for a 'sociology of environmental knowledges', exploring how dominant realist policy formulations, with their focus primarily on nature as setting limits as defined by science, are accompanied typically with a disciplinary and restrictive politics characteristically implemented with a series of don'ts or do less. In its place we set out an agenda that would examine the co-construction of science with societal and political order and forms of life, building on insights from what had been labelled the sociology of scientific knowledge. Next we call for research on 'reading natures sociologically' that would illuminate the socially varied ways in which an environment can be evaluated, alongside an analysis of the social practices (and associated cultural resources) that have facilitated the social reading of the physical world as environmentally damaged. Third, we call for research on the social processes that are currently theorized in sociology (such as consumerism, tourism and globalization) but rarely analysed in terms of their environmental implications. And finally, we ask how sociology could contribute to the understanding of the role that the environmental agenda is playing in the structural formation and cultural transformation of contemporary society. To conclude we argue that the tasks associated with a sociological approach to the environment are both complex and wide-ranging, and embrace many of the issues currently being addressed in sociological inquiry, ranging from questions of political economy and the state, to science, culture, deviance, new social movements and the 'other'.

A couple of years later we were given the opportunity to develop a full book-length treatment of the argument in what became the monograph *Contested Natures* (Macnaghten and Urry 1998). The process of writing the book was typically John, involving a sublime mix of his three key passions: tennis, food and writing. On a typical afternoon throughout the summer of 1997 we would play a highly competitive game of tennis involving at least three sets on a local tennis court adjacent to where I lived in Dolphinholme. John was technically superior but at the time I was more nimble and energetic so we were relatively equally matched (although John typically got the better of me by the close of the game). Then we would frequent a nice bar/restaurant within a 10-mile radius where we would discuss over food one of our chapters. The manuscript itself was completed in the space of a few months. Each of my chapters took at least three weeks to draft while John managed to ease out his in what appeared to be the duration of a few days. Each of mine required endless redrafting while John, having been brought up prior to the days of word processing, managed to produce near perfect drafts at the first attempt. Mine were focused on empirical research that I had been working on over the previous few years while John's were more theoretically driven, albeit informed by large data sets. John, in addition, had the remarkable ability of working with my ideas, of making them more interesting, more crafted, better written and more grounded in current sociological debates.

John was immersed at the time in debates on time, the senses and space, and managed to use these as guiding concepts to frame three of the chapters on which he was lead author. In the chapter on *Sensing Nature*, John investigates the role of the different senses in our knowledge and appreciation of nature, leading to what he considered a more embodied understanding of our relationship to nature. His treatment of the visual was John at his most majestic as he ranged from philosophy, social theory, literary criticism, theology, travel writing, photography and gender studies. The chapter itself contained a number of gems. My personal favourites include the ways he was able to integrate a diverse array of thinkers that ranged from Aristotle, Descartes, Marx, Heidegger, Rorty, Foucault, Berger, Derrida, Novak, Jay and Adler into a unifying narrative to illustrate the primacy of the eye in philosophical and social thought; his analysis of how visual imagery around the sun, moon, the stars, mirrors, night and day and so on have helped make sense of both the sacred (often in the association of naturalness and Godliness) and the profane; his analysis of the historical idea of landscape as (tamed) places to be visually consumed; his account of the 'spectacularization' of nature especially through the visual discourse of the sublime wonderfully illustrated through his beloved Lake District; and the importance of photography (and also of the practice of mapping) as producing various (static) cultures of nature and dominant visual gazes and then into a modality of surveillance and discipline. Rereading the chapter today, the reader gets a sense of how enjoyable it must have been to write and how energizing and innovative it is to read. Indeed, one gets the sense that a whole gamut of points and perspectives contained within the chapter could be (and in many cases have been) developed into domains of inquiry in their own right.

John's subsequent chapter on time is similarly far-reaching. Clearly influenced by the writing of Barbara Adam, John develops a path-breaking analysis of the ways in which time has been configured in the sociological canon as social, and hence separate from and opposed to the realm of nature. This includes a detailed account of clock time as a central feature of industrial capitalism, of time as money, of time becoming a resource differentiated from social space, of how much social conflict has been traditionally structured around clock time, and of the processes of time-space compression in late modern societies. John then moves to an analysis of how nature is intrinsically temporal and of the different times in and of nature. He focuses on two simultaneous and apparently contradictory dynamics: on how time is both speeding up (through in particular communication and media technologies contributing to what John termed 'instantaneous' time) and at the same time slowing down (contributing to what John termed 'glacial' or geological time associated with new sensitivities to the rhythms of the earth or what would now be termed the 'Anthropocene'). These twin dynamics, both of which are a move away from traditional clock time, are seen as presenting complex challenges for environmental policy, citizenship and public engagement, for example in relation to anthropogenic climate change. John concludes the chapter with an assessment of landscape through the idea of dwelling. Building on the ideas of Tim Ingold, John argues how a dwelling approach can help overcome traditional distinctions of nature and culture, and of mind and matter. Using the idea of a taskscape, defined as those social practices which have been embedded in a particular physical environment, John analyses landscape as 'the world as known to those who have dwelt there, who do dwell there, who will dwell there, and those whose practical activities take them through its manifold sites and who journey along its multidinous paths'

(Macnaghten and Urry 1998: 167). John then uses this perspective to develop a dwelling analysis to help explain the strength of local public sentiment that often exists to planned developments, such as new roads; John again: '[s]uddenly paths that have for years demonstrated glacial sedimentation are overwhelmed by instantaneous routes which literally seem to "carve" through the landscape, killing trees, paths, dwellings and their associated taskscape' (168).

In Chapter 6 John and I wrote a joint chapter examining various ways in which nature gets produced as countryside. Building on Lefebvre's account of the social production of space, John develops an illuminating analysis of the historical and cultural processes involved in developing what we now know as the English countryside. Key developments in the late eighteenth century include an emerging set of leisurely practices for the rapidly growing rural elite, especially hunting, shooting and fishing; a new representation of the country-side not as land conceived of practices associated with their productivity but as 'landscape' increasingly cultivated for visual consumption; the increasing power of the large rural landowning class to shape the countryside and so on. Later, in the nineteenth century, the aestheticized English countryside came to be con-trasted with the perceived horrors of the English industrial town, leading to a wider representation of industry and modernity as inherently un-English. As John eloquently states: 'while the countryside came increasingly to be desired because of its visual qualities, the industrial town was seen as thoroughly pol-luted, as unnaturally invading all the human orifices' (Macnaghten and Urry 1998: 175). Through movements that included English Romanticism and the more contemporary conservation and amenity movement, John and I then trace this representation of space to English culture and politics and to dis-tinctive characteristics of contemporary British environmentalism. For example, we show how this representation of space is embedded in national conservation policy and practices, associated with a dominant visual gaze that reinforces dominant logics of discipline, surveillance and commodification.

Contested Natures was an undoubted success. It crystallized and elaborated an argument that extended existing writing on the sociology of the environment. More personally it helped me as a young academic develop a distinctive posi-tion and profile. A couple of years later, at the request of then editor Mike Featherstone, John and I edited a special issue of *Body and Society* (Mike of course was better known at the time as editor of *Theory, Culture and Society*) which we labelled *Bodies of Nature*. The focus of the special issue was on the embodied quality of people's experiences in, and of, the environment, con-centrating in particular on the 'various social practices that are involved in, or passing through, nature, the countryside, the outdoors, landscape or wilderness' (Macnaghten and Urry 2000: 1). The project enabled us to engage with many researchers and thinkers whose work we enjoyed and to ask them to focus on a domain that we wished to further. Looking back on the collection I think we put together a wide-ranging set of articles that included a number of innovative contributions. Perhaps my own favourite is a delightful piece by Tim Ingold and Terhi Kurttila in which they sought to reconfigure the debate on 'indigenous knowledge' by focusing on the practices of inhabiting the land that bring places *into* being and that constitute persons *of* those places, beautifully illustrated through ethnographic research on how Saami people in northernmost Finland perceive their environment, and in particular, on how the Saami experience the weather.

Following *Bodies of Nature* John and I followed relatively independent paths. I became more involved with debates on technological governance, focusing on the challenges of injecting social agency into technological decision making, leading eventually to the development of frameworks of responsible innovation. While John, for his part, developed an interest in complexity moving to his highly exceptional contribution to mobilities research and theory. However, although we moved along different pathways, John's work did continue to focus on matters of the environment and nature with books on *Automobilities, Climate Change and Society, Societies beyond Oil* and *What Is the Future?*. In my view this writing was clearly shaped by our earlier and most enjoyable partnership that had been sedimented in what I still consider my best writing, *Contested Natures*.

Right until his untimely death, John remained a loyal friend and a useful commentator on my own work and trajectory. My last meeting with John was at my farewell event from Durham University in August 2015, which had been organized on responsible innovation and the role of the university. John crossed the Pennines to attend the meeting and was his usual humble, considered and helpful self. I was honoured to have John as a mentor and friend. He was an inspiration to us all.

References

Clark, G., Darrall, J., Grove-White, R., Macnaghten, P. and Urry, J. (1994) *Leisure Landscapes*. Lancaster: CSEC and Council for the Protection of Rural England.

Macnaghten, P. and Urry, J. (1995) 'Towards a Sociology of Nature', *Sociology*, 29: 203–220.

Macnaghten, P. and Urry, J. (1998) *Contested Natures*. London: SAGE.

Macnaghten, P. and Urry, J. (eds) (2000) 'Bodies of Nature', *Body and Society*, 6: 3–4.

Chapter 11

On a pilgrimage
A journey with John Urry

Phillip Vannini

A video of the journey described here, "narrated" by John Urry can be found at: https://vimeo.com/195214454.

December 8, 2016

There are ghosts on the 6:15am ferry. The passengers, the crew, and I have all been wrestled from our sleep much too early and our souls aren't quite awake. Even the *Quinsam* seems to sail through the pre-dawn darkness more like a ghoul than a ship, with hollow groans and moans that reverberate eerily through the pitch-black strait. I ride this spooky sailing about once a month, either to make an early meeting at the university in Victoria or to get on an early Air Canada flight from Nanaimo airport to Vancouver International. Today, it's the latter. Normally I would get off the small regional Dash 8 at Vancouver International and make my way onto a Boeing 777, a Dreamliner, or an Airbus A320 and fly somewhere else, somewhere far. But not today. I am only going as far as Vancouver today and I will be back home sometime in the afternoon.[1] I am on a pilgrimage today.

Followers of many religions embark at some point or another in their life on pilgrimages in order to seek spiritual and moral guidance from higher beings. Filled with hope and faith, they set off on journeys to destinations meaningful to them, their gods, and their prophets. They carry along sacred texts. Along their routes they seek connection and salvation.

I, to be candid, have no religion whatsoever and today's my very first pilgrimage. Mind, it's a pilgrimage in the most metaphorical of terms: an entirely pagan journey driven by the need to find not so much spiritual guidance but rather theoretical and empirical connection by way of experiential inspiration. I carry five treasured texts: four articles in PDF format and a book. The number five – if you happen to be wondering – isn't of particular cabalistic significance, it just happens to be the limit of cited references my editors have imposed on this essay.

Yet the number five presents a unique coincidence: five is also the number of transportation modes I will utilize today: a ferry boat, a car, an airplane, a subway train, and a seaplane. And so along the route I, too, one transport mode after another, will seek a metaphysical connection with someone whose words have left a profound trace on me and my work. John Urry might not be seated next to me today, but he is still here today.

Mobile societies

Back in 2005 I co-wrote a short article based on the comings and goings of the *M/V Quisam*: the same ferry I am currently riding from Gabriola Island to Vancouver Island. The paper was submitted to the *Canadian Journal of Communication* since my co-author and I thought that few people around the world would be interested in a little ship making mundane journeys. I had received my PhD in sociology a year before but my marriage with that discipline was already in deep trouble. Exasperated by the conservativeness of the Sociological (with a capital S) world, I had begun an intellectual affair of sorts with the field of communication. Submitting a short piece to a communication journal, I thought, would be a good way to test the strength of that new relationship. The journal's editor somehow found the piece interesting and eventually published it. "This is neat," I thought, "I can legitimately write about my geeky childish interest – planes, trains, boats, and automobiles – and conceptualize these objects as media of communication, and I am seemingly the first one to ever have thought of this!" Little did I know. It was about two weeks after writing a nearly final draft of that paper that I discovered that John Urry had already thought of that field. He had started, it turned out, a full-fledged mobile turn and laid the foundations for a new mobility paradigm.

I went and grabbed a copy of *Sociology beyond Societies*, read it in a single seating, fell in love with mobilities, and immediately signed my divorce papers with old school sociology. *Sociology beyond Societies* gave me not only a sense of belonging to a young and vibrant cross-disciplinary field but also an arsenal of ideas. Society was no longer to be seen as a static entity. Rather than frozen "institutions," Urry remarked in that book, we should pay close attention to the flows of people, goods, and information intersecting at multiple junctions across the world. Sociology until then had understood mobility to be vertical – as in a metaphorical movement across classes – and neglected to examine it as a horizontal phenomenon based on actual physical movement. It was all I needed to hear. I quit thinking of the ferry boats crisscrossing my region as "media" – which now felt somewhat of a forced metaphor – and turned to the fledgling field of mobilities and its conceptual vocabulary.

On this dark morning I have with me a 2010 *British Journal of Sociology* article in which Urry synthesizes the main points of *Sociology beyond Societies*, a book published ten years earlier. There he summarizes scapes and flows as follows:

Scapes are the networks of machines, technologies, organizations, texts and actors that constitute various interconnected nodes along which flows can be relayed. Such scapes reconfigure the dimensions of time and space ... This creates novel inequalities of flow as opposed to the inequalities of stasis. Graham and Marvin maintain that what is involved here is a rewarping of time and space by advanced telecommunication and trans-portation structures, as scapes pass by some areas and connect other areas along information and transport rich "tunnels" (1996: 60). Social and spa-tial distances are no longer homologous. (Urry 2010: 355)

Thus *Ferry Tales* – my four-year-long ethnography on the roles played by ferry boat flows in shaping the land and seascape of Canada's West – was born. Boats' speeds, rhythms, sailing durations, fares, sizes, and routes created com-plex economic and political inequalities in the Salish Sea. These networks also shaped distinct lifestyles marked by unique senses of place and time.

And speaking of time, we've arrived in Nanaimo and I need to get driving.

Inhabiting the car

Though I have written about roads, I've never seriously written about cars. Yet cars have always been at the very center of nearly all of my fieldwork. Without cars' flexibility I could have never found any of the off-grid homes I docu-mented in my recent ethnography on the subject. Without the complex road systems that link airports, cities, and protected areas worldwide I could never reach the trailheads that take me into the wilderness spaces I am currently studying. Without the complex system of automobility the ferry boats I studied a few years ago would be little more than dinghies shuttling across forgotten waterstops.

Urry (2006) observes that the entire system of automobility is predicated on the simple but seductive power of the freedom of the road. Its flexibility, he writes:

enables the car-driver to travel at speed, at any time in any direction along the complex road systems of western societies that link together most houses, workplaces and leisure sites. Cars therefore extend where people can go to and hence what as humans they are literally able to do ... People find pleasure in travelling when they want to, along routes that they choose, finding new places unexpectedly, stopping for relatively open-ended periods of time, and moving on when they desire. (Urry 2006: 19)

Cars have indeed been extending where ethnographers like me, of all people, are able to go. Indeed, when I read Urry's article "Inhabiting the Car" (2006) a few years ago my thoughts jumped to my fieldwork practice. Different rental cars over the years and the different ways I and my travel companions inhabited them, for example, are deeply emblematic of different fieldwork projects. Rereading those writings exposes the cars I was driving and the atmospheres those vehicles contributed to shaping. As I make my familiar way to the airport this morning the GPS on my dashboard reminds me how GPS-enabled rental cars – with their immense flexibility and full openness to driver coercion (Urry 2006: 19) – have enabled me to quickly and easily reach out-of-the-way places and secluded interview sites. Inhabiting today's cars is a way of dwelling-in-this-world.

There is a line in John's writing that always jumps to my mind every time I get the keys to a new rental car: "automobility is in some respects a source of freedom, the 'freedom of the road'" (Urry 2006: 19). There is a comment on that PDF, a comment I digitally inserted some time ago right next to the word "automobility." It's only one word: ethnography. Ethnography, like auto-mobility and *thanks* to automobility, gives the same source of freedom to me, the freedom of the road. So I have never done research *on* cars. But I think and learn *with* them.

Peak oil and the future of mobilities

At a mere 24 minutes from gate to gate and about 12 minutes in the air, the flight from Nanaimo to Vancouver is the shortest on Air Canada's flight map and undoubtedly one of the shortest in the world. For years Air Canada execs – knowing a full in-flight service during the short journey was impossible – would make the single flight attendant briskly go down the narrow aisle, immediately upon reaching cruising altitude, with a silver plate full of hard candy. Like most of its four dozen or so passengers I would grab a candy, unwrap it, put in my mouth, start sucking on it to cope with my ears popping upon descent, and swallow its last pieces right as the plane hit the tarmac in Vancouver. These days, forced to cut back on perks, Air Canada no longer offers free candy on that flight. But candy is not the only dwindling resource in the air.

Cheap oil has fueled mobilities for decades, Urry (2012) tells us. Oil pro-duction has reached its peak and "thus over the long term oil will be increas-ingly expensive and frequent shortages will occur because of the fall in per capita availability. There is not enough oil to fuel worldwide systems of global consumption" in need of constant expansion (572). It is with this post-carbon scenario in mind that I would fly to meet people who seemed to have found an alternative energy future.

Off-grid home residents offer no solution to the dwindling supply of jet fuel needed to operate this candy-starved propeller jet. Yet they have envisaged a uniquely captivating alternative to non-renewable domestic energy consump-tion. Suburban and peri-urban housing in the Western world has developed without an intelligent link to the geography of urban workplaces and con-sumption spaces (Urry 2012). Those houses have been progressively filled with more and more technologies powered by electricity; technologies supposedly meant to free us from the drudgery of domestic life so that we could dedicate our time to electronic sources of entertainment and leisure travel depending on cheap oil (Urry 2012). This was, and is, an inescapable vicious circle. John Urry has encouraged us to imagine ways in which a "decarbonised society" can be possible (574). And so off I went, sucking more candy, flight after flight, en route to off-grid utopias.

Travelling times, mobile methods

Pilgrimages are supposed to be uncomfortable. Discomfort leads to pain, and pain brings you closer to the healing powers of divine forces. As for my own journey, my key source of discomfort today is coming from the cold. I booked my trip for what appears to be the coldest day of the season and snow – unusual for our coast – is on the ground and in the forecast. I can feel the cold on my skin as I exit the airport en route to the subway. I can feel it on my fingers as I start typing once I find a seat on the train. And I can see it in my laptop and camera batteries, draining energy significantly faster than normal.

Until John Urry and colleagues began to articulate and popularize the notion of "mobile methods" nobody thought much about doing research on the go. I have in my laptop a 2008 piece that John wrote with Laura Watts. In it they write:

> Movement between locations is inherent to ethnography, although it has perhaps only recently become a site for fieldwork ... Much ethnography in mobilities has been located at sites of passage, transfer points, where populations and things are temporarily contained and arranged within stations, waiting rooms, baggage systems ... By contrast, a mobile ethnography involves travelling with people and things, participating in their continual shift through time, place and relations with others. (Watts and Urry 2008: 867)

As an ethnographer, over the years I have traveled with all sorts of people in all sorts of means of conveyance. I have driven on ice roads with patient gatekeepers to Arctic lifeworlds; I have ridden seaplanes with skilled pilots; I have walked and hiked with leisure seekers and lovers of wild places; I have paddled kayaks and commandeered skidoos to remote off-grid cabins. Fieldwork for me has thus become travel time, a time "situated in social and material practices of reading, writing ethnographic notes, using laptops, sleeping" (Watts and Urry 2008: 868), getting lost, feeling homesick, looking for a decent cup of coffee and a reliable wi-fi signal, and desperately looking for outlets to recharge batteries.

Increasingly mobile fieldwork for me has also meant mobile writing. I'm not just referring to taking ethnographic "notes" but rather to the actual articles and books whose drafts and final edits have taken their shape in airports, air-planes, boats, hotels, and terminals of all sorts – just like it's happening today. This is a kind of mobile research to whose characteristics few people are sen-sitive, despite the fact that more and more of us "write up" during travel times. The atmospheres of such sites, our moods, our bodily states, the sensual char-acteristics of these places shape what we think and write in our publications in indelible ways. This is why today I wanted to write this essay in John's memory on the go, like this. There is hardly any pain in my little "pilgrimage" but by being mobile today I feel I can be more open to the ideas of a man who, like me, loved going places and thinking and learning along the way.

Gazing like a tourist

The cold temperatures have brought the sun out. And the sun, in turn, seems to have brought the cameras out. The West Coast sky is seldom this bright blue during the wet months and for shutterbugs like me it's an unmissable opportunity. Cameras are a relatively new passion for me. I've never been the kind of traveler that enjoys snapping pictures to show friends and family back home. I've always enjoyed being in the moment more, feeling immersed into a landscape with more sensory openings to the world than just my eyes. And so *The Tourist Gaze* (Urry and Larsen 2012) has been a relatively recent discovery for me.

Video, more than photography, has become my passion. I take video's sen-sitivity to movement, its capability of conveying sound, and its relation with music as a powerfully affective and more-than-representational performance and so I've turned to gazing through cameras not so much as a tourist, but rather as an ethnographer.

It is perhaps no accident that my discovery of the animating potential of video has coincided with my rediscovery of *The Tourist Gaze*. As I sit inside the seaplane terminal in Vancouver's Coal Harbour the 3rd edition of John Urry and Jonas Larsen's work lays opened to chapter 8, part of an update to their earlier work which puts a much greater emphasis on performance. "The performance turn," they write, "brings forth how tourists are co-producers of tourist places" (Urry and Larsen 2012: 206). It is largely through these per-formances that a place like this terminal – designed to be a transportation hub for ordinary local travel to regional destinations – becomes an exotic magnet for seekers of postcard moments. Even in today's cold air people stop by for several minutes to glance at the floatplanes and patiently wait to video record their landings and take-offs against the ocean and mountain background. In this way camera gazes turn transportation into adventure and commuting into sightseeing.

In 2015 I dedicated a few months of fieldwork to the unique world of floatplane aeromobility, focusing in particular on the planes' atmospheres and pilots. For the first time in my career I decided to do the filming myself.

Following the performance turn, I reasoned, I could use video to bring forth how passengers and tourists are co-producers of place, and to highlight how I, as a filming ethnographer, can take an active role in performing the field. *The Tourist Gaze*, for me, became the ethnographer's gaze. The photographic gaze became my filmic gaze.

Seeing is a relational act and through the tourist gaze, and the ethnographic gaze as well, people – tourists and ethnographers alike – can maintain meaningful relations at a distance with absent others. I never met John. Somehow our paths never crossed and I kept on saying to him through the occasional email that "maybe next year" was finally going to bring us both to a conference or a workshop where we could finally shake hands.

It never happened.

And so I thought I'd bring my camera along on my little pilgrimage today. I figured that by sharing my gaze I might continue my distant relation with him. I left on the internet the video I made today, for readers, for my own memories, and for John too. Hopefully there is a decent wireless signal where he is now.

Note

1 Sensitive to the carbon footprint of travel I took advantage of this trip to Vancouver to accomplish other tasks as well and purchased a carbon offset.

References

Urry, J. (2006) "Inhabiting the car." *Sociological Review*, 54(1), 17–31.
Urry, J. (2010) "Mobile sociology." *British Journal of Sociology*, 61(1), 347–366.
Urry, J. (2012) "Do mobile lives have a future?" *Tijdschrift voor economische en sociale geografie*, 103(5), 566–576.
Urry, J. and J. Larsen (2012) *The Tourist Gaze*, 3.0 London: SAGE.
Watts, L. and J. Urry (2008) "Moving methods, travelling times." *Environment and Planning D*, 26(5), 860–874.

Chapter 12

Remembering my special academic journey with John Urry

Chia-Ling Lai

My first encounter with John Urry: from an admirable reader to his PhD supervisee

I first encountered Urry's *The Tourist Gaze* (1990) when studying in National Taiwan University in 1993 when sociology equalized Marxism and social movements. I was very inspired that such an interesting topic could also be a serious researchable sociological and geographical topic. The book is definitely a long-lasting classic that demonstrates John Urry's academic spirit which always explores new issues and extends the territory of sociology while redefining what sociology could be. It is also a gem that reveals the grand social and cultural change through elaborating newly emergent social groups' habitus and perceptions through some beautiful social episodes. His global research of the middle class and service class at that time with Taiwanese scholar Professor Michael Shaw also gave me great inspiration to study what newly emergent classes and social change can be traced in *Capital, Labour and the Middle Class* (1983) and *Economies of Signs and Space* (1994). Under the supervision of a Taiwanese mentor, Professor Ch-jen Yeh, I explored my MA on museums and social change in Taiwan, drawing upon Bourdieu's field theory and John Urry's globalization and cultural change theory. I met the inspiring writer Urry 'virtually' as a remote admirable reader then.

I started my PhD with John Urry in 1997 after a puzzling exploration on museums after my two MAs. Especially after my MA in interdisciplinary women's studies at Warwick, in which I devoted too much time on feminist philosophy that suffocated me a bit (though my beloved MA supervisor Terry Lovell actually treated me very well), Urry turned out to be a great inspirer. It was John Urry's grand theoretical framework on time-space materiality and very vivid empirical researches that attracted me to work with him and reject offers from LSE and possibly Cambridge. The first time I met John Urry 'face to face' was at a large conference on 'time' in Lancaster University in 1997, where A. Touraine, G. Spivak, Scott Lash and many other great thinkers gathered to discuss cultural value and time, and John Urry was also one keynote speaker. His high interest in time and space was actually influenced by

Giddens. He admired Giddens' research and examined his work closely. Even after Giddens was being criticized for being Tony Blair's spin doctor by many sociologists in 2000, John still defended him, telling me that somebody needs to do what Giddens was doing though John himself wouldn't. John mentioned again that he had carefully read Giddens' later work on the politics of climate change (2009) when we met again in 2010. Time, space, and social change naturally formed the central academic attention of John Urry, so it is understandable that mobility issues and complexity towards future studies became his research interest in this decade. And I was lucky to carry my concern of museums when exploring time-space and social transformation with him all the way!

John Urry: an open-minded supervisor who showed the way but let people be themselves

John was a warm and lovely figure, though a very serious scholar. He was always encouraging, most of the time smiling with childlike curious eyes. It was a great pleasure to work with him, academically rich and amicable. I still remember the supervision time with John Urry: at every meeting, John treated me to a cup of coffee like a ritual and then an hour's efficient meeting followed discussing the paper I had handed him in advance. We also met every three or four weeks with another brilliant co-supervisor, Sarah Franklin. John's supervision was sometimes like a clinic, 12–13 PhD students with different topics and characters piled up for a day or two to impress him and receive his suggestions. We circulated rumours that he could speed-read well, otherwise we couldn't understand how he managed to read our papers and give good suggestions. During six years of supervision, there was only one that he couldn't finish reading my paper in time, because he was reviewing 400 copies of ESRC research proposals as the chair for ESRC!

I share here three outstanding pieces of memories out of numerous great ones while working with John Urry: the first is my French research trip in 1999. He gave me the travel grant instead of giving it to many other British students who studied topics domestically, responding to complaints that 'an international student who explores multiple foreign case studies should be encouraged'. I actually broke my leg before my trip, but I still made the journey and render it a chapter in my thesis. I was more a good speaker than a good writer, and my heavy writing style was often criticized by John. Once I had done my last chapter on the National Palace Museum's travelling exhibition in Paris, he sent me an email that said, 'what a beautiful piece, I enjoy reading it in my garden. What a nice afternoon.' I then understood his standard of writing, requiring both a literary style in description while revealing rigorous sociological theory. His appreciation on French styles influenced me a lot. *Sociology beyond Society* (Urry, 2000) was a less rigorous academic book, a collection of essays on mobile culture that reflected his emphasis on aesthetic and styles in writing and his appreciation on the style of French sociology or Benjamin's arcade projects.

Another memory is about our shared appreciation of Foucault's heterotopia spirit. In the summer of 1998, after my upgrade, I wrote a brief piece and chose Foucault's heterotopia's essay ending as my quote ('The ship is the heterotopia par excellence. In civilization without boats, dream dry up, espionage takes the place of adventure, and the police take the place of pirates' (Foucault, 1967)). John surprisingly told me, 'Chia-ling, look, what a coincidence, I quote the same in my current paper!'. It is probably a common quote nowadays, but a lovely quote that reflects John's spirit. John was a curious and creative spirit who explored without borders, maintaining an environment for academic freedom and cultural creativity being his goal. John's father was in the British navy; the metaphors of sea, freedom, exploration and mobilities in Urry's works, I thought, could come from John's childhood family memories. Coffee, a boat in the sea, a French garden, all become material reminders of those great memories when learning sociological crafts with John.

The final memories I want to share are John Urry's open mind and capacity to create a new framework that converges complexity well. I was not a great follower of him at the beginning, probably a stubborn student who had a feminist psyche to battle against an academic father, but a scholar 'as tall' as him seems to not mind at all. I remember that I drew upon post-colonial feminist theory to challenge his idea of globalization, Bourdieu's field theory to challenge his concept of de-differentiation, digital culture to criticize his concept of co-presence, or time zone to challenge his globalization homogeneous space; worst of all, materiality to challenge his early version of mobility paradigm. Though I actually followed closely his theories of mobile objects and subjects in *Economies of Signs and Space* (1995) and many other theoretical concepts of time, space, global events, global mobilities, and complexity when I was heavily influenced by Tony Bennett's exhibition theory. Every time I stubbornly wrote my heavy materiality essay, he read it carefully and took it seriously before sharply teaching me how to converge and bring complex and multiple mobile academic folders together. My thesis *Museums in Motion* (2004), which genealogically folds materiality and global mobilities in the global museum field and performed as international travelling exhibitions, is one of the academic examples from when I worked with John. Once he told me to 'be yourself! I like the difference. Nobody will be interested in the things that they have already known. Bravely to do the new things, the world is yours!' His tolerance towards different ideas and a great capacity to incorporate new ideas and challenges made him a great sociologist who dared to create new paths and define new sociological territories.

John Urry: a great collaborator who created an intellectual environment

He was an extremely busy scholar, but wisely knew how to use collaborating power, not just for his research team but even for his supervisees. He sometimes arranged a meeting for his supervisees together to get to know each other and let us self-organize study groups and 'counselling groups'. His supervisees shared many research interests. I joined a space study group run by Monica Degen and a consumption group run by Alan Warde. John Urry himself set up a mobility study group in 1998 and formed the centre of mobilities research in 2000, led also by Mimi Sheller. I was enriched by inspiration from the bi-weekly meetings by leading mobility scholars from all over the world. I still remember vividly the tourism team from Kalmar, Sweden, Ulrich Beck's team from Germany, the Roskilde team from Denmark, Tim Cresswell, Dick Pels, Sven Kesselring, Penelope Harvey, Sharon McDonald, Nigel Thrift, Neil Cummings, Bülent Diken, Yoke-Sum Wong, and Kevin Hetherington's talks and discussion in the meals afterwards, of course with some of John's students, Jonas Larsen, Alexander Arellano, Kingsley Dennis, Joyce Yeh, Jennie Germann-Molz, and many more. Later, the CEMORE was officially formed in 2004, now the shining centre of the galaxy of the mobility paradigm (the academic results can be seen in the journal *Mobilities*, co-founded by Kevin Hannam, Mimi Sheller and John Urry in 2005; for Urry's mobility thinking, please see *Mobilities* (2007) and *Mobile Lives* (2010)). I still remember vividly discussing issues such as the metaphors of mobilities, the race/class/gender/age issues of car and transportation, the politics of mobilities of the refugee, the hostage, immigration and garbage, risky stuff, inhabiting cars, the sociology of airports, haunting materiality, and so on. As an Asian female student who conducted research on museums and art, I was immersed in this vivid mobile environment to elaborate my thesis and future research based on dynamics and conflict of materiality and mobilities. His complexity workshop with Bob Jessop in 2005 which extended Urry's thinking in *Global Complexity* and his mobility and Actor Network Theory workshop with John Law in 2007 also made a great impact on my research on Actor Network Theory, complexity, global stages, and events.

I believe John's secret was that he chose to meet up with students and scholars who related to his everyday thinking and research interest at that moment. When I conducted my research on museums, nationalism, and globalization, I found that my peer overseas students on studies of heritages and museums all came from special places, such as Taiwan, Northern Ireland, Quebec, Catalonia, the Basque Country, and so on. He never engaged politically with us, but the natural atmosphere would make people think and explore. Later, I saw that he included David McCrone's *Sociology of Nationalism* in his Routledge edition of Karl Mannheim's International Library of Sociology series, which reflected his thinking then on globalization and nationalism. He was a wise man who was able to form creative environments.

The coordinative and collaborative capacity of John Urry was also evident in the number of famous scholars headed for Lancaster who worked with him for long periods. There were also numerous workshops and conferences that brought together talented minds and set new themes and agendas for sociology.

When I was in Lancaster, there were feminist and cultural study centres, science studies and a policy group, with Scott Lash, Bob Jessop, John Law, Jackie Stacey, Sarah Franklin, Celia Lury, Sarah Ahmed, Mimi Sheller, and many more along with visits by famous theorists, from Donna Haraway, Bruno Latour, Edward Soja, Laurent Berlent, to name just a few. Also, his collaborated co-authoring and works with brilliant scholarly minds from all over the world was an achievement. Once I wrote a paper on 'Art exhibitions travel the world: On international travelling exhibitions', which he kindly included in the book that he and Mimi Sheller co-edited, *Tourism Mobilities: Places to Play, Places in Play* (2004), exploring global tourism based on the concept of 'play' as human-beings' drive to create. It was not just a call for papers and individual writing up, but also a gathering for authors to create related corresponding arguments and dialogues. I was lucky to meet up with Tim Edensor, Kevin Hetherington, Rob Shield, Nailing Sung, Richard Sharply, and many other great scholars and learn how to take part in academic team work. Needless to say, having brilliant feminist and sociologist Sylvia Walby as his beloved wife and lifelong academic companion was probably John Urry's smart pick that would not surprise anybody!

Once a teacher, always a teacher: John Urry as an academic model who leads us to the future

After my graduation, I, as well as many of his supervisees, still kept in frequent contact with him. I stayed in Lancaster as an honorary visiting scholar for one year, when John tried to help me to work in the UK, and I also applied for jobs overseas at the same time. I had done my research, drawing on Actor Network Theory and dealing with how travellers packed multiple materiality under the schemes of anti-terrorism and security checking in the UK, but I chose to work in Taiwan due to family reasons. John kindly treated me to a good Indian dinner with Kingsley Dennis and Jonas Larsen before sending me off home to Taiwan. What a considerate supervisor and friend.

I had special encounters with him on many occasions after graduation without pre-arrangement. One time I remember clearly was the concert of Norwegian saxophonist Jan Gabarek, at the Liverpool Concert Hall in 2005, where I met John and Sylvia and Kingsley Dennis, who was his post-doc and co-author of *After the Car* (2009), and we met in Tate Liverpool before the concert. We all bought the CD 'In praise of dream', which echoed John Urry as a dreamer who always explored while aiming high and far. At John's funeral, Sylvia chose many melodies of Jan Gabarek, it made it an unforgettable music memory piece for me.

Many international conference encounters also surprised me, from the Tourism conference in Kalmar, Sweden 2004; ISA Durban 2006; ISA Gothenburg 2010; Geneva ESA 2011; Centre of Mobility research 10th anniversary 2013; 2016 ISA Vienna (John's final tweet for me was, 'c you in

Vienna! John on 1/2/2016'; it is sad that I won't see him again). When I met John at conferences, he always kindly introduced me to many scholars, from Jon Solomon, Peter Adey, and David Bissell, to name just a few. We sometimes had a meal or coffee together to chat about new academic issues and John enthusiastically found good places for us all to meet up. Apart from my original development on museums/exhibitions and global mobilities, under his encouragement I also later extended my research on global events, from world expos, art biennales to London Olympic/Paralympic Games; CeMoRe and his writings still influence me deeply, now that my research has turned more to Actor Network Theory and assemblage, from museums' technological performances, from audio guides to 3D printing and museums.

John Urry had a free mind, he always encouraged me to be a global/cosmopolitan researcher and to travel far, from Siberia to Dubai. He actually prided himself as being the earliest Western Marxist travelling to China during the 1970s cultural revolution, so he actually travelled to Guang-Dong for a low-carbon innovation conference before he passed away at his Lancaster home. He was supposed to visit Taiwan in March 2016 but this was cancelled due to my busy schedule, what a pity! He was very much concerned about China and Taiwan issues, where my thesis on *Museums in Motion* was based and my research on Shanghai expo has developed. He still encouraged me to do research such as the impact of tourism upon the China and Taiwan relationship, and kindly informed me and even asked for my comments on his new works on China's environment and innovation with David Tyfield. He also recommend Scott Lash's book on Global China when we met in Lancaster in 2012.

I worked at the Institute of Future Studies in Tamkang University, Taiwan for five years (2006–11), taught students what I had learned from my BSc background of atmospheric physics and CeMoRe and its 2004 Alternative Future conferences' multiple mobilities frameworks, on my 'global social futures' and 'mobile social futures' classes. That is the reason I joined Urry's future scenario panels in ISA's RN future studies in Gothenburg (2010), Yokohama (2014), and Vienna (2016, when I launched the commemoration film for Urry's works based on academic tributes of Urry's co-authors around the world). They were based on my research on the sustainable future scenario of world expos, 3D printing, and museums, inspired by Urry's global complexity approaches to disasters and global events as an emergent power and his climate change research. I found out only later that John had actually taken the position as the leading member of UK Foresight for a decade. That led him to explore issues of climate change and society and many complexity issues, such as financial mobilities in *Offshore*. His interest in time that led him from memories, speed, and rhythm to future is not too surprising. So he launched the Institute of Social Futures at Lancaster University in 2015, encouraging multiple dimensions of research for the future, including art and creativities. Also, his son Tom Urry as a famous animator has launched a project to turn academic books into accessible animation – an amazingly creative idea. Needless to say, his final single-authored book, *What Is the Future?* (Urry, 2016), will definitely inspire future sociologists!

In Geneva ESA 2011, his keynote speech mentioned that the future scenario would be like *Mad Max*, a society lacking natural resources and suffering long-term social inequality that would result in severe social conflict and further inequality. In his book, *Climate Change and Society*, there were going to be four scenarios, and I asked him why he mentioned only one scenario. He did not answer then. Maybe he had no time to say the four in full, or he felt it was the worst that could happen. I happened to see the new version of *Mad Max* the week John passed away. I was shocked by the vision and John's talk suddenly came to me. The current emergence of the new Right worldwide and severe environmental disasters worried me even further.

I now work in the Institute of European Culture and Tourism at the National Taiwan Normal University, an institute with close alliances with EU-Taiwan. I probably meet John's wife Sylvia Walby more often at the European Sociological Association annual conference. The second day after John Urry passed away (18 March 2016), Sylvia Walby (the UNESCO chair in gender relations) did not cancel her talk at the European Union, especially after the Brussels attack. According to her secretary, Sylvia said, 'John would not be happy if I cancel my talk at this crucial moment'. Her determined bravery to guard their belief under the pain of losing a significant other is so respectable. She once avowed in the keynote speeches in Geneva in 2011 and ESA 2015 that the European Union is a 'social design' that has gathered so much social energy to make it happen and maintain it, we critically examine its practices with sociology and feminism, but we hope it still survives and does good for all of us. The above story reveals that Urry and Walby are serious intellectuals who care about social equality, cultural creativity, and sustainability. John's sincerely academic engagement with public sociology's debate in 2005 (Urry, 2005), along with many great scholars from Bauman, Beck, and Sassen to Burawoy, also inspired my recent research and writings on theoretical curating and public intellectuals (Lai, 2015). I hope we can make this world a better one through multiple engaging ways, as John wished.

John was always ahead, even with critical thinking and experience of life and death (see 'Death in Venice' in *Tourism Mobilities*; and Lancaster Conference 20–21 January 2016). I was very sad when John passed away and wept like a little girl; worst of all, I was writing a museum essay for *Transfers* about how Czech musicians survived concentration camps during the Holocaust by creating contemporary music, something which reflects Urry's influences on heritage, memories, senses and tourism. However, when this conference on reflexive thinking about life and death occurred to me, I stopped weeping. I imagined John laughing somewhere … and whispering: 'thinking of me, creatively thinking reflexively and sociologically!' As my classmate Alexander Arellano mentioned, humans are mortal, not many people can be as 'immortal' as

Figure 12.1 My final meeting with John Urry at his favorite creative heritage cafe, Atkinsons at Lancaster, Aug 2015. Inspiring and supportive conversations as always.

Photo credit: Chia-ling Lai

John Urry. John often gave me 'gifts' when he supervised me. Once, before my journey home for a summer break in my first PhD year, he said: 'Here are my two newly published papers, 14 hours journey is far enough to finish reading them, enjoy reading!' Though most travellers probably enjoy watching media or falling asleep more than reading academic papers in the inhabiting mobile flight, it was a sweet and serious gift from a beloved supervisor. John Urry left us abundant inspiring publications as 'intellectual heritage', an excellent gift! We will carry on his academic journey, not only through love of his work, but through developing our unique creative work and carrying on influencing future young talent so as to make this fantastic 'academic gift giving' flow!

My last 'corporeal meeting' with John Urry was in July 2014 at Atkinson, his favourite coffee shop, a creatively refurbished 1837 heritage site in Lancaster which is almost a great temporal-spatial-material metaphor of heterotopia as heritage and future creativity. We discussed many academic issues and took a photo at the end. He did not like his photo being taken, but he allowed me to do it three times: once on my graduation ceremony day, the second time at Gothenburg ISA and finally in Lancaster. A piece of memory! I will always remember his academic spirit with a smiling curious face and supporting warm voices.

References

Lai, C. (2004) *Museums in Motion*. Lancaster University, unpublished PhD thesis.

Lai, C. (2004) 'Art exhibitions travel the world', in Mimi Sheller and John Urry (eds), *Tourism Mobilities*: Places to Play, Places in Play. London: Routledge.

Lai, C. (2015) 'Public sociology and theoretical curating as intellectual practices', in *New perspectives for the sociology of art and culture*. Taipei: Tonsen Publications (in Chinese).

Lai, C. et al. (2016) *Journey of Complexity and Mobility, commemoration film for John Urry's work*.

Urry, J. (2005) 'Good news and bad news', *British Journal of Sociology*, 31(3): 375–378.

Part III

Tourism, mobilities, temporalities

Chapter 13

Going places

Jørgen Ole Bærenholdt

From locality to place

Mobility is always about going places. Therefore, it is obvious that Urry was not only a sociologist of mobility but also of place. He was much read by geographers, perhaps as much as by sociologists.

In fact, his interest in tourism emerged out of locality studies; from More-combe and the Lake District, near Lancaster, more precisely. Urry took part in the 1980s major British Changing Urban and Regional Systems (CURS) research programme that became more widely known through its many local-ity studies (Bagguley et al. 1990). Locality studies influenced urban and regional studies internationally. Moving and advancing research away from various dead ends: positivist quantitative research, Marxist determinism and also overly humanistic approaches. In Nordic *Samhällsgeografi* ('societal geography'), locality studies inspired a new interest in how and why localities and places matter and unfold. It opened the agenda for more detailed and theory-informed studies of local and regional development; for example, the present author's 1991 PhD on modes of life and settlement patterns in four villages in Iceland and the Faroe Islands. Thus, Urry took part in the movement that opened and sup-ported studies with more contextual investigations into the complexities of how different localities develop, overcoming both mere ideographic description and the trend of nomothetic reasoning about necessary relations, which had been part of the Marxist legacy. Urry argued against spatial determinism: 'Thus, different areas, towns, agricultural zones, new trading estates, shopping centres, arterial roads, etc. are not merely elements of a given spatial structure and determinative of human activity from outside. Rather they are themselves social, socially produced, and socially reproducing' (Urry 1995: 66).

For Urry, the social and the spatial is co-produced, and it is impossible to think about society and space as separate domains. His engagement with the local and locality and his arguments for richer studies of the complexities involved in urban and regional development was a part of the movement around the CURS programme. But it also became a stepping stone into deeper research in tourism, consumption and place. Much of this work took place in parallel and with reference to the very influential geographer Doreen Massey, who died only a week before Urry. Urry rejected non-spatial sociology and he worked in concert with theory-informed geography.

Locality studies pushed researchers to combine sociology and geography. As part of the Lancaster Regionalism Group, Urry published some of the most important locality studies, where restructuring is approached with much inspiration from Massey (Bagguley et al. 1990). Tourism, especially the decline of tourism in seaside Morecombe, plays a significant role in the empirical analysis of ongoing processes of restructuring. The reader gets a sense of the authors' strong commitment to understanding the empirical details of economic restructuring. The group's conclusion begins by noting that 'Place matters ... What we call society is, in a way, just an aggregate of distinctive local sites and experiences' (Bagguley et al. 1990: 210). At this point place is a concept about the complexity of our world. Thus, they conclude by arguing that 'Place is the intersection of a multitude of processes, the sedimentations of the past, the social practices of the present and projects for the future' (Bagguley et al. 1990: 219).

In another locality book, Urry argued against associating particular interests to localities and stated that 'we cannot simply presume that a given effect (e.g. of increased employment in manufacturing) is necessarily in the interests of all social groups who live and work in a given area' (Urry 1990: 191). On the other hand, he acknowledged the importance of strategies of local political bodies: 'they do show that localities *can* make a difference' (Urry 1990: 203, emphasis in original). His early engagement with local policies and the future can be read as a thread he returned to with his much later engagement with politics of mobility, climate change, off-shoring and the future.

However, place – rather than locality and politics – became much more central in the decade of 1994–2004. The analytical interest in tourism (*The Tourist Gaze*) and postmodernism (*Economies of Signs and Space*) had empirical grounds in locality studies of economic restructuring, and propelled theoretical development around place. In *Consuming Places* (1995), Urry explained the importance of studying place both in a concrete and a theory-informed way, following on from earlier works with, among others, Derek Gregory and Scott Lash. He referred to Marx, Durkheim and Weber, and to Heidegger, Giddens, Castells, Harvey and Massey. But it is no coincidence that when it comes to place, he highlighted first and foremost the contributions from Bachelard, Benjamin and Lefebvre (pp. 23–5), since these three all acknowledged how places are lived and remembered by people.

Bachelard and Benjamin bring deep understanding on how memories are embodied and unfold as traces in tensions between concentration and distraction. And the produced character of space, and of (three) different spatialities (from Lefebvre), became a point of departure for Urry, as for so many other theorists in the so-called 'spatial turn'. Places need to be understood and analysed with qualitative and heterogeneous approaches. Central points for studies in politics, heritage, cultural identities and so on are summed up when Urry shows 'the paradoxical ways in which memories are irreducibly social; that people basically remember together; that the production of shared memory of an event, place or person necessitates cooperative work' (Urry 1995: 27). *Consuming Places* is thus also a part of a mid-1990s paradigmatic reorientation towards the everyday, consumption, experience, memory, place and – although at this point still implicit – mobility.

John, the tourist

John loved to travel and he accepted many invitations to speak and collaborate in places around the world. He also knew the pleasures – and performances – of tourism well. In the beginning of 2000, he arrived in Roskilde and was hired as a visiting professor of Roskilde University for a month a year for the three years of the research project 'Tourism practices and the production of destinations: Representations, networks and strategies'. This led to numerous visits and the co-authored book *Performing Tourist Places* based on the research in Roskilde, the island of Bornholm and Jammerbugten in northern Jutland, Denmark (Bærenholdt et al. 2004). In addition, John accepted invitations to a mobile PhD course in Iceland and to a seminar on the small island of Sommarøy outside Tromsø, northern Norway. In Iceland, John was thinking a lot about his dad's time as a British Army map maker in Iceland during World War II, searching for the people his dad had stayed with. In introducing his lecture at Sommarøy, gazing at the view of the sea, snow and mountains, he began by reflecting 'this is the best view I ever had lecturing – no the second best, there was also one in Rio'! He also made sure to visit Bornholm – and Hammershus Castle, the place of Jonas Larsen's PhD research – together with his partner, some years after our common book on Bornholm and other places in Denmark. He was an early embracer with regards to doing digital photography, as for example when aboard the romantic restaurant ship *Sagafjord* sailing the waters of Roskilde Fiord (see Figure 13.1) around 2001.

John was a great academic traveller, a connoisseur practising his gaze, comparing the best views and snaps to be had. He was a travelling theorist collecting a wealth of cases, mentoring and drawing on the work of so many others. It is perhaps a paradox that he argued for field work with mobile methods while he did not do much of this himself after he began locality studies. But he increasingly established a *bund* (sort of association) of researchers drawing on each other's work. He knew people's life and research well enough to let his new mobility paradigm emerge in contrast to generalised simple sedentary, nomadic or placeless understandings of place and mobility. People go places to meet other people, related through obligations and attachments. And to perform places full of embodied memories. Proximity and co-presence are central concepts here.

While travelling a lot, John moored at Lancaster University, building the social, collective and academic milieu he was so devoted to. He knew how to

Figure 13.1 John Urry doing digital photography on board *Sagafjord*, Roskilde Fiord, Denmark

mentor people, to supervise and suggest while always remembering to do the 'repair work' to make sure that doctoral students and other academics would still feel confident and proceed with their work. But there was also speed in his way of life. He seemed to be a restless writer, read a lot, always had student papers to read with him and sent short speedy emails from around the world. Books came out quicker and quicker, almost as if he knew he had limited time to fulfil his ambitions; he was always looking for new important agendas to address.

From performed place to mobilities

In *Performing Tourist Places* (Bærenholdt et al. 2004), we used the metaphor of the sandcastle to understand how tourist places are 'tangible yet fragile', through mobile materials momentarily melting together, only to erode the day after. Urry himself was on the move, moving his approach, always revisiting and revising his work. This happened when he took part in the performance turn in tourist studies, which emerged through critical reflections on how visual practices could be better understood (see Jonas Larsen's chapter on *The Tourist Gaze*). To approach places as performed provided new insights into how visitors co-produce place in tourism. Drawing on Goffman, tourism then became a mode of relating to the world, and a mode of going places that is not reserved to the extraordinary and far away. Tourist performance also includes everyday practices, laid-back practices and the ordinary, for example in summer houses and homes away from home. But tourist performances are also networked and heavily supported through a myriad of, often somehow dark, mobility systems coming together to produce these light moments of tourist delight. It is only through these forms of networked mobility and performance that places, and tourist places, emerge. The metaphor of the sandcastle was a way to introduce the 'new mobility' to tourism studies.

> This 'place' of the sandcastle contingently stems from various intersecting mobilities. These are imaginative mobilities in which during long winter nights people dream of sun-drenched summer beaches, the globally universal place to play in the contemporary world. These are corporeal mobilities, such as the journey to a holiday region, a day trip, and the dense choreography of a family moving around and building the sandcastle. Then there are mobile objects such as fish, stones and mussels at the shore or on the beach that may have travelled thousands of miles, waiting for their starring role. The tools for building, such as buckets and spades are brought in the family car. (Bærenholdt et al. 2004: 143–4)

We stressed how much this is also a social performance, how tourist places are social projects involving Goffmanian face-to-face interaction (which also became very central in his later *Mobilities* book). Performed places meant a hint of the lively and light, so important in memories, but which is also lost:

> A sandcastle is not fixed and given but is fluid and changing. Tunnels and towers may collapse as the sun shines; the rising tide may cause water to penetrate the ramparts surrounding the moat; the fortifications may get undermined. The work of erosion and sedimentation may slowly alter the sandcastle or there may be certain ruptures as the walls collapse. Erosion and sedimentation are also to be found in tourist practices. (Bærenholdt et al. 2004: 145)

This can be read in more than one way. First, as a continuation of Urry's inspiration from Romanticist modernity, a hymn to the attentiveness of people and places and the beauty of the eroded sandcastle. But it can also be read as hinting at the dark sides of rationalist modernity having produced climate change, sea rise and the erosion of social relations and societies, which appear much more substantially in the later parts of Urry's rich authorship.

Urry was a romanticist and a futurist. He was inspired by classical Romanticism and writers and artists like Wordsworth, Ruskin and Mann, but he also followed Forster's dystopian understanding of how places under cosmopolitanism get desubstantialised and become only 'combinations of abstract characteristics' (Bærenholdt et al. 2004: 142) within that very same Romanticism.

His essay 'Death in Venice' (2004) developed this Romanticist involvement, following Thomas Mann's novel *Death in Venice*. Venice was a place worth dying for; a place one needs to see before one dies. Also, places die or are threatened, like sinking Venice. Studying tourist places of various kinds, even Dubai, Urry approached how tourist places are being designed as scenic combinations, somehow replicating the classical development of tourism in spa towns (such as Harrogate) and other places for medical treatment of the ill.

Based on his keen interest in how tourist places are built and performed, Urry, in a rather futuristic way, engaged with mobility, always interested in scenarios and potential technologies of more sustainable futures. But there was always the darker and more dystopian side of mobility. Often his writings ended with war, terror and Orwell's Big Brother (as in Urry 2004: 214), and increasingly so. Urry was always concerned with nature, environment and planning. He thus ended a paper on tourism and the environment with 'It is not entirely fanciful to suggest that tourism produces some of the *most* difficult of contemporary issues' (Urry 1995: 192). He clearly held mixed views on tourism and the way it shapes the world. And since he went to many places himself, his environmental footprint was not very small.

The early interest in economic restructuring in locality studies can be seen as a backbone he also returned to in his later books dealing with climate change and scenarios of the future. However, Urry's work and life are also complex and point in many directions. Approaches were revised, for example from the very visually dominated *The Tourist Gaze* to the more complex bodily performance of tourism, or from *Economies of Signs and Space* over *Global Complexity* to environmental scenarios of the climate crisis. Urry's way was indeed unforeseeable and irreversible. He certainly left an immense intellectual footprint in this world.

John's trace

To me, John inspired not only the development of research in tourist performance and place design, he also paved the way for my book *Coping with Distances*, on how mobility as a coping practice produced societies in the Nordic Atlantic peripheries, namely northern Norway, the Faroe Islands, Iceland and Greenland. John's approaches did indeed go many places! Thinking critically on how he opened *Sociology beyond Society*, John inspired me to think over how mobility may not only disturb and deconstruct societies but indeed produce societies. Thereby, mobility can be investigated as a practice but also as a strategy exercising power through the movement of people and things. Thus, territorial and mobile practices can complement each other. And mobility is not only in need of regulation and governance. Mobility can be approached as a form of governing people, as *governmobility*, I have suggested, combining inspiration from John with Michel Foucault's governmentality. Leaving the 'conduct of conduct' of the modern self in the concept of governmentality, governmobility is pushing the approach towards understanding societies as 'ruled through circulation and connection'. I mention this just to give the reader an impression of the kinds of thoughts that can emerge from inspiration by John.

But John also inspired through being an academic role model in his way of working. John inspired me to work hard on book proposals, planning and negotiating a publication well, before actually writing it. For example, the way he and Mimi Sheller edited *Tourism Mobilities* was instructive. Potential authors received draft abstracts for their potential chapters, so that they could see what kind of contribution was expected. John was also good at focusing, consciously using book titles and opening sentences to organise more simple, effective writing. In 2004, he became an honorary doctor of Roskilde University, having been suggested by three departments. And we enjoyed his visits a lot.

John had so many promising projects, engagements and ideas, which will keep on setting agendas for change and new practices in society and in academia, across disciplines. He was not only full of ideas, but also an entrepreneur capable of building paths and institutions to make things take place. John was himself an institution, who supported and guided a multiplicity of academic careers around the world. Interdisciplinary work was always a key implicit characteristic of his efforts and enormous academic production.

John made so much change – and made so many move – that his impact will be irreversible and unpredictable in ways deeply consistent with his own philosophy. Therefore, there are so many of us around the world who will carry on researching the possibilities of the world, committed to his respectful, constructive and supportive way of being together while making a difference in making a better world.

References

Bærenholdt, J.O., Larsen, J., Haldrup, M. and Urry, J. (2004) *Performing Tourist Places*, Aldershot: Ashgate.

Bagguley, P., Mark-Lawson, J., Shapiro, D., Urry, J., Walby, S. and Warde, A. (1990) *Restructuring: Place, Class and Gender*, London: SAGE.

Urry, J. (1990) 'Conclusion: Places and policies', in M. Harloe, C. Pickvance and J. Urry (eds), *Place, Policy and Politics*, London: Unwin Hyman, pp. 187–204.

Urry, J. (1995) *Consuming Places*, London: Routledge.

Urry, J. (2004) 'Death in Venice', in M. Sheller and J. Urry (eds), *Tourism Mobilities: Places to Play, Places in Play*, London: Routledge, pp. 205–15.

Chapter 14

John Urry's adventures in Brazil

Bianca Freire Medeiros

The last time I met John Urry in person was in my hometown, Rio de Janeiro, on 10 June 2012, the Sunday before the opening of Rio+20, the United Nations Conference on Sustainable Development. He had arrived the day before as a guest of the Science, Technology and Innovation Forum (sponsored by the International Social Science Council (ISSC), the International Human Dimensions Programme on Global Environmental Change and UNESCO), to speak at the "Global Change and Social Transformation" panel. Organized by Olive Shisana (CEO of the Human Sciences Research Council of Africa and President of ISSC) and Pilar Álvarez-Laso (Assistant Director General at the Social and Human Sciences Sector of UNESCO), the panel aimed to showcase contributions from social scientists to the formulation of more ethical and sustainable responses to global change.

John (he always asked us to avoid the formality of surnames and titles) was particularly enthusiastic. It was a great possibility for discussing his paper, "Climate Change: Bringing in Society," with a regionally diverse and gender-balanced group: Nazli Choucri (Massachusetts Institute of Technology and UNESCO's MOST Programme), John Crowley (UNESCO), Heide Hackmann (ISSC), Úrsula Oswald Spring (National Autonomous University of Mexico), Thomas Pogge (Yale University), and Thomas Reuter (University of Melbourne). Moreover, the fact that the event was held in Rio was key to him: since he started working on what we might call his "post-carbon tetralogy" – formed by *Climate Change and Society* (2011), *Societies beyond Oil* (2013), *Offshoring* (2014), and *What Is the Future?* (2016) – John's interest in Brazil, a country that he considered a major player on the climate change debate, had grown noticeably.

In one of his final articles, co-authored with Carmen Dayrell and published in the *European Journal of Social Theory* (2015), Brazil is identified as "the society apparently most 'concerned' about climate change" and "with less climate change skepticism as compared with more 'advanced' societies." The authors highlight that the largest country in South America has been innovative in developing many non-carbon forms of energy generation and use, while assuming the central stage in international debates on climate change since the

Rio Earth Summit in 1992. For Urry, Brazil represented a unique case through which to analyze the challenges that global warming poses and to think about strategies for action, not only because of its energy potential (both fossil and renewable) and sprawling natural resources, but also for its massive social problems. In this sense, his last books are especially relevant in helping Brazilians face our most daunting task: to match effective social inclusion policies and public services reform with a sustainable economic development.

John had visited Brazil on three previous occasions. In May 2000, he was in Rio de Janeiro as an invited panelist at the international seminar, "The Limits of the Imaginary," organized by Candido Mendes University in partnership with UNESCO. The event reunited several "star scholars," such as Fredric Jameson and Susan Buck-Morss, in order to discuss a topic which was comparatively new back then: the cultural dimension of globalization and its effects. John attended as the author of the classic books, *The End of Organized Capitalism* (1987, with Scott Lash), *The Tourist Gaze* (1990), and *Consuming Places* (1995). If so far globalization was being addressed under the lens of what could be called the production paradigm, in these three books Urry focused on the grey zones between work and non-work time, finding a path to decipher globalization through (then) neglected themes such as leisure, tourism, and consumption. For a nation where democracy was still a novelty and new segments were struggling to be incorporated into the so-called consumption culture, this "cultural turn" was especially inspiring.

Instead of going for the recycling of celebrated ideas, however, John turned the Rio event into an opportunity to test arguments which would be developed from the early 2000s on, and for which, later, he would create (with Mimi Sheller) the term "New Mobilities Paradigm" (NMP). Titled "Inhabiting the Car," his paper exposed the estrangement facing the silence that the social sciences reserved for one of the most exemplary inventions of a globalized technology, which in many ways defined the lifestyle of the twentieth century: the automobile. In that sense, the paper anticipates the debate detailed in an article published with Mimi Sheller in the same year, and which would be revisited another couple of times – especially in the dossier "Automobilities," published in 2004 in *Theory, Culture and Society*, and in *After the Car* (2009, co-written with Kingsley Dennis) – within the context of the NMP.

In May 2007, John Urry made his second trip to Brazil. This time his destination was Recife, where he participated in the XIII Congress of the Brazilian Sociological Association which gathered over 2600 participants at the Federal University of Pernambuco. Alessandro Bonnano (Sam Houston State University), Michel Wieviorka (then president of the International Sociological Association), José de Souza Martins (University of São Paulo), Shen Ming Ming (University of Peking), Maria Stela Grossi Porto (University of Brasilia), Thomas Leithäuser (Universität Bremen), Francisco de Oliveira (University of São Paulo), and John were the keynote speakers. All of them, except Ming Ming, have chapters in an edited book titled "Desigualdade, Diferença e

Reconhecimento" (Inequality, Difference and Recognition), organized by Josefa Salete B. Cavalcanti, Silke Weber, and Tom Dweyer (2009). Unfortunately, the book did not have a wide distribution and John's piece – "Carros, climas e futuros complexos" (Cars, Climates and Complex Futures) – I should admit, is rather unknown to Brazilian audiences. Still, it is important to acknowledge how timely John's critiques on the centrality of the car were for audiences living in a country where road traffic crashes are a leading cause of death, injury, and hospitalization.

That second trip to Brazil marked John in an ambivalent way. On one hand, he was positively surprised at how famous he was, among Brazilian peers, as the author of "O Olhar do Turista" (the Portuguese version of *The Tourist Gaze*, published in 1999), to these days the main bibliographical reference on any sociology of tourism syllabus in Brazil. On the other hand, the contrast between the luxurious structure of Candido Mendes University (the private institution which had hosted him seven years before in Rio) and the precarious state of the Federal University of Pernambuco (a public and non-profit institution located in one of the most unequal metropolises in Brazil), seemed to him "obscene," to quote the exact adjective that John employed. He could not come to terms with the fact that dark-skinned waiters, wearing white gloves, served dishes on silver plates in Rio while, in Recife, the university lacked basic infrastructure. A former student of the prestigious Cambridge University, he was no stranger to academic ostentation; but it was, more than anything else, the unevenness between the two environments that he found unacceptable.

The "obscene" socio-economic inequality, that in a nutshell defined Brazil for John, was to be experienced on even more radical terms on his following visit to Rio in September 2011. The main reason for the trip was the project, "Emerging Middle Classes and Low Carbon Mobilities: Setting Long-Term Foundations for Transnational Research," which we designed together (with Javier Caletrio) in 2009, during my stay at Lancaster University's Center for Mobilities Research (CeMoRe) as a visiting fellow. Financing from the British Academy (to which, later, Brazilian educational institutions added resources) allowed us to put together two events – the first, at Lancaster University; the second, at the Center for the Research and Documentation of Contemporary Brazilian History, at the Getulio Vargas Foundation, where I was an associate professor before migrating to São Paulo. At that point in time, Brazil was, more than ever, the "land of the future" and our president, Luis Inacio Lula da Silva, was "the man." A new category had emerged, not only in the media, but also in the academic vocabulary: "new middle class." Our aim was to think about the dramatic growth of that supposed new middle class, and its aspiration to emulate the energy-intensive, mobile lifestyle first initiated in the rich North, having four key themes – imaginaries, practices, networks and infrastructures – in mind.

When I went to pick him up at the airport in Rio de Janeiro, I expected John to be exhausted due to his previous busy schedule at an event in Santiago,

Chile, and at least indisposed after having squeezed his nearly 1.90 meter height into an economy-class seat. But there he was, bubbling with enthusiasm for what he called his South American adventure, ready to be with his "mobilities gang," as John affectionately nicknamed us (Javier Caletrío, Saulo Cwerner, Sven Kesselring, and myself).

As part of the workshop, we organized a guided tour to Rocinha, advertised in the tourism market as "the largest favela in Latin America" and where I conducted field work for several years. John had patiently listened to me talking about how Rio de Janeiro favelas, territories historically associated with poverty and violence, had been turned into a commodity, a tourist destination, and a mediatic landscape. While I was putting together the manuscript for my book, *Touring Poverty* (2013), John and I discussed how mobile images of a desubstantiated favela – i.e. a geography of imagination that lacks empirical specificities – were produced and shared, resulting in what I ended up naming "the traveling favela." It was finally time for John to turn what so far had been "imaginative" and "communicative" travels to him into an embodied one. The tour impressed him on many levels, especially because socio-economic inequality was there, once again, in a very tangible and obscene way. On the following day, in his keynote speech at the opening of the seminar, John referred to Rocinha as an empirical reality capable of giving complexity to his possible future model, demanding a deeper examination of the links between poverty, resilience, and sustainable futures.

The Rio+20 episode marks the last "corporeal trip" John Urry took to Brazil. Fortunately, that doesn't mean we, Brazilians, have seen his last incursion among us. As I write this piece, hundreds of volumes which comprised his personal library are being packaged by Lancaster University to cross the Atlantic Ocean and land at the Florestan Fernandes Library at University of São Paulo. I am at a loss for words to express how honored I am to be part of the mobility of John Urry's ideas in this vast Global South. It is not only a major gain for all of us who are interested in John's legacy and the NMP, but it also represents an important step forward in designing a different map for the geopolitics of knowledge, one where concepts flow in all possible directions.

This new map is far from being an arbitrary or artificial invention as there is a clear convergence between several epistemological categories proposed by the NMP and what Latin American authors, who are less well known due to language barriers, have long defended. Authors such as Raquel Rolnik, Milton Santos, and Walter Mignolo, for example, have insisted that in contemporary times space combines flows and fixed aspects, systems of objects and of actions; that interactions with and within space take place both based on specific places and on new global information and communication technologies; and that the dichotomy between territories or networks is fallacious, since what actually exist are network territories. On the other hand, concepts such as network capital enable us to better understand what is taking place in different megacities of the global South where high levels of socio-economic inequality go hand in hand with all sorts of apps and technological devices that enable disenfranchised and urban poor to carry on their mobile lives. It is in this sense that I and other colleagues who, inspired by John's legacy, are committed to spreading the "mobilities word" down here believe that time has arrived for a more horizontal mobility of ideas and concepts between all of us.

I wrap up by once more evoking that Sunday which I mentioned early on in these notes. In the company of mutual friends and fellow sociologists, Licia Valladares and Edmond Préteceille, we had lunch at my house and watched a Euro 2012 match on television. As the game went on, I tried not to get lost in the flow of a wide variety of topics, a typical effect of conversations – formal or informal – with John. The same thing had happened, for example, when I had the pleasure of interviewing him for the Brazilian journal *Estudos Históricos*, in the company of Sergio Benício de Mello, a professor at Pernambuco Federal University, who was also a research fellow at CeMoRe. Like our many informal conversations, the interview with John captivates us not only for his erudition, but also for his ability to articulate apparently disparate themes – cinema, Vikings, petroleum – in a continuum of meaning. He always gave forth a line of argumentation – not always direct, but never too twisted – able to tie together lessons from history with speculations about possible future scenarios. From this fine stitching emerged key concepts turned on their head, or "under erasure," to use the expression of Stuart Hall, a thinker much admired by John. For Hall, operating with concepts "under erasure" means balancing them on the dividing line between the original form and complete deconstruction. In the writings of John Urry, even the concept of society appears "under erasure": a concept that is no longer serviceable for present challenges, but that has not yet been superseded by an entirely new idea. It is no accident that the book published in 2000, from which the idea of the mobilities turn largely emerged, was provocatively titled *Sociology beyond Societies*.

I am unable to trace in my memory the avenue of themes we covered that Sunday afternoon. I remember well, however, John's enthusiastic recommendation of *Solar*, by Ian McEwan, the "first novel about climate change" according to his brief yet provocative description. When I heard that John had passed, I went ahead and bought the book as a way of paying him a private homage. I could hear echoes of John's frank laughter as I read the comical misadventures of scientist Michael Beard, McEwan's misogynist, swindling, vain anti-hero. Pathologically selfish, incapable of any sort of moral or physical sacrifice, Michael Beard embodies the sins of capitalism which have driven the planet to its current crisis. Extremely generous and utterly unattached to academic deference, always loyal, and deeply committed to the principles of a fairer world, John Urry embodied the virtues necessary to stand up to the sins of any Michael Beard. This confrontation is necessary and urgent, inside the academy and out, in Brazil and elsewhere, because futures, as John taught us, are battlegrounds in the present, and they approach us increasingly fast.

Chapter 15

After the end of tourism

Jennie Germann Molz

John Urry was fond of starting his books with evocative quotes, and so it seems appropriate to launch this essay with a quote that reminds me of John's notion of the end of tourism. Now that we have lost the old tracks of tourism, where do we find ourselves? What wonders are here to be revealed?

Well, at this very moment I find myself writing this essay about John Urry in the kind of café where many of you are probably sitting while reading it. This particular coffee shop occupies a renovated warehouse in a gentrifying post-industrial American city. A chalkboard near the front counter informs me that my coffee today is from Kenya and that the bread of the day is olive and herb. The décor is typical: exposed brick walls, weathered hardwood floors, and optimistically large tables meant to be shared with strangers. Instead of sharing my table with a stranger, though, I'm sharing it with my laptop computer. On the screen I have half a dozen windows open: my email inbox with unread messages from colleagues around the world; an airline website displaying the price of flights to Amsterdam (conference this winter; should I bring the family?); a social media site where I'm intermittently chatting with a friend in Italy while watching videos from protests at the Philadelphia and Boston airports flow into my news feed; the draft of this essay. This is a snapshot of a relatively privileged lifestyle, to be sure, but it offers a glimpse of what life looks like after the end of tourism.

But before we come to the end let's go back and start at the beginning. For me, it all started with the first edition of *The Tourist Gaze*. It is no exaggeration to say that reading *The Tourist Gaze* changed my life. After spending several years of my 20s backpacking around the world, I knew that I wanted to delve further into the study of travel and tourism. I assumed I would go the anthropology or history route, and I was already investigating PhD programs in the U.S. when I first picked up *The Tourist Gaze*. I had no intention of moving to England or becoming a sociologist, but I ended up doing both because of the way John wrote about tourism in that book. He made a case that tourism was far more than an industry of escape or a practice on the margins of everyday life. Instead, he saw tourism as a symptom and a symbol of the modern condition. The idea that studying tourism could reveal the complexity of our changing world sparked my imagination.

In the opening chapter of *The Tourist Gaze*, John defines the tourist gaze as a socially organized way of consuming landscapes and townscapes that contrast with the mundane scenery of our everyday lives. By definition, the tourist gaze is a quest for something out of the ordinary. But he ends the book on a somewhat different note, suggesting that the extraordinary has become ordinary while the ordinary has become extraordinary. As evidence, he offered the case of Glasgow. Named the 1990 European City of Culture, Glasgow had been remade from a "rough and depressing place" into a tourist attraction. This transformation suggested to John that there was no limit to the reach of the "endlessly devouring gaze" (1990, p. 156). John didn't use the phrase "end of tourism" in the first edition of *The Tourist Gaze*, but he anticipated the concept in the book's final sentence where he predicted the unrelenting "democratisation of the tourist gaze and the spectacle-isation of place" (ibid.). He recognized that the tourist gaze bore the seeds of its own demise. As the world is remade to satisfy the tourist's insatiable appetite for difference, there would be nothing different left to gaze upon.

In *Economies of Signs and Space*, published with Scott Lash a few years after *The Tourist Gaze* came out, John articulated his notion of the "end of tourism" more fully. His argument was not that people would stop traveling or that the tourism industry would crumble. On the contrary, he foresaw – and rightly so – substantial growth in the practices and business of tourism. What was ending, he claimed, was the notion of tourism as something out of the ordinary. If anything, our daily lives were becoming more touristic – more organized around sites of consumption and themed environments and visual spectacles – to the extent that "people are tourists most of the time, whether they are literally mobile or only experience simulated mobility through the incredible fluidity of multiple signs and electronic images" (Lash and Urry, 1994, p. 259).

By the time he published the second edition of *The Tourist Gaze* in 2002, the social and cultural effects of globalization had borne out his prediction. We had arrived at the end of tourism and entered a globalized world. Here, distinct tourist times and spaces had given way to a post-Fordist era in which the distinctions and dichotomies that previously held the social order together begin to melt away:

> There are increasing similarities between behaviours that are "home" and "away" … Tourist sites proliferate across the globe as tourism has become massively mediatized, while everyday sites of activity get redesigned in "tourist" mode, as with many themed environments. Mobility is increasingly central to the identities of many young people, to those who are part of diasporas and to many relatively wealthy retired people who can live on the move … And "tourist reflexivity" leads almost every site – however boring – to be able to develop some niche location within the swirling contours of the emergent global order. (2002, p. 161)

And that is where I find myself today, in a boring post-industrial warehouse that has been remade in the swirling contours of the global order. I am immersed in a world of what John called "aesthetic cosmopolitanism," where exotic commodities (like coffee from Kenya) and artisanal breads become everyday menu items. My mediated and imaginative mobilities overlap with my physical mobility, including my upcoming trip to Amsterdam where I will be traveling for work *and* pleasure. And as I gaze at my computer screen, I see a video feed of a political drama unfolding against the backdrop of the arrivals hall at the airport. Tourist and refugee mobilities become intertwined with social movements and calls for mobility justice in airports that look like shopping malls. This is life after the end of tourism.

In the transnational and post-Fordist world John was describing, tourism is no longer discernable from other ways of being in and moving through the world. As the tourist gaze becomes thoroughly integrated into the everyday, a host of other dichotomies also collapse: home and away, work and leisure, authenticity and simulation, local and global, proximity and distance. And this is especially true when we consider the technologies of travel and communication that make it that much cheaper, easier, and faster to be here, there, or elsewhere. Instead, social life becomes organized around people, objects, and images that circulate between faraway and nearby and it involves intermittent moments of mobility and immobility, of dwelling-in-motion, and of being together and being apart.

By the time I arrived at Lancaster to begin my PhD studies, John had published *Sociology beyond Societies* (2000) and given a new name to what came after the end of tourism: *mobilities*. Between the unraveling dichotomies of the old sociology and this emerging mobilities paradigm, John unlocked a new empirical world. As the supposedly fixed anchors of social life were set in motion, how were we to make sense of the kinds of socialities, subjectivities, intimacies, and citizenships that were circulating in this new mobile world order? I quickly embraced the questions John posed in that book and carried them with me into my own research.

If *The Tourist Gaze* had validated my desire to study tourism, *Sociology beyond Societies* made it seem urgent and important to do so. The sense of urgency I felt was fueled, as well, by the proliferation of the internet and the pace of technological innovation that was making networked social lives ever more prominent in the early 2000s. In my doctoral thesis, *Destination World*, I studied the phenomenon of round-the-world travel through the websites that travel bloggers were just beginning to publish online. I was initially interested in understanding round-the-world travel as a performance of global citizenship, but I soon discovered that this particular intersection of tourism and technology – of backpacking and blogging – involved a constant navigation between home and away, distance and attachment, and escape and belonging. When John and his collaborators Jonas Larsen and Kay Axhausen wrote in *Mobilities, Networks, Geographies* that tourist travel represented "not just an escape from home, but also a *search* for home(s)" (2006, p. 44), I nodded in agreement. The travel bloggers in my study were not merely escaping from home or from their daily social obligations; instead, they were marshaling new technologies to stay in touch, to meet up with friends and family members while on the move, to extend and maintain their social networks, and to make themselves at home on the road and in the world.

In many ways, the internet was accelerating the de-differentiation John associated with the end of tourism. It allowed backpackers to bring home with them on the road; it enabled tourists to work while on holiday; it brought the faraway nearby and allowed travelers to create a buffer that kept local realities at arm's length. I tried to capture these practices of mobile attachment and detachment with concepts like "global abode" – the idea that home can be multiple and mobile – or "cosmopolitan belonging" – the notion that global citizenship is not necessarily about floating around freely, but involves an embodied and embedded way of inhabiting the world. In other words, I was trying to make sense of what John referred to as "dwelling-in-mobility."

My interest in this home–mobility nexus eventually extended to the world of hospitality exchange networks. After I completed my PhD, I stayed at Lancaster as a postdoctoral fellow in the newly founded Centre for Mobilities Research where my project was to study couchsurfing and similar online platforms that enabled travelers to find local hosts willing to let them stay in their homes for free. In these blurred spaces between home and mobility, I found hosts and guests enacting moments of "mobile conviviality," a kind of embodied togetherness-on-the-move inflected with aspirations of cosmopolitan community. It all sounds so lofty when I summarize it like that, but I was – and have remained – conscious of John's steady reminders to pay attention to the inequalities, violence, and oppression that persist amidst mobility. For example, as much as couchsurfers claimed to be creating a better world, theirs turned out to be a fairly exclusionary vision of a global community.

Couchsurfing represented the de-differentiation of home and mobility or of hosting and guesting, but it also revealed the way online and offline worlds were blending together. This became the focus of my next project, *Travel Connections*, which explored the way travelers use technology to connect to – and disconnect from – people and places while on the move. In that book, I subjected the prevailing theories in tourism studies to a makeover, the idea being that many of these theories – about landscape, hosts and guests, authenticity, escape, and even the tourist gaze – had been developed prior to the arrival of the internet. But my contribution in that book was equally inspired by John's call to theorize the forms of mobile sociality and mobile lifestyles that emerge at the end of tourism.

That is the same call that brings me to my current research on worldschooling. Worldschoolers are families who take their children out of conventional schools and educate them while traveling the world. With the internet at their disposal, they lay claim to location-independent lifestyles funded by remote work and justified by the belief that the world is their classroom. The sedentary categories of social life have almost completely collapsed in these performances of life on the road: home and citizenship are multiple and mobile; family life and gender relations are fluid; and work and leisure are so thoroughly entangled that for many of these families, especially the ones who make money by blogging or consulting about worldschooling, their lifestyle *is* their livelihood. Worldschooling mobilities flow and diverge alongside a host of other mobilities that make the world go round – business travelers, expats, retirees, diplomats, travel nannies, backpackers, migrants, refugees – in search of the "good life" or at least a better life. But this is just one example of many, many ways of what life looks like after the end of tourism.

As I study worldschoolers, traveling with them online and in person, I aspire to move as deftly as John did between the biographical specificity of their "mobile lives," the title of his book with Anthony Elliott (2010), and the broader social, historical, political, and economic contexts that shape the lived experiences of globalization and mobility. John's theories were comprehensive, but they were always attuned to the messy, complicated realities of life in a mobile world; to the threads of daily life – commutes and traffic, shopping and working, meeting up and saying goodbye, or traveling for work or for pleasure or for survival – that weave together a social world. He had an eye for these personal experiences as symptoms of larger trends and truths. I never had the chance to talk with John at length about this project, but I suspect that he would not be at all surprised by this new permutation of a mobile lifestyle. It's what he always told us to expect after the end of tourism, at least for as long as the oil holds out.

It's hard to imagine a more welcoming – and stimulating – intellectual home for a project on worldschooling than the new mobilities paradigm that John spelled out in *Sociology beyond Societies*, and later in articles and editorials co-authored with Mimi Sheller and Kevin Hannam. Tourism studies has traditionally been on the margins of more serious sociological pursuits, and the alternative travel practices I study – backpacking, couchsurfing, worldschooling – are even further on the margins of tourism studies. But the new mobilities paradigm opened a door onto a world where these practices mattered. The mobilities paradigm gave me the conceptual and methodological tools to think about tourism's complex entanglement with various other embodied, imaginative, and mediated mobilities and to parse the power relations that bring tourists, migrants, and refugees into one another's orbits. It pushed me to think about tourism in terms of mobilities as well as immobilities, blockages and frictions, and the conditions of movement or stillness. It challenged my assumptions about free and frictionless mobilities and gave me good reasons to place tourism at the center of consequential debates about politics, energy, or the environment. But it didn't tie me to tourism. In this sense, the mobilities paradigm has been not so much a home as an intellectual mooring; something that both anchors and propels new ideas.

But it is not just with the mobilities paradigm, as a set of ideas or a scholarly agenda, that John has created a mooring for our work. It is in the constellation of people who gravitated toward John, inspired by his work and enlivened by his mentorship. It is in the many connections he choreographed among us, in my case with Mimi Sheller and Anne-Marie Fortier, who supervised my PhD thesis, with the cohort of brilliant doctoral students and postdoctoral fellows who also came to Lancaster to work with John, with the eminent guest speakers and visiting scholars he persuaded to spend an afternoon or a few weeks or months in northwest England, with the dedicated scholars who launched CeMoRe and sister centers across Europe and North America, many of whom are recounting their own stories in the pages of this book. I guess it turns out that I'm sharing my table with all of you, thanks to John, after all.

References

Elliott, A. and Urry, J. (2010) *Mobile Lives*. London: Routledge.

Larsen, J., Urry, J. and Axhausen, K. (2006) *Mobilities, Networks, Geographies*. London: Routledge.

Lash, S. and Urry, J. (1994) *Economies of Signs and Space*. London: SAGE.

Urry, J. (1990) *The Tourist Gaze*. London: SAGE.

Urry, J. (2000) *Sociology beyond Societies: Mobilities for the Twenty-First Century*. London: Routledge.

Urry, J. (2002) *The Tourist Gaze*, second edition. London: SAGE.

Chapter 16

Tourism, mobilities, geopolitics, events

Kevin Hannam

Introduction

On 28 April 2017 the prime minister of the UK, Theresa May, mistakenly commented that she wanted to prevent 'tourism' instead of 'terrorism'. Given the political climate this was an unfortunate slip but it does highlight the fact that tourism and politics are intimately connected. It also demonstrates that words can somehow slip and the importance of clarity of communication. John Urry is sorely missed both for his ability to communicate difficult ideas and to bring forth new concepts concerning how we understand the societies we live in currently and in the future – so that we might not be sad about the future. Although he was always a sociologist, his work spanned many disciplines and had a wide-ranging influence in the social sciences, including geography, tourism studies, science and technology studies, as well as the arts and humanities. In this essay, I wish to consider the influence his work has had in particular on tourism studies and the development of mobilities research. But in relation to these more obvious aspects of John's work I also want to reflect on wider aspects of his influence of geopolitics, artistic work and the study of events.

Tourism

My first ever publication was in fact a book review of John Urry's seminal book *The Tourist Gaze* (1990) which he told me he wrote based on the course he taught at Lancaster University – a place he made his intellectual home, or rather 'mooring'. He never expected this book to be 'a big thing'. For him it was perhaps a sideline to his central focus on the transformation of societies, but this book was to be a significant influence in the mainstreaming of tourism in geography and social science. Rather than the 'end' of tourism, his analyses made it more important to study tourism as part of the wider transformations in society.

His book *Consuming Places* (Urry 1995) engaged with tourism in the place he was embedded within – the Lancashire countryside and the Lake District in particular. In this text he examined the making of the Lake District and concluded that it

> has had to be rescued from itself. Culture has been necessary to save nature in the Lake District and to produce a very distinct and 'civilised' place for consumption (especially for the white service class). It is a place that is simultaneously valued for its culture and civilisation and for its naturalness and relative wildness. It is a hybrid landscape. (Urry 1995, 210)

He also emphasised how embodied practices of 'walking' were socially and historically constructed: 'Walking gradually came to be viewed as a positive choice. Since ordinary people did not now always need to walk so walking travellers were not necessarily thought of as poor' (Urry 1995, 201). Indeed, his reading of the embodied practices of walking in the Lake District would subsequently influence the development of practice theories in tourism research but also more implicitly artistic engagements such as the exhibition Walking Poets, organised at Grasmere in the Lake District in 2014 (Collier 2014; see Figure 16.1).

Writing in the catalogue for the exhibition, Carol McKay explains that in his 'creative reworking, Collier has deliberately selected journal entries that describe favourite routes Dorothy followed – and ones he has walked a number of times: an ascent of Fairfield foiled by weather, followed two days later by a walk "upon Helvellyn, glorious, glorious sights"' (Collier 2014). In the book *Envisioning Networked Urban Mobilities* (Kjaerulff et al. 2018), we seek to further develop John's work through an examination of the connections between various artistic practices and social science methodological debates that 'envision' the urban future, as relatively little critical work has been published on what happens when artistic work and artists become mobile and their influence on possible futures.

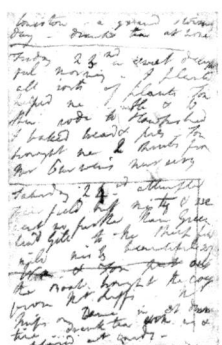

Coniston—a grand stormy day—drank tea at home.
Friday 23rd. A sweet delightful morning. I planted all sorts of plants, Tom helped me. He & W then rode to Hawkshead. I baked bread and pies. Tom brought me 2 shrubs from Mr Curwen's nursery.
Saturday 24th. Attempted Fairfield but misty & we went no further than Green Head Gill to the sheepfold—mild misty beautiful soft. Wm and Tom put out the Boat brought the coat from Mr Luff's. Mr Simpson came in at dinner-time—drank tea with us & played at cards.

Figure 16.1 The Texture of Thought: Fairfield, from Dorothy Wordsworth's journal entry, 23 and 24 October 1801, unison pastel onto digital print, 2014, 35 x 65 cm

Mobilities

Somehow John also found time to attend many conferences around the world and I would spend some time with him at many of these. Indeed, I once sat next to him on a lengthy bus trip from Hamilton to Rotorua in New Zealand as part of the Taking Tourism to the Limits conference in 2003, where he was variously described as being the John Lennon or Michael Jackson of tourism studies – something he was more than a little embarrassed about. On this bus journey we also discussed ideas concerning tourism and mobilities which sub-sequently led to the establishment of a new journal – *Mobilities*, now in its eleventh year of publication. Although he was initially reluctant to be an editor of the journal given the many projects he was involved in, without his support and vision this would never have been realised.

His direction in terms of the mobilities paradigm and the journals *Mobilities* and *Applied Mobilities* have substantially influenced the direction of mobilities research and will remain a long-lasting legacy as he has helped us to understand the transformation of societies. However, his last projects were devoted to cri-tiquing and developing an analysis of our environmental problems in particular, with a focus on manufacturing, urban transport systems and climate change (Urry 2016). In this sense, the advent of a more applied aspect to mobilities research was particularly poignant as we seek to find complex solutions to complex problems, even as these problems seemingly multiply through our actions and inactions – as we see below in the discussion of the very real 'problems' of geopolitics and events.

Geopolitics

In his final book, *What Is the Future?*, John demonstrates that futures are often con-tested and saturated with different interests, especially in relation to future generations (Urry 2016). The contemporary debate over 'Brexit' from the European Union provides an example of how geopolitical futures may have significant consequences for those that are yet to have the power to vote. He shows how analyses of social institutions, practices and lives should be central to examining potential futures and issues as to who owns the future. He argues that there are multiple 'causes' and 'solutions', long-term lock-ins and complex interdependencies, and social groups having radically different time frames for understanding what is at stake. Mobilities research advances an agenda that thinks relationally about the geopolitics that hinders, encourages, regulates and informs mobilities at various scales, from the micro-biological to the bodily to the national, the mobility of information and non-human objects, as well as how these are represented in the media.

For example, since September 2015 the issue of refugees and/or migrants has entered centre stage in terms of the geopolitics between Western Europe and Eastern Europe, with the centre being reimagined as a space of transit for those seeking a new life away from the fragility of becoming human in Syria,

Afghanistan and elsewhere. However, the complexity of the reception was frequently portrayed in the media as a division between those that welcomed these new arrivals and those that expected their government to enforce the borders and prevent so-called abuse of the EU's system of asylum. This became focused on the 'mooring' for many potential migrants at the main train station in Budapest, Hungary – a geopolitical space which was subsequently framed and reframed by both the international media and international tourists as either a place to avoid or, conversely, a place to visit and offer voluntary help. Mobilities theory helps us to critically think about such events as events in progress, as the consequences of diverse planning and unplanned geopolitical decisions and indecisions are worked through complex systems.

Events

An event may be commonly understood at its most minimal level as something out of place, something shocking that interrupts the normal flow of things. It may be planned for or may be somewhat unexpected. Events can take hold of the imagination though, such that it takes on a life of its own and thus unfolds through time and space. Sporting events may seemingly take place in defined spaces and times but have much wider spatialities and temporalities as well as geopolitical consequences – we only have to think about such 'hallmark' events such as football world cups and Olympic Games to understand the complexity of these spatial and temporal mobilities. Moreover, we also need to recognise the ways in which films and other social media commonly frame our under-standings of events and the places of events. Fundamentally, fiction and reality thus become blurred in contemporary events as we witness the postmodern parody of 'fake news' being played out across the world, often for geopolitical causes.

We can go to an event, but the social nature of this event may lead us to become obligated to attend further events which we may not (really) want to attend (such as another political meeting). Tourism, events and mobilities co-exist in various foldings and unfoldings through time and space which are difficult to control through contemporary scheduling as much as they are subject to national and international geopolitical structures. Events may also serve as contexts that provide meanings and purpose to a distinct action – from frantically leaving one's home to escape from a mudslide, to embarking on a protest march.

The amount of events as well as the different scales of them also leads to various stresses: in terms of transport systems through congestion, in terms of security through geopolitical systems of control, as well as in terms of indivi-duals' abilities to cope with attending multiple events at the same time (should I attend my son's birthday party or go on a protest march through London?). John's work also emphasises how people find meaning in temporality, in events, something we have tried to recently draw attention to in discussions of 'event mobilities'. Events are unpredictable and uncertain but are key to understanding the future through notions of irreversibility, lock-in, thresholds, feedback loops, tipping points and phase transitions. John further discusses how more 'clumsy' rather than 'elegant' solutions may help us to solve our contemporary 'wicked' problems, but that these may of course have unintended and often unwanted consequences as the many examples of research into the ambivalences of mobilities testify (including the amplification of migration as well as the impact of the use of smart technologies) (Urry 2016).

Conclusions

In *What Is the Future?*, John explores contested mobilities in cities and the futures of energy and climate change, noting that what is preferable may actually turn out to be the least probable. He notes the dilemma of the classical Cassandra syndrome whereby we know the problem but try to ignore it. In particular, he was critical of any technological determinism of the future, against any simple e-solutions to our contemporary problems (as advocated by many in tourism studies) as well cognisant of the dangers of a dive into catastrophism. Instead, he argued for an active planning for future alternatives based upon critical social science and complexity systems analysis: 'A complex systems approach brings out how the future cannot be reduced neither to the actions of individual actors nor to persisting social structures' (Urry 2016). In his recent discussion of the future of urban transport systems, the founder of Tesla and Space X, Elon Musk, stated that he was inspired to consider a tunnel system to alleviate congestion because he found being stuck in traffic 'soul destroying'. His vision is to have 'no limits' to the amount of tunnels, but to find ways to cut the cost of boring and to speed up how quickly such tunnels could be created: 'We have a pet snail called Gary, and Gary is capable of moving 14 times faster than a tunnel boring machine – so the ambition is to beat Gary' (Wakefield 2017). While we may not agree with the development of a life underground using tunnels, we do need to think about alternative systems to the ones that have been created thus far drawing upon the insights of mobilities research. Contemporary tourism, geopolitics and events reflect many of the problems of global complexity that John highlighted in his many publications.

References

Collier, M. (ed.) (2014) Wordsworth and Bashō: Walking Poets, Sunderland and Grasmere: AEN and the Wordsworth Trust.

Kjaerulff, A. A., Kesselring, S., Peters, P. and Hannam, K. (2018) *Envisioning Networked Urban Mobilities*. Abingdon: Routledge.

Urry, J. (1990) *The Tourist Gaze*. London: SAGE.

Urry, J. (1995) *Consuming Places*. London: Routledge.

Urry, J. (2016) *What Is the Future?* Cambridge: Polity.

Wakefield, J. (2017) Ted 2017: Elon Musk's Vision for Underground Road System. Available online: www.bbc.co.uk/news/technology-39741094, accessed 30 April 2017.

Chapter 17

Running away from, or with, the tourist gaze

Jonas Larsen

Introduction

The Tourist Gaze (1990) made John Urry a world-famous tourism scholar and the book quickly became a seminal text. It is John's 'best-selling book and more or less most cited book' (personal email). Few tourism concepts are cited and commented upon more than 'the tourist gaze'. Its massive impact dazzled John as it was one of his first pieces on tourism, and he never devoted himself fully to tourism studies. As John often told me, *The Tourist Gaze* taught him the importance of an excellent and cite-able title and he was grateful to his editor who suggested that title as an alternative to 'The Sociology of Tourism' (Larsen 2014).

In this essay, I revisit the 'tourist gaze' through three small tales about the concept and how it came to influence my and many others' academic thinking and career. These tales also unveil how John Urry invested enormous trust in the younger scholars that he worked with. The first vignette explores the birth of the 'tourist gaze' and how it eventually came to define the sociology of tourism and, many years later, my formative years as a tourism scholar. Drawing on emails, notes, scribbles in old *Tourist Gaze* books, track changes in manuscripts and my memory, the second vignette explores how John Urry and I wrote *The Tourist Gaze 3.0* (Urry and Larsen 2011). In the final vignette, I briefly explore how the tourist gaze is part of my new research project on geographies of running mobilities.

Vignette 1: 1990–2004

John Urry was always ahead of everybody else in discovering new and exciting research fields; *The Tourist Gaze* is an early example of this. Prior to this book, few sociologists had taken tourism seriously or noted its growing significance around the world. Tourism, it seemed – this frivolous world of pleasures and carefree leisure – was not an appropriate subject matter for a serious sociologist. John Urry was clearly aware of this. On the first page, he almost apologizes for writing a book about this seemingly trivial subject matter, and yet he speculates, 'that sociology might have great difficulties in accounting for holi-day-making' (1990: 1) as sociologists struggle to write about pleasure and fun. I think this knowledge gap and intellectual challenge triggered John Urry's interest in tourism. However, John Urry was also now aware – in part because of his 'locality studies' in the 1980s (see Bærenholdt, this volume) – that tourist travel was increasingly central to much social, cultural and economic life as well as to the rise and fall of cities and the built environment. Travel and tourism were already a significant phenomenon and their impact would only increase in the decades to come. While John Urry did not use the term 'mobility', we may say that *The Tourist Gaze* develops his interest in mobility and is a forerunner of the 'mobilities turn'. While tourism arguably played a smaller but nevertheless consistent role in John Urry's later work, it still sparked his interest in travel and mobility.

The Tourist Gaze is essentially an account of how modern tourism became organized around a core set of new institutions, ideologies and practices, and not least how vision and new visual technologies such as photography pro-duced new and exciting ways of looking at and visually appreciating landscapes and architecture as aesthetically pleasing and spectacular. Tourism became materially and discursively designed as a 'way of seeing' and this mirrors the general Western preference towards vision, as discussed by Foucault and others. The 'system' approach that was so central to John Urry's later mobility thinking is also present here as different tourist gazes are said to be organized, patterned and systematized by various discourses, material relations, social groups and environments. Tourists do not gaze by chance.

I first discovered John Urry and the 'tourist gaze' when, as a second-year BA student in the mid-1990s at Roskilde University, Denmark, I took a course on modernity and postmodernity and wrote a project on postmodern consump-tion where *Economies of Sign and Space* (Lash and Urry 1993) played a key role. A year later, I found myself enrolled in an MA course in Cultural Studies at Lancaster University. I was disappointed that Scott Lash had left Lancaster a month earlier but that did not alter my excitement of studying sociology at Lancaster University. It was such an intellectually and socially stimulating place.

I particularly enjoyed John Urry's class on tourism. The class took place late in the afternoon and the 20 students were from all around the world. Few were native speakers and many – including myself – were not brilliant at English. We easily got lost if the lecturer was talking too fast or using academic jargon we did not fully comprehend. As far as I recall, John taught in much the same way as he would conduct a seminar or keynote talk; sitting behind the desk, with a warm and relaxed composure, he would read out a manuscript that was lying in front of him. This may sound boring and aloof to some, but it worked for us as he was never going too fast, his pronunciation was clear, and brevity has always been a trademark of his writing. In his class, we did not get lost. I was particularly interested in the lecture on gazing in relation to tourist photography. I volunteered to do a presentation about the wonderful *A Dream of England: Landscape, Photography and the Tourist's Imagination* by John Taylor (1994), which explores the history of the English landscape seen through the development and later mass popularization of tourism and photography. In my MA thesis – supervised by John Urry – I was concerned with the tourist gaze in relation to the built environment and architecture in my 'reading' of the then newly built and lavishly appointed Trafford Centre shopping centre in Manchester (Urry and Larsen 2011: 129–32).

I left Lancaster after completing my degree but we met a few months later as John Urry became a visiting professor in a research project about Danish tourism at Roskilde University (see Bærenholdt, this volume), where I was appointed as a PhD student. 'The tourist gaze' framed my PhD and John Urry eventually became my second supervisor. I wrote about tourist photography as a commercial and vernacular practice, but I also developed and indeed criticized John Urry's take on the tourist gaze, for being too static and too concerned with sights. I developed the notions of the 'travel glance' to capture how landscapes are viewed through motorized, framed movement and the 'family gaze' (with Michael Haldrup) to discuss the crucial role of family photography within much vernacular tourist photography. Eventually I questioned the explicit tendency within *The Tourist Gaze* (1990) to portray gazing as a monolithic, all-encompassing tourism practice; there is more to tourism than gazing. In this critique, I was inspired by Tim Edensor's amazing book *Tourists at the Taj* (1998) (which, ironically, was based on a PhD supervised in the later stages by John Urry) that gives a rich account of the multiple practices – including gazing – and sensuous engagements that tourists perform while visiting a place like the Taj Mahal (see Edensor, this volume).

Vignette 2: 2009–11

John Urry was (in)famous for his extremely short text- or twitter-like emails that got straight to the point in one or two sentences, with no unnecessary chit chat or formality – indeed, why write 'very' when 'v' does the job? Wordy emails seemed to annoy him; they were a waste of one's time to write and read. I was therefore puzzled when I received a substantive email from John one day in 2009. The content was mind-blowing, too, with John asking me to be the co-author of the next edition of the classic and much cited *The Tourist Gaze*. The email was – despite its many words – characteristic of his email style as well as his generosity and humbleness. He wrote that SAGE had approached him to do a new version but that he wasn't sure whether he wanted to do it because he thought the structure of the book was cracking somehow and he was not fully up to date on the current debates in tourist studies.

Then he told me that he had thought to himself with whom have I worked on tourism most in recent years and with whom would it be fun to make the new edition with? It turned out that I was apparently that person! In addition to some general editing, he suggested that I could add two extra chapters: one on tourism and photography and one on tourism and multiple mobilities/types of performances. In the end, he told me that we would share 50/50 advances and earnings, although the publisher would probably insist that he figured as the first author. Finally, he wrote that he would not be at all offended if I declined the offer.

Jubilant, I promptly replied: 'I would love to co-write the new edition of *The Tourist Gaze* with you.'

I knew from my time as a research assistant (2003–2004) at Lancaster University that John and I were effective and productive together – even when I moved to Roskilde University and we wrote together at a distance. There was no meeting, no phone or Skype call to agree upon this project and outline the main tasks ahead – we knew each other well enough to rely on emails, and emails and digital networking were crucial throughout as we never phoned or Skyped and we only met face to face on two occasions during the two years in which we wrote the book. We must have sent hundreds of emails where we talked through problems with, and changes to, specific chapters; and emails 'transported' our track-changed word documents with our edited and new chapters. This allowed us to write *together*, despite the fact that we never rubbed shoulders in front of a computer. This is somewhat striking given the significance of intermittent meetings and verbal talk in much of John Urry's writing on distanciated social networks. In contrast, affordances and practices of digital co-working, of emailing, sharing documents electronically, and co-writing and co-editing a text through 'track changing' in a shared Word document are less discussed in his work.

However, we did meet on two occasions and these 'meetings' were crucial as they, in direct contrast to our brief emails, gave us a couple hours to discuss the book in its entirety and work with *printed* documents, correcting and scribbling on them with pencils, which was something that John Urry really appreciated. We never worked with computers on those meetings; they were devoted to talk, paper and pens – and a drink and meal afterwards where football and tennis were frequent topics. In contrast to his fast and succinct emails, in the flesh John was the master of the slow, a very convivial person to be in the company of.

For our first meeting, John Urry prepared himself by reading and scribbling a book version of the second edition on a long-haul journey. It turned out that John's scribbles suggested much deletion, rewriting and new ideas and studies to incorporate. He realized that the first two editions focused on the northwest of England and contained outdated case studies that ought to be replaced with new cases from around the world. As he was also supportive of my substantive list of suggested alterations to the existing chapters, we began to realize that we would probably end up significantly revising the existing book as well as adding three new chapters. The key challenge, as we saw it, was to find the right balance between defending and yet rethinking the tourist gaze in light of the recent 'performance turn' that suggested that the tourist gaze was outdated and ought to be replaced with more dynamic, processual and multi-sensuous concepts. I was in the middle of this discussion, as I had argued strongly for such a 'performance turn' in my own research. This concerned me. The way forward, it occurred to me, was to integrate the paradigms of gaze and performance within a single framework. John agreed. So, *The Tourist Gaze 3.0* ended up rethinking the tourist gaze as performative embodied practices and we also noted that there were limits on how much the gaze can explain.

John Urry was a perfectionist and it was very demanding to work with him for the simple reason that he always met our deadlines and his writing never failed to impress. He worked so fast and effectively, with emails arriving at all hours. I repaid his trust by working harder than ever. Part of John's academic success – and legacy – was his ability to instil faith in people, and in that process, empower those he worked with, giving them freedom and responsibility, which allowed him to work on several projects simultaneously. However, John was not into micro-management and control. At our first meeting, John handed me the scribbled book and told me do certain changes as well as *all* the changes *I* found necessary. John wanted it to be *my* book too. From that point onwards, we had equal say, and it became a co-authored book where John never used his superior status to triumph ideas or obstruct my substantial revisions and changes to his seminal work.

John Urry could not refrain from correcting some of his old writing. He crossed out surplus words and simplified wordy and convoluted sentences. He clearly found some of his writing from the 1990 version rather laborious and in need of shortening and editing. Over the years, John Urry became more and more preoccupied with writing in a lucid and brisk fashion. His academic success was partly down to the fact he could write fluently and accessibly about complex issues and difficult theories. Even non-native English speakers, students and non-sociologists, found him relatively easy to read and understand.

My writing was always what he called 'Urry-washed'. John corrected convoluted, wordy sentences and wayward language. I still recall an email where he pointed out that the content of my chapter was fine but that the writing was a bit wayward and in need of Urry-washing. It had an element of proofreading but it went beyond that: it was his way of teaching me to become a good writer and ensure the flow of the book. John's writing was relatively light but he did not take writing lightly; writing simply and to the point is hard work. It is a craft that takes time to develop and every new piece requires many, many revisions and edits.

Vignette 3: 2015–20

How did you write The Tourist Gaze 3.0 together with John Urry?

Do you feel a responsibility to keep the tourist gaze alive, to defend it, and develop it, now that John has passed away? Will there be a version 4.0?

These questions were posed to me in the summer of 2015 at a master class at Wakayama University, Japan, where I presented my recent article *The Tourist Gaze 1.0, 2.0, 3.0* (Larsen 2014). I paused, unsure how to respond, and then said:

> There will be no fourth edition without John. It was such a pleasure writing the book with him. Do I feel responsible for keeping it alive? That's a difficult question. I somehow hope that the tourist gaze is strong enough to look after itself and continue to be relevant for tourism scholars in the future – and not just because it is a seminal text.
>
> I'm seriously running a lot these days – and seriously thinking about mobilities, events and practices of running; it will be my academic topic for the next five years. I still haven't figured out if this means that I will be running with, or away from, the tourist gaze.

A couple of days before this event, I made a keynote presentation in Japan, this time for a conference on 'tourism mobilities', organized by the Japanese Society for Tourism Studies.

As much as I enjoyed these two events and the overwhelming hospitality, I could not help but feel like a poor substitute for the real thing – a John Urry-lite. Initially they had probably invited John Urry, and he then suggested me; both parties saved my face by not revealing this fact. On the long journey home, I said to myself: it is time to move on, to run away from the tourist gaze.

While this chapter is indeed going to be my final piece devoted to the tourist gaze, I am now sure that I will not run away from it completely. The tourist gaze will continue to be part of my future mobility research on cycling and running. However, it will not play a lead role, and it will travel outside the domains of tourist studies. In a recently completed project on urban bicycle mobilities and everyday commuters, we also explore how cycling affords specific embodied, multi-sensuous and kinaesthetic gazes. I will also run with the tourist gaze in my current and future writings on marathon running. On the face of it, gazing is an ill-suited metaphor for understanding long-distance running where somatic and kinaesthetic sensations seem far more significant than aesthetic immersion and visual apprehension. Yet I am coming to realize that urban marathon running also embraces the tourist gaze. In parallel with this essay, I am writing an article on urban marathons where I discuss the selection of spectacular tourist sites being integral to the planning of urban marathons and how major marathons, such as those in London, Paris, New York and Tokyo, are huge international events that attract many international participants that combine running and tourism. It seems that more and more tourists gaze upon the world while 'on the run'.

Last night when I was out running, I became excited about writing an article about (tourist) gazing and running. It was dark and I ran fast. I could not see much. However, the article made perfect sense; I sped up and I could not help but to strike up an imaginary conversation with John about the idea.

References

Edensor, T. (1998) *Tourists at the Taj*. London: Routledge.

Larsen, J. (2014) *The Tourist Gaze 1.0, 2.0, and 3.0: The Wiley Blackwell Companion to Tourism*. Chichester: Wiley Blackwell.

Lash, S. and J. Urry (1993) *Economies of Sign and Space*. London: SAGE.

Taylor, J. (1994) *A Dream of England: Landscape, Photography, and the Tourist's Imagination*. Manchester: Manchester University Press.

Urry, J. (1990) *The Tourist Gaze*. London: SAGE.

Urry, J. and J. Larsen (2011) *The Tourist Gaze 3.0*. London: SAGE.

Chapter 18

It's about time ...

Juliet Jain

Mobilities are all about temporality.

(Urry 2000: 105)

Time underpins my research into the organisation of travel, the experience of travel and the impact of travel. John Urry initiated this research trajectory and became a collaborator and supporter. Time and travel of course are usually expressed with a spatial dimension, and the relationship of these three elements is critical to the narrative here. In reflecting on this personal career journey, I consider the ways in which John, as a fellow traveller, shaped my thinking about time expressed through research connected to three locations: Lancaster, Bristol and Washington, covering the period 1998 to 2016.

Lancaster: the beginning of time

Two decades ago a train carried me north from Bristol to Lancaster on a dreary October day. I arrived slightly late in the university term, perhaps a suitable start for someone studying the future of the British passenger rail network post privatisation; a network troubled with delays to services and infrastructure projects. The studentship title 'Networks of the Future: Time, Space, and Train Travel' was collaboratively supervised by Elizabeth Shove and John Urry, and co-funded by the Association of Train Operating Companies. The following months unfolded multiple concepts of time and space over which I hovered uncertainly. Intellectual development was a long durée, in which John kindly told me I was unlikely to become an expert on time, but I would be the expert on trains!

Time was inescapable. Trains demand temporal ordering primarily for operational safety. However, the railway and the railway timetable changed society. As John argues in *Sociology beyond Societies* the railway operation not only generated a need for standardised time (GMT in Britain), but by opening up travel to the masses ensured a new culture of commuting and leisure shaped by the railway timetable (Urry, 2000). I am sure that John loved such geeky railway history, and he introduced me to Schivelbusch's account of Victorian rail travel, which sets out Victorian fears of the passengers' experience of speedier travel, and how time use on the train was exploited as a commercial opportunity by WHSmith book retailers (Schivelbusch, 1986).

Rail travel in Britain in the late 1990s was central to the New Labour political discourse of 'integration', as it was recognised (at that time) that more road building was unlikely to meet travel demand, and there was an opportunity for a 'rail renaissance'. The post-privatisation period saw an unprecedented growth in rail travel; but it was an industry wrought with challenges, particularly expressed through the rapid succession of rail crashes that culminated in a five-week suspension of the rail timetable following the one at Hatfield on 17 October 2000. Amongst this operational mess, I was trying to make sense of how the future of the rail network was being envisioned, and how the passenger of the future was constituted within the planning process.

Given that the car was the dominant mobility paradigm, rail travel needed to be set within the context of the car and society. It was a time when John, Elizabeth Shove and Mimi Sheller were driving car debates in sociology, and connections between automobility and temporality, networks and the urban form. These ideas coalesced with my train research, and often shaped the PhD supervision discussions.

Cars are inescapably attractive; they enable time-space flexibility and suggest freedom – that is until you want to park. In those days John lived in Leeds and commuted to Lancaster by train. He was thrilled when my research found itself at Leeds railway station investigating how visions of the future passenger were being enacted through the station upgrade (Leeds' first). John kept reminding me about station parking; the lack of parking, the need for a parking space proximate to the station and how annoying it was to have to park somewhere else when there were only minutes to catch a train.

I considered the discourses coming from central government at the time of the seamless journey, and argued that the experience of all travel time was now directed by a car driver's perspective. I called it 'the time-space template of the car', and got a tick from John in the margin. This idea also connected with another one of John's pet interests at the time, which was the concept of path dependency. My argument suggested that the policy intention to change travel behaviour (not my subject expertise) was to replicate the experience of the seamless journey (by car) through seamless integration, thus dependency was not so much a mode but a way of being in time and space.

Flexibility and freedom, however, was emerging in the late 1990s–early 2000s in a new way. Mobile phones were becoming more prevalent, with ownership rising rapidly for personal and business use. Mobile phones and the ability to text created new opportunities for people on the move, and to manage schedules more fluidly, and these devices were about to revolutionise society in a way the railways had in the 19th century. The rail industry and the Department of Transport were developing new web-based travel information systems, but other innovators were looking ahead to the early smartphones, 3G and the opportunity to deliver real-time information to such devices. For the first time ever you could have an extra ten minutes at home knowing your train was delayed! Thus, technology was offering an interface between the strict scheduling demands of a fixed network, and the opportunity to have more fluid arrangements or ensure a seamless trajectory.

Alongside path dependency, John seemed to have another new interest at the eleventh hour of completing my thesis, which was complexity theory. He was keen that I considered it in relation to articulating the possible variants of future outcomes, and I grudgingly conceded with some additional paragraphs. Looking back now, the opportunity to acknowledge multiple future outcomes was quite right. Questions are now being asked that connect the flexibility of mobile travel information alongside using time while travelling through mobile devices as some of the reasons young people are less likely to drive. Could the rail industry have imagined back in 2000 the need for data on the move and the emergent policy aim for all trains to offer free WiFi for all passengers?

Bristol: time on the move

Time was inescapable trajectory. Some five years after leaving I returned to Bristol to join Glenn Lyons at the recently formed Centre for Transport and Society, University of the West of England, to work on a collaborative project with John Urry (a period in which the Centre for Mobilities Research also emerged as an official entity at Lancaster) and Laura Watts. The research project 'Travel Time Use in the Information Age'[1] not only challenged the concept in transport studies that travel time had zero economic value, but pushed the debates in sociology about the experience of travelling, particularly on public transport, and developed innovative mobile methodological approaches.

The social context of travel time connected back to those debates of time explored early on at Lancaster with John. Time is given an economic value that forms the basis of valuing travel time savings within the cost-benefit calculations of public policy. Thus, clock time, the measurement of time, and attributing time to paid work and non-paid activities underpin the discourse of travel time. A project hypothesis was set very much in this paradigm, suggesting that if time was being used productively (i.e. for paid work) then the values of travel time savings should be revisited.

However, John, with his former economics hat on, railed against the term 'positive utility' of travel time, and supported the need to explore beyond productive time as work output-orientated. The idea that time was embodied and experienced outside of clock time was critical to developing an understanding of how travel connects multiple temporalities. These were ideas I had touched on during my PhD research, but not fully explored from a traveller's perspective. With particular encouragement from John, Laura and I travelled around the UK experiencing the travel environment and reflecting how fellow travellers used and experienced travel time through observations and ad hoc conversations with fellow passengers. Our field notes illustrate how time could stretch out and speed up; the anticipation of arrival in the moments of waiting for a free platform; the dullness of sitting in slow-moving traffic. Experience collided with clock time and the need for productivity. Sitting on a delayed train causes frustration because of the impact on schedule; an equipped passenger is able to repair this loss of time with other activities (whether work or pleasure), and with the advent of mobile technology communicate the delay. Later we sat with John and Glenn discussing and interpreting what this all meant for transport studies and the development of the field of 'mobilities', and John explored many of these issues in writing *Mobilities* (2007).

Within the early discussions of travel time use, John particularly encouraged the development of the idea that travel time could connect with theoretical ideas of gifts and gift giving, and told me to read Malinowski and Mauss. I began to question how time is embedded in social and economic relationships, and the need to give time to commuting, visiting friends and relatives, as well as to business relationships. In this respect the idea of giving 'travel time' strongly connected with John's ideas of the social obligations of co-presence driving travel demand. Yet at the same time individual benefit could be gained from travel time. The paper 'The Gift of Travel Time' developed this concept of reciprocation in response to travel time (Jain and Lyons, 2008). We argued that people often want time between activities, and travel time could be a temporal opportunity. Travel facilitates time for transitioning between roles (e.g. work and home); it creates a space for specific activities (paid work, reading a book); and time away from other demands (e.g. work, children, family and responsibility). Thus, in this liminal space travellers can become something else. Despite the project being interested in mobile technology in the early 2000s smartphones had not yet emerged, and WiFi was only available on board one train line. The gift of travel time therefore predicated on escape from other demands, and home and work were not continuously connected in a pocket device.

Increasing mobile connectivity may be further transforming the experience of travel time, and this is an area that we have continued to work and take forward the ideas from this collaboration. However, connectivity on the move for me connects with another of John's interests and collaborations – that of business travel, elites and the compulsion for proximity in the work context.

Washington: the lobby of hyper-connectivity

International business travel is male-dominated; far fewer women with caring commitments choose to travel with work. The Association of American Geographers' annual conference was my first international opportunity for some years. I had rather glibly argued that leaving my 4-year-old twins for five days would be fine, what could possibly go wrong? I arrived in Washington, DC shortly before the Icelandic volcano Eyjafjallajökull disrupted air travel into, and within, Europe for around six days in April 2010.

The planned relaxing few days focusing on a conference suddenly transformed into endless international communication by phone, Skype and other social media, seeking possible ways of returning home and where to stay in the interim. The conference hotels' lobbies became hubs of digital flow making use of free WiFi; while stories were shared within the co-present stranded community. I walked corridors watching people catching up with spouses and kids on video calls, carving a time and space for family intimacy from a distance, and started to consider the broader implications of what being absent from family life in the digital world really meant for workers and their families. Yes, we academics felt obliged or desired the richness of co-present encounters at a conference, but what was happening to the richness of life back home without us?

John had suggested that in the age of digital technology absence can become a mediated presence as the absent worker/traveller dips in and out of 'life' as well as 'work' and boundaries between realms blur (Urry, 2007). My research had begun to consider the blurring of work–life boundaries in examining people's technology use in everyday life. In Washington it was obvious that technology was transforming the experiences of people who travel away from home for work.

An opportunity to take forward this idea arose with gaining funding for the research project Family Rituals 2.0,[2] which considered how absence could be digitally reconfigured to manage work–life balance and connect to family rituals within a broad set of work-related travel (from air crew to oil rig workers). It aimed to explore the 'opportunities' as well as the 'burdens' articulated by Elliott and Urry (2010) in their exploration of 'mobile lives'. However, while John and Anthony Elliott discussed how moments of family intimacy may be articulated and co-presence scheduled around mobile lives, Family Rituals 2.0 explored digital opportunities to virtually pop home while away with work. In particular, it considered how existing family rituals could be reconfigured digitally and new ones might emerge.

John had made sure I understood that time was socially constructed, and concepts of work–life balance are situated in the temporal organisation of capitalism. There is an assumed division between work and non-work activities (i.e. life). Generally, work is configured around a 9–5 routine, sandwiched by a commute, and life happens in the other bit. Mobile workers shift into a different temporal structure where their absence takes them not only away for longer than the working day, but international travel may also take them into different time zones. Different temporal working patterns and places can sit awkwardly for digital reconnection within the organisation of time back home. For instance, back in Washington and four hours behind London time, finding a 'good' time to synchronise was a bit awkward. The slippage between my evening (US) against home evening (UK) found me seeking moments to step out of 'work time' commitments, or rising much earlier, to seek a good time to talk. There might have been something rather contrived about having a shared virtual breakfast with the family given the time difference, but eating together is an exemplar of a family ritual that could be digitally configured.

Intimacy for mobile workers requires effort, and being on the road can be a lonely time as John intimated in various writings. Digital technology can open a virtual window on life back home where the absent member can join in conversations and share the moment at a distance, but mostly this is another scheduled moment in the busy diary. Family Ritual 2.0 research participants articulated scheduling as a challenge particularly where children were concerned, but there were some who had it sorted as these two examples illustrate: (1) calling in to chat on the speaker phone as the children were being driven home from school; and (2) a mother who had developed a virtual relationship with her son and read him a bedtime story via FaceTime. However, increasingly, the visibility of online presence of specific network connections can create opportunities to fluidly digitally 'drop by' for a few minutes, as one of the Family Rituals 2.0 participants described. He said he would see his teenage son was logged in and would just drop in to say hello – a bit like putting his head around his son's bedroom door. No need for an in-depth conversation or shared breakfast for a moment of intimacy. Thus, technology facilitates a continuum in the relationship.

John suggested that digital technology creates a flickering of absence and presence and Family Rituals 2.0 developed this notion to argue that people are glimpsing or peeping into life at 'home'. For those who travel for longer periods, there is the potential for the digital to connect simultaneously shared experiences (e.g. drinking or eating together-apart), which is less of a glimpse or flicker but still reliant on the visual and aural. Physical proximity remains the essence of intimacy and is the challenge for those who live mobile lives (Elliott and Urry 2010). John's work was formative in shaping this articulation of absence/presence, and will continue to do so in developing the conceptual framings for this research area.

Back in 2010 I hadn't imagined that talking about travel time in Washington would develop a new research direction that connected and utilised so many of John's interests. The last time I saw John at a workshop in Lancaster we briefly talked about the emerging findings from Family Rituals 2.0, and as ever he was encouraging and enthusiastic.

Kairological futures: going forward

I didn't get around to talking about a lot of things that John put his stamp on, but I want to briefly finish with the concept of Kairos. John stated: 'Kairological time is based on the experience of the past in order to develop the sense of when a particular event should take place in the future, of just when it is the right time for something to occur' (Urry 2000: 112). In contrast Chronos (or clock time), as I noted earlier, dominates the structures of modern society, and is perceived as critical for the scheduling and planning of activities against which 'progress' can be measured (e.g. the delivery of an infrastructure project on schedule). There appears little room for working with the 'right time' in planning futures that are complex and could have many outcomes. It is perhaps too fluid and risky, and suggests a lack of certainty especially for measuring outcomes, yet the 'right time' is highly relevant to innovative research and practice.

In my own research career there has been a strong element of Kairos – the coming together of academics to challenge the value of travel time perhaps being a good example. Certainly, a PhD with John Urry at the time of a new sociological paradigm shift was not consciously planned! Looking forward to a continuum of research at the intersection of technology and travel I hope there will be Kairological opportunities in which the essence of John will be made present.

Notes

1 'Travel Time Use in the Information Age' was funded by the Engineering and Physical Sciences Research Council from 2004 to 2007 (GR/S58270/01).
2 Family Rituals 2.0 was funded by the EPSRC from April 2013 to September 2015 (EP/K025678/1) (see also www.familyrituals2-0.org.uk).

References

Elliott, A. and Urry, J. (2010) *Mobile Lives*, London: Routledge.
Jain, J. and Lyons, G. (2008) The gift of travel time, *Journal of Transport Geography*, 16(2), pp. 81–89.
Schivelbusch, W. (1986) *The Railway Journey: The Industrialization of Time and Space in the 19th Century*, Berkeley, CA: University of California Press.
Urry, J. (2000) *Sociology beyond Societies: Mobilities for the Twenty-first Century*, London: Routledge.
Urry J. (2007) *Mobilities*, London: Routledge.

Chapter 19

Ice-fishing with John Urry – and other Finnish episodes of ontological importance

Soile Veijola

I met John Urry before I knew him.

Unknowingly, he played a part in a Pork Feast episode in the article *The Body in Tourism*, which I wrote with Eeva Jokinen already some time ago in our youthful, feminist recklessness regarding the codes of literary academic comportment.

Here is a more detailed account of this encounter.

> Dear Diary. Tonight we are attending a Pork Feast … We arrive at the manor, and I wonder aloud if it is authentic, real – that is, if it has any referential validity as a thought and experience. Your glance seems to question my intellect, or yours (but here we *are*, can't you *see*, you mutter), yet I save my face by spotting John Urry, a front-row tourism analyst from Britain. Unsuspectingly, he takes a seat opposite to us, with his back against the wall. We can't miss out on this chance. Before I manage to cook up a sophisticated opening line, you burst out impolitely, "What are you gazing at?"
>
> "By considering the typical objects of the tourist gaze one can use these to make sense of elements of the wider society with which they are connected … Thus rather than being a trivial subject tourism is significant in its ability to reveal aspects of normal practices which might otherwise remain opaque." (Urry 1989, 2, in Veijola and Jokinen 1994, 131–3)

In retrospect, with this statement John brings tourism-related phenomena beautifully to the heart of social analysis. We certainly had enjoyed his article *Cultural Change and Contemporary Holiday-Making* (1988) when the ink was still fresh on it. Along with Judith Adler's work *Travel as Performed Art* (1989), John's book *The Tourist Gaze* (1989), Daniel Boorstin's (1964) *The Image: A Guide to Pseudo-Events in America*, and, last but not least, Dean MacCannel's *The Tourist: A New Theory of the Leisure Class* (1976), it provided a serious (!) research field for us to step into – at a time when serious minds perhaps found leisure to be a far too trivial aspect of life to be given a second glance. Nothing to do with culture, society, or politics.

Yet, we were eager to bring *the body* onto the scene and were thus not very good listeners, holding up John to hear out more feminist exclamations: "The typical objects of the tourist *gaze*? Isn't it rather the tourist *body* that breaks with the established routines and practices?" (Veijola and Jokinen 1994, 133).

In the storyline, we trapped John in a corner, continuing with the view of tourism being largely "arguing for and by the bodies present, the collective body" (Veijola and Jokinen 1994, 134) if one wants to have a good party. The episode ends with self-admonishments: "We turn back to our cavalier but he has disappeared. We figure we earned it. After all, we did not even ask him for a dance!" (134).

The next episode with John, however, takes place in real life. Well, the academic life, to be more exact. (Come to think of it, what is real? We cannot escape the power of perceptions, yet we so often disregard them in academic writing, acting as if we simply know things.) So, anyway, having finished the manuscript of *The Body in Tourism*, we presented the paper at the Annual Meeting of American Anthropologists in Chicago in 1991 and at the ISA Working Group of Tourism, Le tourisme international entre tradition et modernité in Nice 1992 (no, not in French) and then sent it to all but one of the other author protagonists who were placed in different episodes of our travel narrative on Mallorca, asking if it is OK for them to have been included in it. (For some reason we failed to send it to Jost Krippendorf. As if he would live in a different time zone or on another planet just for the fact that he wrote about tourism as an everyday utopia and that his name sounded German!)

John's answer came without delay: "I do not feel mistreated."

He did not feel mistreated! He acknowledged the point we made, he did not have his ego in the way when making a judgment and he also had sense of humor. Who *is* this guy?

Well, eventually, no one else objected to their free vacation on the Canary Islands, either, and the piece got swiftly published in *Theory, Culture and Society*, with Mike Featherstone adding an encouraging note to his letter of acceptance: "I like the idea of people laughing when reading TCS." At this point, we were absolutely certain that *no one* would *ever* speak of tourism – nor of anything else, for that matter – from an *un*embodied, *non*-gendered position again. Little did we know …

How could we be so naïve? We had no doubt been reading too much critical theory – in the 1980s and 1990s there still was time to read, you see – which had led us to believe that everything, even gender, is a topic and a concept that can and should be critically assessed rather than taken for granted. Especially if there are power relations, injustice, and violence involved – as is often the case. We had also figured that speaking is an act, an enactment of agency for the self and the other. And since we are women and men, also sexual difference, which Luce Irigaray has written about, needs to be given a chance to be a fruitful and respectful one – even and particularly in Academia. (Today we know, of course, that we are not only women and men, but also other genders and that some people think they have no gender at all, yet not even they can ignore the impacts of the prevailing gender orders in social life.)

When digging even deeper into the various discourses of tourism research, we noticed that there clearly was an air of unarticulated indisputableness regarding the perspective of a subject speaking through the male body and through the male position in society. Age did not seem to matter: young and old men alike did not appear to have gender, neither epistemologically nor ontologically, while women did. Women seemed to be loaded with gender and men entirely devoid of it.

But where did we leave John? In the meanwhile, growing impatient with our male peers, we met John at the ISA meeting in Bielefeld in 1994.

The Bielefeld gig was interesting. Eeva and I had decided that it was time to travel in a more masculine way than taking a charter trip to Spain. In a more Kerouacian style. Hence, we jumped into Eeva's white BMW sedan (do BMW wagons for families even exist?) and drove all the way from Finland to the conference hotel in Bielefeld. No navigators, mind you, just a big book of maps and road signs.

We brought along a session to which we had invited speakers. It was titled *Rewriting the Tourist: Embodied Landscapes, Encounters and Mimesis at Work.* (So very nineties.) Not only did Judith Adler, Dean MacCannell, and Juliet Flower MacCannell speak in it, but John attended as well! The seminar room was full, but I remember the joy when noticing a certain, long-legged, British gentleman next to the door. The paper on *the disoriented tourist* that we handed out tried to make sense of a variety of metaphoric travelers in social theory. It later found its way to a book called *Touring Cultures: Transformations of Travel and Theory* (1997), edited by John together with Chris Rojek. In the paper, we claimed that the imagery of travel also needs feminine social figures, such as *au pair* and babysitter – not mere male morphologies of the tourist experience.

To fast-forward a decade or so, as full-time university teachers and later on professors in our respective universities, Eeva in eastern Finland and I in Lapland, Rovaniemi, both of us drifted into studying a more serious theme, namely *work*. Eeva had noticed the precarious nature of work, the labor market, and everyday life, while I had lacked visiting teachers who could talk about tourism as work in my courses. So, I fixed the problem by launching a largish, four-year project in 2006 under the very title *Tourism as Work* with colleagues and PhD students at our university and by picking up co-thinking with Eeva through the notion of the *hostessing society*. But there was a stepping stone before it, and John stood on it in a winter overall.

By way of finishing my previous project, *Amenity Landscapes: Spaces of Mobility and Immobility*, I organized with Sami Moisio (international relations) and Anne Keskitalo (art education), a winter academy in 2004. It entailed a formula for cross-disciplinary academic meetings spiced up by a serene and cheerful approach to social programs as part of its intellectual commonality, and an emphasis on engaging local scholars and students on an equal footing. I invited

John to attend the event. It was entitled *HOSTILITIES AND HOSPI-TALITIES. Encounters with the Strange in the International Relations of Tourism and Travel.* Our Call for Papers argued (language check added) that states, multinational companies, privately owned enterprises, tourists, tour operators, and voluntary and involuntary travelers form an intensified and complex network of relations of power and intimacy which has an impact on places and cultures. Through these processes friends and enemies are made; milieus, territories, and communities are transformed and acknowledged, be they place-bound or mobile.

Hmm. One can say that again. A wave of nostalgia hits me when I remember how fun it was in the good old days to "hit the lines," as they say in the French Open, between disciplines when setting up conferences instead of focusing safely (and unsurprisingly) on one's own.

Well, as always, event-wise, the golden ratio of a human-friendly conference hushes the participants out of the lecture rooms at some point – not only outside but also *on ice* when in Lapland in winter. We went *ice-fishing* on the Kemijoki river that runs through Rovaniemi city center, and camped at a riverbank that hosted a publicly maintained *lavvu*, a lean-to, which is a half-open wooden shelter facing benches on two sides of a campfire in front of it. It was a cloudy afternoon in March and we wore black and red overalls and turquoise knit caps rented from a local snow mobile safari company. Not me, though. Being vain, I wore my elegant black coat and a furry, white scarf around my neck. Then again, I knew how to dress according to the weather when going ice-fishing.

Two of our invited keynoter ladies had parted company with us and chosen the commercial fun of husky safaris. Typical tourists! I was afraid that the next speaker, John, would also withdraw to his room in order to finalize his presentation – like an ordinary academic – but he did not. Being a good sport he showed up, accompanied by Joanne Sharp and Costas Constantinou. With a wry smile barely noticeable on his face (as shown in a number of photos taken during the event) he used his camera, too, to capture the peculiar local customs and surroundings, learned to make a hole in the ice with a special tool called auger, reached his hand to take a fishing rod from a student, and sat there, on a reindeer skin, on ice, next to Joanne, waiting for a sign of a fish down below. Afterwards, we all sat around the campfires, had coffee and grilled sausages – a Finnish combination of outdoor refreshments that cannot be explained semiotically – and chilled out.

Fittingly, all the invisible hostessing work invested in the gathering had worn me out to the extent that I wanted to skip my own talk on the contemporary guest situation. I remember John lamenting my decision, saying my title had sounded like the closest to the conference topic. That was encouraging! But I cannot recall if I restored myself or not.

Soon after, either John invited me or I invited myself to visit Lancaster and the Centre for Mobilities Research in April 2005. I spent two wonderful weeks there, dwelling in the campus guest room and meeting lovely and hospitable people in and out of corridors – whilst being hit by a heavy spring allergy affecting my intelligence, which, during the teaching terms, was not really much to brag about to begin with. After the doctoral seminar, in which Jennie Germann Molz presented her final touches to her brilliant thesis on contemporary mobilities and hospitalities, John shook his head at the fact of there being only two bestseller textbooks in tourism studies, MacCannell's and his own, and urged us to go out there and make new ones.

Two other special events during this visit spring to mind. Firstly, Elizabeth Shove realized her moment had come to get her colleagues to play floorball ("sähly" in Finnish and "innebandy" in Swedish), with an authentic floorball ambassador from Scandinavia visiting the unit. She had been baptized by Mika Pantzar to this silly team play invented in the early 1980s in order to make team sports more accessible and serendipitous to all regardless of skill, size, or gender. Six or seven people showed up, possibly with mixed feelings. John had excused himself this time. I recall someone arriving late and asking on whose side he should be. I told him to play on both sides. He did, but not very fervently, so it did not disrupt the game too much. Not that a game made out of disruptions could easily be disrupted. Elizabeth seemed very happy afterwards. She was by far the most energetic figure on the field!

The other moment I will mention is when I visited John at his office. It was the only time when I ever saw him angry. Really. Angry. I do not remember the details but a decision had been made by the university headquarters to turn down a research proposal made by John and his colleagues, and he felt it would have been a very important project to carry out. Nevertheless, he sat down on his sofa in front of his bookshelves and smiled for the camera when I took a photo of him.

So, how to wrap up these memories of John being hosted in various acts of conferencing? I suspect you might have a story to tell, too. Let me share with you a few more encounters with John of some of my Finnish colleagues in sociology. I received these notes while excusing myself for not joining the annual meeting but writing this essay instead. The question I asked was, "I went ice-fishing with John. What did you do with him?"

Lena Näre replied swiftly:

> Elina Paju and I hooked up with John who looked lonesome at the reception of the Nordic Sociological Association in Lund in 2014. The remarkably asocial Lundians had left all the speakers on their own. In the first evening, keynoter Michael Burawoy was left to cope on his own in the "get together" event until we saved him to have dinner at the table of Finnish sociologists; and at the reception, we kept company with John. We talked about Lancaster and John spoke very enthusiastically about researching oil, an issue he had just published on and wished to dig into even deeper, which brought us to discuss Antti Silvast's thesis on electric

infrastructures. I remember John also praising the theme issue of *Mobilities* on childhood research.

Risto Heiskala picked up my opening question and its tone, too, adding:

> Jari Aro and I, for our part, kept company with John during the evening entertainment program at the meeting of Italian sociologists in Napoli because the hosts had completely abandoned their foreign guests. The only thing that could be done was for the sociable Finns to patch up the situation. John gave his keynote in the chapel of the University of Napoli, which – with its marble walls, ceiling murals and cupolas – was without a doubt the most ceremonious space for a plenary session I have ever attended. We got along fine, even though we nagged a bit at John about the points the panel he had chaired had given to our unit in a research assessment. The year was 2015, so this was a little before John passed away.

Harri Melin finished the series with stories from two other remarkable conference cities.

> John visited Tampere at the annual meeting of sociologists Anno Domini. We went up to the top of the Pyynikki observation tower to have coffee and sweet pastry ("munkkikahvit" in Finnish). John thought the pastries were especially tasty. At the world conference in Brisbane, John and Sylvia gravitated to the circle of Finns at the beach party to drink beer with us. They said that the company of Finns is cultivated in a relaxed way since we are not prone to show off so much.

It is indeed fun to have a bit of a laugh at national stereotypes, like the famous Finnish silence turned into sociability every time John is around. Yet, if we embrace *conferencing* as "bringing together, deliberate, talk over, in the act of conferring" (www.etymonline.com), then we can always meet John in his own stories, as well as in all the stories about him, be they fiction or real. Besides, at the end of the day, what *is* real? Where are we and where will we always be if not in the minds and memories of other people, in the intellectual and emotional spaces we have created together with them?

John, I hope you do not feel mistreated.

References

Urry, J. (1988) Cultural Change and Contemporary Holiday-Making. *Theory, Culture and Society*, 5(88), 35–55.

Veijola, S. and E. Jokinen (1994) Body in Tourism. *Theory, Culture and Society*, 11(3), 125–151.

Part IV

The mobilities turn

Chapter 20

Mobilities without weight

Peter Adey

It is odd to write about John Urry and mobility in the context of weight or lack of weight. It seems somewhat incongruous to put them together. John, of course, oozed levity. He would laugh often and regularly at himself. Indeed, I'd heard him joke how much time he would spend in the air in an aeroplane's cabin, moving between the many different collaborations, conferences and research networks he was part of. But his patience and spirit, his work and his words were anything but light – at least in any kind of superficial or partial sense. In lots of ways John's contribution to thinking about mobilities railed against lightness. Mobilities were not frothy, superfluous movements, skimming across the surface of society and space, but were rather embroiled in social structures, limited by capital, time, poverty or affluence, deep-rooted relations and familial, work or other commitments. Urry and many others were particularly keen to reject the putative nomadic celebration of mobility that expressed romanticised notions of free-flight, as if mobility were simply an escape from relations and structures of power.

In his later work, Urry's examination of climate change, oil, off-shoring and new systems of production in the form of 3D printing saw mobilities as more sticky and viscous than the fluidic metaphors others have been fond of (Bauman 2000). Indeed, Anthony Elliot has characterised Bauman's work as having a concern with 'light mobilities'. Instead, John saw how mobilities are reliant upon the resources and resource mobilities of substances such as oil. Mobilities leave deep tracks in the landscape and surfaces of the environment, from concrete and asphalt to the carbon emissions released into the air. Even the apparently footloose and semi-invisible mobilities of the super-rich, and the capital that accumulates and moves with them, Urry would suggest, depend upon spatial locations and fixities within complex geo-legal and territorial arrangements, and even information systems to keep their transactions and assets moving, sometimes still, as well as secret. In essence, the tension between mobility and what seemingly holds it down, as Urry and others have written elsewhere, is what produces so much of life on the move: Urry called these moorings.

Led by this line of thinking, I would like to propose that mobility studies could begin to account for other examples and imaginations of mobility that are considered to be literally, and often figuratively, without weight. Such a line of enquiry takes us into mobility studies and its continued engagement with the humanities, especially the visual arts, as well as an address of mobility from outside of the preponderance of Westernised and global North contexts and perspectives. When I gave a contribution to a panel at the The Royal Geographical Society (with the Institute of British Geographers) conference on this topic last year, I showed various imagery of medieval and Christian representations of levitating figures, and a day before we remembered John at quite a moving memorial special session, someone joked that I had become an art historian! Of course, the point is that we should be able to move between different settings and contexts where mobilities are produced, and this might mean the visual arts, where arts practitioners and performance artists have begun to provide rich ground for mobilities research (Witzgall et al. 2016), whether they are creative performance and video works at the borders of Europe, tapping into migration flows from Sub-Saharan Africa, or experimenting with weightlessness in zero gravity. Indeed these other settings, contexts and mediums might be much more ready – much more sympathetic – to the possibility of the kinds of light mobilities I am thinking of.

What I'm thinking of are curious instances when humans and things are believed to have flown, somewhat unaided. This might include superheroes, mystics, artists, fashion models, astronauts and cosmonauts bestowed with privileged knowledge or powers. But levitators do not often or always occupy the position of the powerful. Some of what I am hinting at here is a parallel and counter-history to the aeromobilities research that John, myself and many others have been involved in advancing. That is, there are other aeromobilities within the cultural, scientific and spiritual imagination, wider tendencies in religious belief, art history, psychical investigation, popular cultural representations of science and technology, and many other genres. These contexts have long celebrated lightness, but particularly in the form of the figure of the levitator who can somehow overcome gravity and experience a form of weightless travel, both from the ground and through the air.

Of course the tension I mentioned at the beginning is just as at play here. The above do not present superfluous issues, but mobilities which are entirely embedded within deep-rooted and felt social, cultural and political relations. Just as Sheller's excavation of the light substance of aluminium – a material revelling in what she calls the 'light modernity' of early 20th-century cultures of speed and consumer capitalism, is revealing of much more earthly concerns: namely the toil and exploitation of embodied labour, the environmental and social inequities of heavy resource extraction and the durability of colonial structures. Going further, however, we could recognise other cultures of lightness, which are not so aligned to the 'aesthetics of aerodynamic speed, accelerated mobility and modernist technological futurism' (Sheller 2014: 87).

In laying some of these out, through the levitator, I will outline what we might take forward from the study of such light mobilities, that are always already heavy with the weighty baggage of culture, social context and meaning.

These are not so assertive forms of mobility, but much more tentative, slower and even more fleeting. We will come to see the critical import of such a focus, too, and take light mobilities and the figure of the levitator as potentially quite disobedient.

Spirituality, belief, misogyny

There is probably much more to be said about spiritual mobilities, which could build on the fascinating research on spiritual journeys, pilgrimage and climbs that writers such as Veronica Della Dora, Richard Scriven and Avril Maddreell have advanced so far. As already mentioned, levitations have a crucial hold within religious belief, their histories, practices and forms of representation. And yet, levitators have often been marginalised, castigated or objectified. They have been the subject of sartorial humour, especially in Jewish representations, stories and literature of the luftmench, a figure that derides and portrays the rootless and wandering Jew. The art work of Marc Chagall is probably the most famous of these. The levitator's strange mobility is a continual expression of otherness which we will come to later.

European visions of the Orient frequently accounted for exoticised and eroticised women levitated by a male magician. Some of the first moving images from India were filmed by Thomas Edison in 1902 in a film titled *Hindoo Fakir*, showing a woman levitated by a magician before being transformed into a butterfly. As Italo Calvino has suggested, this trend for lightness or levity may well be a response to the 'precarious existence' of potential levitators, expressed perhaps in racism, a form of sexual exploitation or poverty. Levitation is not always wilful either. Their bodies succumb neither to gravity or the oneiric impulse to float away but are held in suspension by others, sometimes tentatively for a while, and at others, unwittingly. The idea of ascent is a common forebear of levitation, especially within the infusion of Neoplatonic thought in Christian doctrine. Spiritual development has been commonly thought of as a journey, a path inwards and an ascent via a ladder or a mountain. Rising up vertically, for many, has become the natural metaphor of many faiths, symbolising a communion with god, in heaven, to the point that such metaphors seem to have taken hold. Unsurprisingly, the first balloon ascents tended to be portrayed in such terms – their flights were a mixture of scientific and technological innovation, but also spiritual rapture and even sexual excitement.

Even religious inspired ascendance could be turned and twisted through patriarchy and male misogyny. Teresa (1515–82), from Ávila near Madrid, who became so influential as a female mystic and gave lucid accounts of levitating in an act of possession, was soon derogated, characterised as drifting towards nymphomania and hysteria by early psychiatry.

Of course, there are more recent associations between aeromobility and spirituality. Historians of aviation hold that promise of flight cannot be conveniently divided from other myths of ascension. A messianic yearning for aerial mobility took such a hold in the United States, launching barnstormers and a general aerial craze – an airmindedness – in all corners of the country. In the United States, Russia, Germany, France, Britain and elsewhere, pilots and early aviators took on almost godlike properties, just as astronauts would do later. The Italian Futurists would draw similar conclusions, finding in flight a collusion of technology and religion or a new spirituality. Indeed, Sheller shows how Alcoa, pairing the light modernity of aluminium with flight and mobility, were beckoning to a new age of lightness by claiming: 'The swan song of needless weight is being sung'. However, light mobilities – so involved in vertical perspectives and the promise of living above the ground – were not only couched in capitalist systems of production and consumption, and the soaring cities that would represent the zenith of technological innovation and consumer capitalism in the popular imagination of so much science fiction and urban planning. Utopian socialist imaginations of cities in the air would emerge in Soviet Russia too through experimental designs for public housing, their connection to the ground made through the tenuous connection of flying pods. And so rather than lightness being the summit of the capitalist pyramidal system, it would rather mark a socialist revolutionary break – its crisis – from the ground.

Failing to levitate and subversive mobilities

Levitations and the light mobilities we could examine should be seen as inherently volatile and potentially disobedient. As Jason King writes so eloquently on the tropes of rising and falling in social and lateral mobility of Black Americans, a kind of 'insurgency' has been embodied within the metaphors and connotations of Black mobility. 'Uprightness,' King argues, has been a common enough refrain in the civil rights movement and Black power so that ascension and the common phrases of 'getting up' and 'standing up' become chief registers of political potency. Moreover, within different representations of levitation we tend to find light mobility as a kind of resistance or subversion. Scott Bukatman sees Christopher Walken's 'embodied kinetic incursion' as inhabitation and trespass in the Fat Boy Slim music video *Weapon of Choice* (2001). The video depicts Christopher Walken as an alienated business type, sitting exhausted or perhaps just impassive in the lobby of a hotel. The video slowly but surely accelerates Walken as his movements pick up speed, his burgeoning animation combined with the track sampling Fat Boy Slim has become famous for. Walken's body excites towards dancing, which soon sends him airborne, gliding and pushing off from walls. His motion is both enlivening and surprising.

But could levity's powers not be about levitating at all, but a more ambivalent, stuttering kind of force that comes from failure, as in the way Bruce Nauman's artwork 'failing to levitate in my studio' has been interpreted? In this vein we see a variety of efforts to mobilise levitation in political movements through ritual and ceremony that ultimately fail to levitate, well, anything. From the failed attempt to levitate the Pentagon in the peace march in Washington in 1967 (copied by protestors even at my old university Keele to levitate the vice chancellor's residence), and Occupy's chant around the Koch bros' Georgia Pacific building in Atlanta (the Koch bros are infamous for funding right-wing organisations and think tanks). These are efforts of rupture.

Perhaps we can see this nowhere more direct than in one of the best books I have read all year by the writer and Royal Holloway lecturer in creative writing, Kei Miller's *Augustown* (2016). The book weaves post-colonial critique around a story of a preacher, Alexander Bedward, a real figure who proclaimed that he and his followers would ascend to heaven from Kingston, Jamaica in 1920. Bedward promises to return in order to smite the colonial regime with lightning bolts. In Miller's book, Bedward really does levitate – using chains as a gesture to colonial slavery to keep him down – but he only rises so far, the smile slowly leaving his face as he goes nowhere near to heaven, and he is brought down as the government's men use a pole to hook him.

In spite of Bedward's failing levity, Miller wonders at the promise of this kind of writing and why we might want to tell stories such as this, of the levity of affective life, which in many senses is not preachy but provoking:

> there really was a time in Jamaica, 1920 to be precise, when a great thing was going to happen, though they desperately needed it to happen, it did not … Look this isn't magical realism. This is not another story about superstitious island people and their primitive beliefs. No you don't get off that easy. This is a story about people as real as you are … You may as well stop to consider a more urgent question; not whether you believe in this story or not, but whether this story is about the kinds of people you have never taken the time to believe in. (Miller 2016: 114–15)

Surreal and magical mobilities

Levitators, as you might expect, conjure up imaginations of the bizarre, strange and the magical. It is not incongruous to expect their popularity within early cinema and stage magic as well as artistic and political movements such as surrealism. Within parallel histories of stage magic, and in cinema, from Edison to Melies, the magician's assistant has been floated, raised, transformed and trans-figured, in highly sexualised clothing and repose among the stage craft of excitement and drama. Melies' *Les bulles de savon animées* (*Soap Bubbles*, 1906) demonstrates an advancement in his cinematic magic but a continuation of the levitation and objectification of women. A woman seemingly condenses out of the steam a magician lets rise into the air. Standing the woman on a table or altar, the magician then blows bubbles from a pipe, except the bubbles are the levitating heads of women, hovering in the air.

We can see continued the objectification of women levitators, even within literature. The famous magic trick the Trilby, a levitation trick performed by Robert-Houdin, Houdini and many others, of course bears a resemblance to the hypnosis- and mesmerism-themed novel *Trilby* by George du Maurier. As several critics have made clear, much like her stage counterpart, the Trilby of du Maurier's book is an aestheticised and sexualised object throughout. She is Svengali's Trilby, an object of capture, becoming an accomplished operatic singer only when hypnotised by Svengali, so coining the name's association with misogynist possession. Within these traditions of cinematic and stage magic, women's bodies are frequently levitated and moved at will.

Other artists have explored the relationship between levitation, femininity, magic and spirituality. The Spanish artist Remedios Varo (1908–63), who, with other women artists (such as Leonora Carrington), would escape to refuge in post-revolutionary Mexico during the Second World War, is one example. Like Carrington, Varo's works on levity turn to a variety of belief systems, folklore and alchemy, as well as experimental science. Indeed, levitation is common to many female surrealists within Varo's circle, Carrington famously devoting her convent school days to rebellion and eventual expulsion through her efforts to levitate. In Varo's many numbered works we see solid bodies becoming light, losing weight. But while expressing domination, women also take the place of men in Varo's works, embarking on journeys on strange machines, impossibly small wheels, or they take flight on their own. As Whitney Chadwick writes of her imagery: 'the women in Varo's paintings ... are alchemists, magicians, scientists and engineers who travel through forests, along rivers, and above the clouds in jerry-built conveyances that run on stardust, music, and sunlight'.

Many female levitators would be characterised as light in spite of their body size, exciting sexism but also a common relationship between light mobilities and the apparent incongruity of a fat or unhealthy female body (I am very conscious of the potential allusions with some of the excellent work on Flying While Fat and the politics and experience of mobility and body size). There was the famous medium Mrs Guppy, known best for her transportation and levitation from a friend's home in Highgate to Holborn on 23 June 1871. And there was Eusapia Palladino, exposed to the witnesses and scientific measurement of psychical investigation. Both are highly sexualised figures, both taunted and ridiculed for their mass. Many characterisations of Guppy's flight played upon the size and weight of her body, repeating some of the tropes of fatness and supernatural flight associated with the witch of early modern Europe. Weight and lightness were a prime object for satire, making her levitation seem somehow more absurd, while hinting at her apparent low class, low morals and yearning for sex and ascendance, both social and material. Palladino would be equally subject to insinuation. In the context of the séance, darkness provided the grounds for rising urges that would undermine her and she would openly describe 'trembling' under the scrutiny of a male scientific gaze.

Post-gravity mobilities

Finally, levitators might point us towards a new genre of mobilities research, which authors such as Bron Szerszynski (2016) have already begun on extra-planetary mobilities. In this sense we need to ask, what might our mobilities look like inside different sets of gravitational conditions? How have our mobilities been utterly conditioned by weight, and what would it mean to us if weight no longer mattered in the way it once did? How, moreover, to consider light mobilities from outside of the human, where gravity acts differently on bodies of different sizes, where weight may be experienced very differently?

One place to turn for advice is space flight, and the technologies that have mimicked it such as the Zero Gravity Corporation's simulated zero-g environments. These flights, produced by aircraft flying in continuous parabolic arcs, have inspired a large and interesting movement of post-gravitational artists. Just as the absence of gravity disturbs those who experience it with their sense of self, their position in space, as well as longer-term physiological issues to deal with, our arts practices have experimented with the possibilities of creative expression under conditions all but without gravity.

Painters have experimented with the differences zero-g environments provide. Paint takes on a movement, force and a contingency far outside of the usual parameters as artists do more letting go than directing the paint onto any kind of surface. Similarly, other art works have been set into almost infinite motion, sculptures set spinning and bouncing – and even a CD – during such flights and on the International Space Station. There is the important mechanical matter to contend with here that mobility without weight and frictionless inertia could mean relatively limitless and uncontrollable movement, sometimes with terrifying results.

Conclusion: depletion

The above may mean an embrace of a wider research field, or rather the ethos, that others have called medieval. That is to say, some of the contexts where the light mobilities of the levitator may be found in the spiritual traditions of the Middle Ages could soften some of the stricter boundaries we place on our claims to knowledge, the role and pathos of belief in our research and disciplinary lines. Nicolas Masciandaro, in a wonderful piece of writing, describes this ethos as a kind of medieval possession that takes hold of *him*, and encourages an 'unknowing' of our established ways of thought or writing and an embrace of the strange.

Tackling light mobilities and other mobile bodies that appear to move and rise without weight may force us to reconsider other relatively well-established debates. If we are used to seeing the plane and the drone in the context of state and military power and technological innovation, we might account for aero-mobilities that are much less certain and are forced and passive, rather than force. In this sense, the mobility of a rising body may be a submission, a diminishment, a lessening of capacity, what we could think of as a depletion of identity, will and self.

On the other hand, perhaps even in accordance with notions of drift, and Studio Saraceno's experiments with future air flight, mobilities research could focus more attention to mobilities that are possible merely by the weak forces of the sun and the wind, forms of mobility that are not necessarily weightless, but are less weighty in order to move without power, carbon emissions and the depletion of other resources. Future light mobilities could accord with Urry's concern for the post-carbon, post-car world, because they move without the heavy and sunk costs of energy and matter. They may appear to levitate.

References

Bauman, Z. (2000) *Liquid Modernity*, London: Polity.

Miller, K. (2016) *Augustown*, London: Weidenfeld.

Sheller, M. (2014) *Aluminum Dreams: The Making of Light Modernity*, Cambridge, MA: MIT Press.

Szerszynski, B. (2016) Planetary mobilities: Movement, memory and emergence in the body of the Earth, *Mobilities*, 11(4), 614–628.

Witzgall, S., Vogl, G. and Kesselring, S. (2016) *New Mobilities Regimes in Art and Social Sciences*, London: Routledge.

Chapter 21

Time

The particular and the universal

Malene Freudendal-Pedersen

> [D]ifferent senses and different mobilities are organised in, and through, and sometimes against, various times and memories.
>
> (Urry 2000: 104)

So, how did I become interested in everyday transport? It's a difficult question to answer. I'm quite sure, though, that encountering John Urry's work on the framing of mobilities had a great deal to do with it. In this chapter, I will trace my interests back to John's first comprehensive writing on mobilities – *Sociology beyond Societies* – and, in particular, his chapter on time.

When *Sociology beyond Societies* came out in 2000, a lot of pieces fell into place for me, in that John provided a way into understanding the bigger picture of what frames and enables everyday life mobilities. A societal framework, situating mobilities as an all-compassing creation of societies and the individuals inhabiting and (re) creating these societies, provided me with the link between the particular and the universal and almost everything in-between. Particularly pertinent to my work on everyday mobilities was the underlying premise that time 'often engenders enormously powerful emotional sentiments' (Urry 2000: 105). In this sense, John, for me, (re)installed emotions as an important issue within everyday transport praxis.

Time as an individual feeling can be interpreted in all sorts of ways. Since the passing of time is not visual, the eye needs different indicators, as well as temporal divisions of time into specific purposes, such as day, week, month, year, etc., for it to make sense. Apart from these diverse systems of measurement, we also have social control systems qualifying time. Expressions like 'waste of time', 'so much time', 'trapped in the past' are all expressions not based in clock hours but more on sentiment, emotion and a social ordering of what 'good' time is. These different measurements, meanings and emotions are used by the individual when describing and qualifying everyday mobility praxis, while at the same time being produced and reproduced in policy and planning in an ongoing process of structuration and reification.

In *Sociology beyond Societies*, John primarily takes an outset in the differences between instantaneous time and clock time. Clock time is the ordering necessary for the industrialization of societies where a synchronization and measurement of time is essential for the production system. Clock time is essential in all shared physical mobilities systems. Virtual mobility, together with the developments in physical travel, has produced an increasingly mobile world; this has prompted an instantaneous time characterized by simultaneity and fragmentation that has become part of modern life. Instantaneous time symbolizes a time regime where individuals and institutions constantly need to be ready to respond to impulses and snippets of information surrounding them. Cars, trains and planes carry us increasingly faster, and modernity represents a continuous accelerating process towards the speed of light, which cannot be halted. This fragmentation of time has also meant that activities in everyday life are less collectively organized, being replaced by more individual patterns. When community is presented as a contrast to freedom – and freedom today seems to be related to the ability to move either virtually or physically – slowing down the acceleration of time becomes a form of resistance to instantaneous time. John frames this as 'glacial time', a slow-moving time intrinsic to dwelling.

Understanding everyday life within the time regimes John lays out provided me with a way to understanding the stories about, and the rationalities individuals ascribe to, the car. Together with Kingsley Dennis, John formulates this quite rigorously in the book *After the Car* from 2009: 'this car system overcomes a public timetable by enabling car drivers to develop their *own* timetabling of social life' (Dennis and Urry 2009: 28). We live in a time characterized by instantaneous time – but clock time still plays a vital role in everyday lives. Organizing and planning everyday life with work, kids, friends, parents and other diverse activities, and the mobilities this entails, are most often guided by clock time. While obeying clock time, everything the individual expects to achieve and do in order to meet the requirement for 'the good life' is guided by instantaneous time. Navigating and moving an everyday life while constantly being able to commute between these two concepts of time does not leave much flexibility for changing the organization of this puzzle. Thus, asking people to change their everyday life mobilities praxis is the same as asking them to change their everyday life puzzle – a puzzle they carefully orchestrated in order to fulfil not only their own but society's expectations.

Time is related and measured in all our transport modes. Time is an essential parameter in socio-economic traffic models, where transport time is still perceived as wasted time. We know from the multiple research done on this topic the last few years that it is not. It is a qualitative time that is highly valued – a glacial time, a dwelling encased in a moving technology. The way policy and planning describe meaning to time clashes with the 'powerful emotional sentiments' that people experience and this affects their praxis as well as the way they describe and rationalize praxis. In Denmark in the 1990s, there was something called 'the traffic and environment fund' initiated by the Ministry of Environment – it was later taken over by the Ministry of Transport and became 'the traffic fund'. The fund money was aimed at municipalities around Denmark who wished to make improvements to the environment and traffic safety. The majority of the money was used for infrastructure changes, such as roundabouts, bike paths and bus lanes. But a few of the projects also aimed at working with individual praxis related to traffic modes – trying to get people to use bikes or buses instead of cars. These projects were actually quite successful, but unfortunately the effect wore off a couple of years after the projects ended and people fell back into their old habits (using their car for all their journeys, for example). From the outset, I think I had a clear idea that one of the main reasons for this was the quite simplistic view of individuals and their everyday lives, pretty much based on the economic rational man. Thus, from my first step into this field, I struggled to find a way to argue that everyday movement was much more than a rational system inhabited by rational individuals making choices based on accessibility, economy and speed. Basically, what John expounded in his chapter on time (and also later in diverse writings on the different systems of mobilities) is that: 'There is too much transport in the study of travel and not enough society and thinking through the complex intersecting relations between society and transport' (Urry 2007: 20).

Part of the syllabus in my university education was, among other things, looking at technologies through the multi-level perspective (MLP) together with the social construction of technology (SCOT). I guess this was my way into making a project on the electrical car (in the mid-1990s there was yet another attempt to introduce the electrical vehicle into the transport system). I think this piqued my interest in the meaning and significance of the car not as a form of technology but in all the meanings, ideas and emotions embedded *within* the technology. Today, several mobilities scholars are being inspired by MLP and SCOT and I recognize the usefulness of these concepts, but at the time I was introduced to them, before the mobilities literature started emerging, my problem was, in hindsight, that their everyday or praxis perspective was too simplistic. The emotional, philosophical and embodied elements of everyday life that are constantly diffused into politics, planning and business didn't play a big enough role for these concepts to be pertinent as a response to my research questions. In this sense, John's work on time pushed my drive to elucidate how the emotional and ethical ideas of late modern lives needed to be understood and respected if there was ever going to be a way of breaking through the path-dependent characteristics of movement into more sustainable mobilities.

Based on my empirical work over the past 20 years, I would claim that individuals struggle to find ways to act upon ethics in relation to (more sustainable) mobility praxis; they felt an inherent 'response-ability' to the future of this planet. And yet there still exists a large gap between the ethic and the ability to respond to changing mobility praxis. The problem is in the ability – the ability to respond to a common good in a world where individualization is a main driver seems, from an everyday life perspective, to be increasingly challenged. The way that the mobilities turn, with John in the forefront, frames ways of, and reasons to, travel, as much more than a rational thing, opens up the opportunities to analyse mobilities praxis in new ways. Nevertheless, the technocratic view still poses a challenge when much planning of infrastructures and systems for travel still has way too little 'thinking through the complex intersecting relations between society and transport'. And this is where my focus on the relations between the individual and the universal comes from. The concept of the structural stories was my attempt to understand this relationship and also to discuss how the rational technocratic way of arguing for everyday life mobilities praxis is an ongoing reification between individuals, institutions, the media and politics. The philosophical, and thus almost always ethical, questions that shape emotions became my way into understanding everyday life mobilities praxis. And what my empirical work has shown is how present reflections, and the significance of ideas of time, freedom and community as something substantial is in people's lives.

These days I am working to understand the significance of communities and the essential ontological security they provide to everyday lives. Recently I was presenting my preliminary work to colleagues; one of them asked me why I kept to the word 'community', when my claim was that it had changed. Why not use 'assemblages' or 'networks' or one of the many other newer concepts available? My answer was a little bit blurry but nevertheless coloured by an unwillingness to give up on the word community. When I came home, I took out Bauman's (2001) book on *Communities*. I have read it several times and, like with *Sociology beyond Societies*, it is for me one of these books I return to again and again because it stimulates my sociological curiosity. And when I opened the book, the first lines of the book gave me a clear answer to the question. Bauman writes 'Words have meaning: some words, however, also have a 'feel'. The word 'community' is one of them' (Bauman 2001: 1). Time also has a 'feel' as a quote at the beginning of this essay show, and this goes for my work on freedom as well.

What John's work on mobilities helped me to understand and frame is how everyday life and its mobilities are not isolated units but constantly challenged and interacting with the surrounding world. Understanding and changing mobilities praxis and the rationalities formed to support it in everyday life is not simply a question of everyday life. Global and local news, commercials and politics play a decisive role in how this is handled. Everyday life praxis is practical but also influenced by significant ideas of late modernity and emotions related to time, freedom and community.

Today, it seems that the power of individualization as the pathway to freedom has outruled the power of people, communities and institutions as drivers of change. As a consequence, lived lives are often given little significance in relation to change when people are only seen as individualized consumers. There is no doubt that to a great extent modes of thought and possibilities in everyday life are influenced and guided by the capitalist system. Lived lives have different expressions, also decided by factors such as class, gender, education and location. Besides all of this, however, values emotions and dreams of everyday life are, generally speaking, very much the same for most people.

Behind the individualized, there is still a need for an ontological security based on wants and desires, security, safety and communities. However, using dreams, utopias and imagination to inhabit the kind of world we want, endangers the fragile irrationalities holding everyday life together. But, without imagination and aspiration, another more real and significant menace is born when these imaginings, dreams and utopias disappear, and we subsequently forget how to play and live life beyond the frames already existing.

And finally, on a personal level, John actually also made a big difference in my professional life. The first time I met him in person was at a seminar at Roskilde University in 2005. At this time, some of my colleagues were involved in a research project on tourism where John was included. They needed someone to present their work and discuss with John, and they asked me to do it. At this time, I was only a year into my PhD and not that experienced with getting into an academic debate like this. I don't remember much from the seminar but what I clearly remember is that when we were done, John turned his head towards me and very discreetly nodded his head and whispered, 'Well done'. This, I know today, was a typical John way of doing stuff: laconic, no fuss, but in a very respectful and supportive way, making sure I came out of this situation feeling good. And this actually shouldn't be underestimated. Working with everyday transport in Denmark from a mobilities perspective was a quite lonely experience. I was already often used as a speaker at several events – I was one of the few who actually knew something about behaviour (as it is called in the transport world). And let's face it – I was so used to being criticized or patronized (depending on the situation), but I always had John to back me up. His work and his recognition of what I was doing helped me to stay on track. And, very importantly, it made me look for other researchers that also found inspiration in the mobilities literature. This is how I ended up in my first Cosmobilities workshop in 2005 and found a network of people where respect, curiosity and a drive to understand our mobile world was at the core. In Chapter 24, Sven Kesselring tells the story of the network, and I can fully support the significance this network had, and still has, for a lot of people, myself included.

John's work was, and still is, highly significant to my writing and to my thinking. I use vast amounts of his texts in teaching and I would love nothing more than to have the opportunity to talk, laugh and discuss with him again.

References

Bauman, Z. (2001) *Community: Seeking Safety in an Insecure World*. New York: Polity.
Dennis, K. and J. Urry (2009) *After the Car*. Cambridge: Polity.
Urry, J. (2000) *Sociology beyond Societies: Mobilities for the Twenty-First Century*. London: Routledge.
Urry, J. (2007) *Mobilities*. Cambridge: Polity.

Chapter 22

A long conversation

On meetings, travels, and conversations with John Urry

Ole B. Jensen

Introduction

This essay describes how the mobilities research and turn from the hands and mind of John Urry has influenced the emerging research area of mobilities design. The story is autobiographic and I touch down on some critical moments in my interaction with John Urry to see how these formed my trajectory into mobilities research. From 2000 and until John Urry's premature death in 2016 we had multiple conversations in often rather odd places – from universities to train stations, from airport lounges to my patio. The common denominators to these conversations were a mutual interest in mobilities, and always with me as a learning novice. At the end I shortly discuss the field of mobilities design as an emerging research field under the strong influence of John's work. The essay uses the personal narrative and our many conversations to show how my academic work was influenced by John's ideas and thoughts – and as such carries the imprint of a 'long conversation'.

The early days

The interaction with John's work started for me with reading *Economies of Signs and Spaces* (co-authored with Scott Lash in 1994). This particular book was one of two books I bought in the very first week of my new job as a PhD student in 1996. Since my supervisor had a keen interest in Marxist economy and critical geography I was mainly exposed to the works of David Harvey, Ed Soja, Mike Davies, and the like. However, the critical (and spatial) sensitivity that social science had experienced from the mid-1980s in writers such as Anthony Giddens (*Constitution of Society*, 1984) and John's work attracted my attention. I remember coming across a book with the compelling title 'Consuming Places' by John from 1995. The book was a collection of individual papers all circling around a critical, geographical understanding of the valorisation, appropriation, and consumption of places by social agents and institutions. The book fuelled my geographical interest to say the least. Also this was the time I became aware of John's most famous book until that date, the agenda-setting *The Tourist Gaze* from 1990 which since has taken on iconic status. John's work fitted into my emerging interest in the relationship between space and society that grew as a function of my thesis work. Another of the books that really caught my interest as a vivid expression of his cross-disciplinary insight was the book *Contested Natures* (co-authored with Phil Magnathen) from 1998. I was particularly intrigued by the ways in which often mundane and taken-for-granted dimensions of the socio-spatial dynamics were taken apart analytically in this book. The consummation and aesthetization of the English countryside through a mix of 'countryside codes', social practices, and materials for enabling this (e.g. hiking gear, countryside pubs, hiking paths, etc.) was a great source of inspiration to me. So was the clashing of different types of temporality excavated in a dispute over road planning through the countryside. I was so keen on the book I wrote a book review for the Danish Social Science Journal *GRUS* on which I was an editorial board member at the time. I assume one could argue that the early traces of the mobilities turn was already present in much of this work. However, it was only with the landmark book of 2000 that things really started to take on momentum.

Beyond societies

Finalizing my PhD thesis in 1999 on Danish and European urban and regional policies I went into a position as assistant professor in a university planning department. It is safe to say that I had now developed the practice of monitoring whatever came of new publications from the hands of John. So in that sense it was little more than an act of routine check when I ordered a copy of a new book titled *Sociology beyond Societies* in the year 2000. However, as I read my way into this book a sense of change happened. I will not pretend to claim that I sensed the profoundness this work would have on the academic scene. Rather, I sensed a deep resonance on a personal level – this research programme was just so compelling and motivating! As I dived deeper into it I got even more excited than with the *Contested Nature* book and I went on to, once again, write a review for the *GRUS* Journal (for all I know this was the only review in Danish of this book – and at least it was the very first one). I do not think my fellow editorial colleagues (who were predominantly from political science and sociology) really agreed with me when I agitated that this was a 'new way of seeing the social'. I remember having rather heated arguments with my peers on the abolition of the fixed notion of 'society' and having a bit of a job persuading them to see the value in putting flows, movements, and mobilities first. In hindsight, I do not think I really understood just how profound a change of mind-set in the social sciences John was advocating at the time. I just had this gut feeling that this was richer, more open-minded, and explorative than anything I had read before. Just the sort of thing a newly appointed assistant professor with a huge appetite for research was looking for.

Meetings and PhD courses

Until here, my tale has been without any interaction with the main character. This changed when I met John personally for the very first time in Aalborg in 2002. The finer details of this meeting are eloquently described in Claus Lassen's essay elsewhere in this book. The reason therefore is that I asked Claus (whom I supervised as a PhD student) to come along to a lunch meeting organized by sociology professor Jens Christian Tonboe. Suffice here to say that it was a very small gathering! The important thing was that it inaugurated the start of a long and very friendly relationship. The 2002 lunch meeting spurred an explicit interest in following up on the new mobilities turn and contributing more directly hereto. Furthermore, it gave me the confidence to ask John to come to Aalborg to participate in a PhD course I organized with my colleague Tim Richardson in 2004. The title of the course was 'Critical mobility studies: the politics and sociology of planning in a mobile world' and John gave a talk on 'Meetings and networks' (drawing on recent empirical work with Kay Axhausen and Jonas Larsen). The number of participants was about ten and during the conversations in the group, John gave not only the PhD students sound advice. I presented a draft version of a paper on the relation between the works of Georg Simmel, Erving Goffman, and the mobilities turn. I think I casually noted that I could not quite understand why no one had ever written a journal paper on this, to me, obvious and very important relationship. John's immediate response was simply: 'Well, why don't you do it?' In retrospect, this may sound silly, but the thought had never crossed my mind. Having John asking in such a blunt and straightforward manner totally side-tracked all my defences and excuses. This became the paper 'Facework, Flow and the City' to be published in *Mobilities* in 2006. It was also during this PhD course that I noticed John's keen interest in, and sharp eye for, short and precise titles. As often happens PhD students tend to make titles of their dissertations stretch out in endless detail. John targeted this quite head-on and asked the students to minimalize their titles. In the beginning I thought of this as more of an aesthetic ideal, but as we discussed it dawned on me how important is to be short and precise in one's academic communication. 'Telling your story short' has since become a key beacon for my own work (I will let others judge if that succeeded). John was very clear on his stand on the theme of clear and short titles and kindly advised me when we had a conversation about one of my books: 'If it was my book I would call it DESIGNING MOBILITIES which is short and snappy'. I followed John's advice even though I actually ended up using that title for another book! Obviously his own production with titles such as *The Tourist Gaze, Consuming Places, Mobile Lives, Mobilities, After the Car, Offshoring*, and *What Is the Future?* all bear witness to this interest in coining your message with needle-pin-precision. This phase of my acquaintance with John also contained a nice car trip with John and his partner in the summer of 2008. John was invited to speak in the sociology department of my university and we organized an additional meeting. Next to this, I offered to take the two of them on a car trip to the rough nature on the Danish west coast. We saw the countryside and enjoyed lunch at the famous seaside hotel in Svinkløv, only to end up with a cup of afternoon coffee on my patio. Again, I recall a joyful and relaxed company sparkled with the constant references to concepts, theories, and research ideas. John truly experienced the details of the world and lived the moment, as much as he analysed and reflected theoretically about what he saw.

Travels, conversations, and more meetings

I cannot quite recall the precise event but sometime in 2010 John asked me rather directly if time had not come for me to publish a book in the ILS series? John was the long-time editor of the International Library of Sociology Series at Routledge and I suppose he was scouting for new entries. What might have been a routine enquiry on his behalf became a pivotal point in my academic carrier. Such a direct request made me rethink a few things. I remember the emails going back and forth between the mid-English countryside and the northern region of Denmark as some of blunt testing. In one of the emails, I proposed a very long book full of many photos, diagrams, and visualizations (I suppose I could have ruled this out myself, but I got carried away in the conversation). John replied politely and gently that such a book would stand absolutely no chance in this series! However, when I reiterated with an idea for a shorter theory-framing book titled *Staging Mobilities*, John was pleased. Not only had I managed to shorten the book length, but I had also accommodated to his interest in 'short and snappy' titles. The book was published in the ILS series in 2013 and I am pleased with the many sound pieces of advice John offered me 'en route'. In this period, I had the opportunity to travel, talk, and dine with John on numerous occasions. One trip stands out though and serves as an illustration of how the travels and conversations all come together as mobile practices and thoughts. We were both attending the AAG in Washington, DC in 2010. This particular conference is well remembered by most attendants since it coincided with the eruption of Icelandic volcano Eyjafjallajökull that sealed off global airspace between North America and Europe (and actually became the subject of my paper 'Emotional Eruptions', *Mobilities*, 6(1), 2011, which I keenly discussed with John during the whole event). We had the usual conference talks, coffees, and dinners along the event. However, what really stands out was the train trip to the inaugural symposium of the Drexel University Center for Mobilities Research and Policy (the mCenter) in Philadelphia. John, Mimi Sheller and myself were joining company on the Amtrak train from DC to Philly. Conversations about systems, globalization, and mobilities were abound as we were not merely contemplating mobilities, but actually 'doing mobilities'. As I recall our departure from DC Mimi Sheller had to see someone before the train left and the small travelling fellowship of John and myself went looking for lunch at the train station. John spotted this circular and wood-cladded restaurant elevated from the ground. It looked very posh and expensive. However, for John this was just another diner and I remember him talking excitingly about the global disruption of airspace as we had our nice club sandwiches with sparkling water. I also had the great fortune of receiving the CeMoRe 2013–14 Visiting Fellowship and I subsequently spent four weeks split into two trips at John's home base at Lancaster University. This was again a great time for seminars, improvised coffee talks, and dinners.

A very special doctoral defence

The listing of stories, anecdotes, and events could go on, but I think I have proven the point of illustrating that having a conversation with John was possible across vast time and space scales. Retrospectively, what was a disrupted series of events across continents and countries takes on the character of a 'long conversation'. I shall move towards a close but I will mention two events. The first requires a little contextualization. In the Danish academic system, we have annexed a German tradition. We do therefore not only have the internationally recognized doctoral degree awarded with the PhD title. We also have a much rarer and historically traditional 'doctoral degree' (which used to be mandatory in order to get professorial tenure). I mention this since it is important to understand the event I want to present. In 2014 I decided to opt for the doctoral degree and I had developed the theoretical arguments for situational mobilities analysis with the *Staging Mobilities* book (2013) and the design and materially oriented empirical case analyses with the book *Designing Mobilities* (2014). Therefore, I submitted the two books for the defence of the classic Danish doctoral degree. An assessment committee was established and provided they would vouch for the work it would be defended at a public defence act. Enough said about context. The members of the assessment committee for my doctoral defence were Arne Remmen, Aalborg University, Rob Shields, University of Alberta, and John. In the light of this essay, I need not explain to a very long degree the honour and pride I felt by submitting my work to the scrutiny of these scholars. As some readers will know, Rob Shields had in fact himself had John as a PhD supervisor when he wrote what later became the eminent book *Places on the Margin: Alternative Geographies of Modernity* (1991). To complete the picture, I should mention that *Places on the Margin* was the other book I bought during the first week of my PhD study in 1996. If the reader senses 'circle closed' I have succeeded in my account. The defence act took place on 4 November 2014 and lasted for many hours, as is the Danish tradition. After the defence, we enjoyed a beautiful dinner at the new House of Music on the quayside of Aalborg Harbour. Today I am thankful that I had the devoted attention of John to my work at this special event.

I shall end with an event that actually never took place. For the last two years, I have had a seat on the academic advisory board to the Copenhagen Metro. For the last year, we have been discussing future mega-trends within transportation and urban development. In the light hereof, I proposed a seminar where we would invite John as the keynote speaker. This connected to his work on 'futures' as published in the books *Climate Change and Society* (2011), *Societies beyond Oil* (2013), *Offshoring* (2014), and last but not least his posthumously published *What Is the Future?* (2016). We had a couple of emails bouncing back and forth and all was set for John to come across and give a keynote on 'Future mobilities' in Copenhagen on 7 April 2016. I was in my summer cottage taking a short Easter break when I received the news about John's untimely passing in an email of 22 March circulated through the CeMoRe email list. The shock was petrifying, and as many of the readers of this book surely know, the email list shortly turned into a generous forum of condolences and anecdotes in the days to follow. Sitting alone in my rural retreat my own immediate reaction posted to the list was this: 'This is horrible … I have just planned a joint seminar with John on April 7 and he seemed very fit. I can't believe it! We have lost an academic giant and a fantastic person. My warmest thoughts goes out to John's family and dear ones'. I need not say much more.

Impacts on my research into situational mobilities and mobilities design

It is quite evident that I hold John to be a great source of inspiration, as well as a sensitive mentor and supporter of my personal attempt to carve out a niche and contribute to the new mobilities turn. John eagerly supported the early ideas about situational mobilities that I based on Goffman's work. This predominantly came across in his encouragement of me to write the 'Facework' paper but also in his direct asking for a manuscript to the ILS series. The work around the situational mobilities theory is in many ways still relatively traditional in a sociological sense. However, the following development of my research into design and architecture I term 'mobilities design' research represents a much more explorative and uncertain trajectory. The book *Designing Mobilities* is evidence of this effort to explore and establish a new and emergent field. As mentioned, the book carries the title directly proposed by John. The many talks we had around the development of mobilities design research furthermore has strengthened my understanding that not only did he endorse this work, but he also viewed it as an example of how someone takes on the core ideas within the new mobilities turn in a double act of appropriation and creative exploration. In short, the development of mobilities design research is my attempt to establish thinking and research inspired by John, but as an act of personalized and independent contribution to the expanding research field.

Epilogue

When we had the International C-MUS Conference on 'Materialities and Mobilities' at Aalborg University at the end of November 2016 we organized a plenary session titled 'Commemorating John Urry'. At this session Claus Lassen, Monika Büscher, and myself first shared memories of John and explained how he influenced each of our works in profound ways. Hereafter the floor was open and a very warm session of sharing anecdotes and personal experiences framed John's legacy in the best possible way. Besides being a testament to the huge academic impact of John, there were also joyful moments shared and great stories about John's deep sense of humour. The assessment, the impact, and the aftermath of John's life and work will be in momentum for many years to come. In that lecture theatre of the commemoration session on that November day of 2016 (the very same venue wherein John scrutinized my doctoral work exactly two years earlier) it really started to sink in more clearly: John is not with us anymore! However, we must do our best to remember him as well as to take on the huge task and responsibility of carrying on (as well as transforming) the mobilities turn. I am left with a huge influence on my scholarly work as well as with many, many warm memories of an 'academic friend' with whom I just seem to have had a very long conversation.

References

Dennis, K. and J. Urry (2009) *After the Car*, Cambridge: Polity.
Lash, S. and J. Urry (2004) *Economies of Signs and Space*, London: SAGE.
Urry, J. (1995) *Consuming Places*, London: Routledge.
Urry, J. (2000) *Sociology beyond Societies: Mobilities for the Twenty-First Century*, London: Routledge.
Urry, J. (2016) *What Is the Future?*, Cambridge: Polity.

Chapter 23

Europe beyond mobilities

Vincent Kaufmann

The sociology of a world in movement

John Urry's work on mobility provides a means of interpreting societies from the myriad movements and flows that traverse them. More specifically, it allows us to start with that which moves and to go towards what is inert; in other words, Urry's work invites us to use mobilities to describe social issues, even in the most static institutions. This is an original, refreshing perspective in a field largely built on the study of what is instituted, a perspective that was likewise met with resistance and controversy. Ultimately, John Urry's work on mobility has found large echoes in the post-structuralist currents of sociology.

But the earthquake may be yet to come. In this chapter, I will illustrate the heuristic value of John Urry's approach to the future of European societies and, in so doing, address the ideology of mobility in the European construction. But before embarking on this intellectual exercise in the pages that follow, I would like to relate a few anecdotes that have marked my experience as a researcher and likewise seem essential to John Urry's position.

Discovery of a world and a man

It was on Patrick Le Galès's recommendation that I contacted John Urry for a postdoc at the University of Lancaster. After a few epistolary exchanges, John wrote me a glowing letter of recommendation, and I received a grant from the Swiss National Science Foundation to spend a year at Lancaster. That is how I arrived there in March 2000, the year *Sociology beyond Societies* (Urry 2000) came out. My postdoctoral period at Lancaster was largely spent writing *Rethinking Mobility*, an enterprise in which my many exchanges with John deeply marked me.

My original scientific culture is French sociology and, by extension, the Francophone networks into which it delves. Marked by this habitus of strong links to philosophy – and hence powerful theoretical and conceptual debate – and a tradition of oral argumentation, my contacts with John Urry taught me several important things about my work as a researcher.

To welcome me upon my arrival in Lancaster, John took me to lunch at a small country inn, taking the time to introduce himself, to introduce me to his team and — something that intrigued me at the time — insisted on explaining the rules of scientific debate within his team, underscoring the imperativeness of discussing colleagues' work in a "fair" way and never attempting to destroy a speaker. He also stressed his commitment to cordial discussions and constructive debate. Accustomed to scientific debates where one pushes one's peers to their last bastions to find out what they're made of, I was suddenly confronted with a whole new way of debating, and I liked it — a lot.

Constructive debate, to which John Urry was very much attached, allows people to express themselves more serenely and dedramatizes taking the dais because the rules are less definitive and formal than in France. The circulation of ideas and the emergence of pearls of thought are thus fostered. Transposed to writing, this approach has, among other things, the advantage of freeing one from the trench warfare to which I was accustomed in the pragmatic, strict, structured approaches that are the basis of French sociology. But does not some kind of intellectual mush ensue, you ask? On the contrary; it is often raw criticism that impedes nuance and subtlety of analysis.

A few months later, I submitted a theoretical text to John Urry for discussion, a first draft of a chapter of *Re-thinking Mobility*. From the start, he didn't seem very comfortable with the text; he had annotated it and seemed puzzled. Finally, after a few formal, jolly remarks he asked me, "Why so much theory?" The text was full of references and theoretical arguments from numerous authors. I spent pages justifying my position relative to those of other authors, discussing the differences between their understanding of mobility and territory and my own. The text was convoluted and ultimately unclear: the mere density of its "theory" made it essentially inaudible. In the exchanges with John that followed, I learned that parsimony is an essential ingredient of a good theoretical argument in sociology.

I was deeply marked by these episodes which, in my opinion, underscore the essential framework and power of John Urry's thinking (the clarity and purity of his arguments which give apparent simplicity to his texts, a writing style imbued with literary accents — a mark of good humor and enthusiasm rather than dull criticism). Such qualities have contributed to the influence of his thinking; many authors draw inspiration from it due to its creativity, particularly for anything related to mobility as a social fact, from which it is possible to infer a social dynamic. The dynamic, refreshing approach to societies, in my opinion, enables researchers to overcome much of the antagonism that plagues holistic, pragmatic, and post-structuralist currents in the social sciences when one considers Urry's proposals with regard to the mobility turn broadly. The journey into the social sciences and various scientific approaches which John Urry's work invites was, for me, a key source of inspiration in developing the notion of motility, like a Swiss Army knife one brings along on a trip.

Europe as a case study

My exploration of the mobilities that traverse European societies – be it daily life, high mobility, cross-border relations or companies' motility for tax incentives – has convinced me that Europe is prime testing ground for John Urry's theories. If a paradigmatical case study of theses on the mobility turn exists, it's the European construction. Effectively, the European Union (EU) is essentially a mobility project, when one analyses its founding texts, and the economic and institutional crises it has been mired in since the late 2000s glaringly raises the question of governability of mobility.

To demonstrate the advantages of a flow-based approach to societies for general sociology, the current crisis in Europe provides a perfect case study. With Ander Audikana our approach was based on the popular Swiss vote "against mass immigration," an analysis of the ins and outs of this referendum that clearly targets the free movement of people, and raises questions that go far beyond Switzerland alone (Kaufmann and Audikana 2017).

On 9 February 2014, Switzerland adopted the popular initiative known as "against mass immigration," with a 55 per cent participation rate and approval by 50.3 per cent of the population. The result was stupefying: the bilateral accords between Switzerland and the EU were challenged, particularly that which concerned the free movement of persons. Given the vote result and Switzerland's refusal to apply the extension protocol of the Free Movement Agreement to Croatia, the EU suspended Swiss participation in mobility and European academic research programs.

The Swiss vote also brought to light a certain unease; above and beyond a vote that denotes a political climate specific to Switzerland, it tells us something about Europe more generally, that being its construction and the tension that permeate it. Mobility is now at the heart of a number of issues directly facing contemporary European societies. The February 2014 Swiss vote was merely the local expression of a series of more structural upheavals currently affecting the European continent.

Moreover, the result of the vote appears paradoxical given that on February 9, 2014, a federal decree aiming to invest 6.4 billion Swiss francs to "sustainably finance the operation, maintenance, and development of rail infrastructure" was overwhelmingly approved by 62 per cent of voters. While the popular movement "against mass immigration" aimed to regulate the mobility of persons and migration towards Switzerland more specifically, the second measure clearly marked the desire to increase Switzerland's mobility potential. Confronted with these two mobility issues, Swiss citizens expressed two very different opinions the very same day: the majority said "yes" to "less mobility" while at the same time saying "yes" to "more mobility."

To analyze this vote and the debates it reflects, we did an in-depth analysis of European texts on mobility in all its forms and the debates surrounding the February 9, 2014 Swiss vote. We then conducted a series of interviews with the presidencies of the six major political parties in Switzerland.

The aim of these investigations was to think of mobilities as a system and thus sought to highlight the links between various types of flows of people, goods, and capital. As a result, several central issues in terms of mobility policies were identified.

The political importance of communicating on the imaginaries of mobility dynamics: Mobility is as much a daily reality as a mediated perception; it is both a concrete phenomenon and a part of our individual experience.

Public authorities' capacity to intervene vis-à-vis mobility dynamics: To what extent are mobility flows controllable through public regulatory tools? Two extreme positions stand out: on the one hand, the capacity to regulate mobility flows is largely surpassed by the dynamics at work. Mobility flows far exceed institutional frameworks and governments' intervention capacity. In other words, we are simply condemned to "laissez-faire." The second position considers that mobility is a controllable phenomenon that can be structured, limited, and promoted. Some public policies designed to influence mobility flows aim for this. However, our analysis does not allow us to confirm either of these positions. In this sense, overestimating the government's ability to intervene or defending radical resignation are both politically comfortable but difficult to prove.

The unequal distribution of the benefits and disadvantages of mobility dynamics: Certain groups and individuals – as well as territories – can benefit from the advantages associated with mobility. Mobility, however, is problematic for other populations: newcomers are often perceived as a threat by poorer populations; increases in traffic disturbs residents; and low taxation of the rich irritates certain taxpayers.

From the outset, the different forms of mobility are a powerful analyzer of societal dynamics in these three political issues. This aptly illustrates the heuristic virtue of considering different types of flows and mobilities together, not separately, and thus the relevance of John Urry's refreshing approach of exploring movement to describe social dynamics down to its very institutions. More fundamentally still, they show that the controversies surrounding the issue of flows and mobility concern the solid world of institutions and structural social positions. The issue therefore is recognizing the importance of the injustice and inequality represented by or experienced through mobility, and providing appropriate answers lest the instituted edifice collapse from within.

Deconstructing the ideology of reversible mobility

The three political issues briefly described from the analysis of the Swiss vote also suggest that ideological tensions regarding mobility dynamics in Europe are based on a fundamental dichotomy: considering mobility as a priority response to societal problems or, on the contrary, the main source of these problems – mobility synonymous with freedom and creative force, or mobility as a threatening, destabilizing force. This fundamental dichotomy thus contrasts positions favorable to mobility with those that argue for anchoring policies.

If one rereads the European integration process based on this mobility/ anchoring dichotomy, it is clear that the EU was fundamentally designed, in recent decades, as a unilateral mobility promotion and proliferation program.

Mobility should help eradicate old entrenchments, implicitly considered as residue, to promote functional integration similar to that of large cities, and ultimately to strengthen the European scale to a new perimeter of anchorage. The four freedoms of movement have often been exercised painfully, through competition between territories, economic actors, and people. It was the market that served as a unifying instrument, and the old national systems of protection and anchoring were the guardians of diversity and difference. The European Commission thus far has not been ready or appeared able to act as a guarantor not only of mobility, but also of anchoring.

Mobility between European countries requires a capacity for uprooting and rerooting much greater than the one between the constituent states of the United States. It implies changing health systems, education systems, labor markets, languages, and even lifestyles. The reference to the United States as an inspiration for the European construction must undoubtedly be cast aside to make way for a new balance between mobility and anchoring.

But does not such an undertaking inevitably fall into an ideology that is as totalizing as that of promoting flows? No, because the critique of free movement applied to different types of mobility is not necessarily reactionary or anti-liberal. It is not a question of criticizing the principle itself but of determining how it is implemented. The need to consider mobility in its various forms, to focus on the advantages versus the disadvantages or to consider the tension between individuals and mediated experience are essential ingredients of a mobility policy.

Thinking about mobility naturally means thinking about immobility and anchoring. Here again John Urry's works are a source of inspiration. Considering societies based on flows and the mobilities that characterize them does not mean ignoring that which does not move (Urry 2007). Mobility forms are key here. European policy has, until now, focused on encouraging reversible mobilities, meaning the ability to cross space without having to confront otherness. Given the perverse effects of this policy and the opposition it encounters throughout Europe, promoting free movement based on the ability to uproot and reroot elsewhere – rather than reversible mobilities – has become essential. Such a broad political program that rethinks flows and mobility together – not separately – could be fueled by works on the mobility turn.

The importance of breaking language barriers in research

The work and ideas of John Urry have been decisive for me in designing my research on mobility in Europe, and particularly for analyzing the practices and values conveyed by the EU for mobility in a global perspective.

From this example and to conclude, I would like to come back to the Anglo-Saxon and Francophone traditions, not from the standpoint of cultures of debate and the positions they entail, but rather in terms of the "migration" of authors. Mobility research in the French-speaking world is strongly marked by the idea that mobility is a social and spatial phenomenon that involves both a change of role or position and movement in space.

This notion undeniably has heuristic qualities that clearly highlight the relationship between spatial mobility and social integration; from this perspective, Francophone sociology made its mobility turn long ago, in the 1980s. In this research environment, the discovery of John Urry's approach to mobility greatly enriched my work, as it complements the mobility turn sparked by Francophone sociology and geography by fundamentally challenging the static boundaries of its conceptual framework. Introducing John Urry's work and ideas in research arenas where he had no founding role is extremely stimulating. It has led me to reflect on the "mobility" of authors from one language to another many times.

In fact, translated into French, John Urry occupies another position, becomes part of another set of debates and brings new ideas on mobility beyond merely those of the Anglo-Saxon scientific world. The above discussion concerning the book I wrote with Ander Audikana on the principle of free movement and its application is undoubtedly a good example of this, as it is built on a combination of references from different scientific worlds built around different languages.

The symbolic importance of "uprooting" an author's work and rerooting it in debates in other languages is fascinating to me. I have tested it with John Urry's work. More generally, however, doing so builds a strong case for a veritable mobility turn in scientific literature between languages. All authors do not lend themselves to this, but for intellectual heavyweights like John, this seems to me a highly creative approach and therefore a good one! There is still much work to be done (in French, at any rate …).

References

Kaufmann, V. and AudikanaA. (2017) *Mobilité et libre circulation en Europe. Un regard Suisse.* Paris: Economica.

Urry, J. (2000) *Sociology beyond societies. Mobilities for the twenty-first century.* London: Routledge.

Urry, J. (2007) *Mobilities.* Cambridge: Polity.

Chapter 24

Mobility – why actually?

Sven Kesselring

As long as I can think back I was somehow intrigued by mobility. One of the first papers I wrote at the university was an attempt to find out which social scientists have been working on different aspects of mobility and who had some theoretical and conceptual work to offer to better understand what mobility actually was. But even when mobility has almost been part of my academic work the question why actually it was something special to me often gave me a hard time. In fact, when John Urry's *Sociology beyond Societies* came out in 2000 I already considered myself as a mobility scholar. But I still couldn't give a satisfying answer on the question. My colleagues and I worked hard on deciphering what was later called the "mobile risk society" (Kesselring 2008). But in some ways John's book suddenly placed a new language and a reference system that allowed us – together with the Beckian theory of reflexive modernization – to describe and analyze the complex relationships between mobility, individuality, and emancipation in modern societies. And still this is the underlying rationale for most of my work: as Bauman puts it, mobility is an ambivalent, Janus-faced phenomenon, promise and threat at the same time. Being mobilized can set you free. It has a disembedding energy, which can be liberating. Moving around, being on the move, and traveling can open up horizons. Sometimes it provides views and opportunities not even imagined before. But it can also scare you, frighten you, and the mobilization of the own self is full of risks and jeopardizing. There is always the biographical risk of "drifting" (Sennett) instead of navigating.

This ambivalence of mobility is structural. It belongs to modernity. Recently, I came across the high risks of mobility again when I was reading Didier Eribon's extraordinary self-reflexive autobiography *Returning to Reims* (2007). Maybe this also brought me a little bit closer to answering my own question why mobility came to me as a topic and why it is so important to me and to most people in the world. In fact, Eribon's strong essay made me aware – and this time more on a biographical than on a seriously scientific level – how immensely true John's credo is that "there is … too much transport in the study of travel and not enough society and certainly not enough thinking through their complex intersecting processes" (Urry 2007: 19–20). I am coming back to Eribon soon, but first I want to mention that in particular those amongst us who are engaged in questions of sustainable mobility often get stuck in staring at the figures of mobility behavior. The "brute facts" (Cresswell) take over much of our attention. And by doing so we often forget that mobility is a deeply social phenomenon, a process in constant motion, not a given or stable fact. Mobility performance is learned on the one side, "cultivated" on the other, and connected to the opportunity spaces and imaginaries that individuals have, that they conquer themselves sometimes, and that are habitualized and somehow scripted/inscribed into people's practices and even their whole life courses.

In this sense, I need to admit that publishing *Aeromobilities* with John Urry and Saolo Cwerner in 2009 was not only driven by the motivation that this is a key topic for the future of modern societies. It was also biographical – an investigation into a topic, which has bothered me all the way since pre-academic times in my life. I remember clearly my first flight ever. Unfortunately, I need to say, tongue in cheek, it went to Brazil. I must have been about 20 and I was part of a youth delegation heading there to set up a collaborative partnership between young people in Rio de Janeiro and my hometown in Germany. Until then, I had not even thought about taking any flight somewhere else and the idea to travel in the air for 16 hours scared me to death. The opportunity to be part of this adventure came to me by surprise. From the moment I said yes to the final departure to Rio I had only four weeks to prepare myself. Nevertheless, immediately I sensed I had to take this chance. At the same time I felt a huge unease, actually a sort of shame for it. Coming from a working-class family my emotions were more than ambivalent. And at some point I needed to learn that this ambivalence of mobility that I experienced in 1987 should never go away again. Not even today, since I have done research on it for more than 20 years, I can think of mobility as something unambiguous. It was and it still is the blessing and the curse of modern societies, the hope for a better, more tolerant, cosmopolitan world and the biggest menace for the survival of mankind. Well, as I said before, this flight to Brazil was so much more than transport. It was, as John Urry put it, more than just changing from one place to another. It was a social move and it had a lot of socio–cultural implications. It was actually a kind of social mobility. And the fright I felt while sitting on this plane was not only due to the fact that I found myself suddenly 30,000 feet above the Atlantic. It was also because I sensed that this flight might push me somehow into a new direction.

In some ways the experience was life changing. At least, it marked an individual turning point and – symbolically speaking – the "departure from Reims." In Brazil I met a lot of people, saw many places, entered awesome landscapes, and cruised exciting cities – all this I had never foreseen for my life. It was the beginning of accumulating new social, cultural, and network capital. With some of the people I met I am still connected, some as friends, some more as acquaintances, some as part of my social "cosmos." And of course, many other people might also never have thought about flying to Brazil. I am not saying this is unique at all. But Brazil hasn't even been on my social map, wasn't a real place, and definitively not part of the opportunity spaces I imagined for my life. This has to do with social class, with the place and the people one comes from. Didier Eribon describes his life as one which has been shaped by the constant "discomfort that results from belonging to two different worlds, worlds so far separated from each other that they seem irreconcilable, and yet which coexist in everything that you are" (Eribon 2013: 18). People like him crossed the boundaries between classes but still have one foot in each, the working class they originate from and the academic middle class they grew into. But at the end of the day his book is a document of a life that never arrived somewhere, never experienced the feeling of being perfectly at home. It is a story of hybridity and an ongoing unfinished travel, somehow rooted in two irreconcilable worlds, a life mobilized at its core and somehow resonating to what songwriter Billy Joel calls a state of mind that "could be the Pennsylvania turnpike." This experience Eribon describes is a deep and highly ambivalent mobility experience. In the way he explains it is comparable with a unidirectional migration from one continent to another. He was happy to break up and escape his narrow, homophobic, and increasingly right-wing radicalized French Front National milieu. It saved him in some ways. And it gave him the opportunity to become an intellectual figure in contemporary France and a celebrated sociologist.

While I am writing this I am sitting, again, on a flight. This time I am not heading to Brazil, but to New York instead. And I am on the way visiting friends I met some 30 years ago in Brazil and who are now living next to New York in New Jersey. And I am rethinking John's words, "there is … too much transport in the study of travel."

Seen from today the flight at the end of the 1980s doesn't symbolize such a dramatic act of liberation as in Eribon's case. But it was an eye opener and maybe also a door opener for a life and a career, for unintended but meaningful social relations and networks, etc. which had never been on the radar, not for me, not for my parents, not for anyone in my whole family. Spending a professional life on cosmopolitan mobilities and the like – what a crazy idea! Not even words existed in a world where it happened from time to time that people felt sorry for me, because I still had to learn something. I wrote "unfortunately" at the beginning of this text and what I mean is that at this time not only the fact that I was sitting on an airplane made me sweat, the whole trip into an uncharted territory; a different culture with unknown manners, everyday routines, etc. scared me. It was the whole sense of flying into the open (which actually wasn't as open as I thought it would be) into a world of uncertainty and into my semi-private and personal clash of cultures.

I cannot say if the definition of mobility we developed later in a research project on mobility pioneers has been influenced by this early experience. But retrospectively this would make sense (even if we know that we have the tendency to straighten out inconsistencies and cognitive dissonances). Mobility as the capacity of individuals to co-navigate and co-shape their life courses, as we called it, probably reflects this somehow. While I am now getting closer to the US and its somehow awkward and conflictual political situation under its recently elected President Trump I recognize the sense of flow all passengers including me are in, the socio-material and digital networks, the coded and digitalized mobility spaces surrounding us on which we travel and the power of technoscapes and the infrastructures of mobility which prestructure, enable, and limit our capacities to navigate ourselves within modernity today. There is a power of mobility. There is also the violence within and spreading out from the massive mobilities and the movements that modern societies generate. While sitting on this plane to New York and getting closer to old friends, a meeting with a publisher, and a congress with almost 10,000 scientists, I am in the middle of the ambivalences of a mobilized modernity, the liquid modernity as Zygmunt Bauman put it. "Consuming the Planet to Excess" (Urry 2010) perfectly grabs this ambivalence, the pervert beauty and the dark side of the moon in the mobile risk society.

John loved to travel, even more he loved to meet and talk to people and see the academic people that he was working with grow, develop, and mature. He had an amazing ability to connect with people, intellectually but also personally. I have seen it a couple of times and experienced myself that a short intimate conversation with him after someone's talk had a lasting impact on the work and also the course of the work of this person. Mobility – and here I am talking about the old Latin meaning of it as *mobilitas*, as the capacity to move (and also change) – in this sense can also depend on someone else's mobility, traveling and the proximity it creates. Meeting people and places can change lives, open up the horizon for new ways of thinking, of seeing, of designing, and connecting things.

Flashback: it was in 2001. Two years before, in 1999, we had started the mobility pioneers project in the Munich Reflexive Modernization Research Center. We had this vague idea that we wanted to research how people who are expected to be highly mobile work-wise, flexible, and manage their jobs and social relations (we didn't use the word networks at this time yet) through different forms of mobility. Surrounded by sociologists (while being one myself) I argued that there are at least physical, socio-cultural, and – attention! – virtual mobilities. In particular for the use of the notion "virtual mobility," a term that can be found everywhere today, we almost got slaughtered. There was actually little understanding for an interdisciplinary approach and not even a few of our colleagues thought at this time we should focus on social mobility and stratification instead of giving so much attention to aspects which might have been better dealt with in other disciplines such as geography, transportation research, computer science, and others.

In this situation I had the opportunity, strongly supported by Ulrich Beck, to invite John Urry to Munich for three months. Apart from John having discussions with Ulrich in particular and other colleagues we had a couple of meetings with him in our research project. At this time we had heated internal discussions about the question of how much space social mobility, class mobility, and questions of social inequality should have in the project. There was a tendency to give in to the pressure and to conduct the project more towards the sociological mainstream. In the end it was also one of John's short remarks after one of the meetings, which helped to become more secure in keeping track towards an interdisciplinary concept of mobilities. He said something like, the way we handled the mobility questions sounded quite German to him, a bit too tidy maybe. And he argued from a complexity perspective that we should maybe give a bit more space to the fact that there is no Weberian pure social space but spaces and scapes of interdependency and the intermingling of different mobilities and different forces of modernization.

At this time we found the mobility pioneers project seriously challenging and somehow pioneering itself. There was no such thing as a grand mobility theory but we actually needed one. *Sociology beyond Societies* and the work on the mobilities of the 21st century was for me as for many other scholars the right book at the right time. Suddenly there was the terminology, deeply rooted within modern sociological thinking but far beyond disciplinary limitations. This made it possible to express, analyze, and understand what we tried to find words for.

Ulrich Beck also sensed this at the time. He was aware that a competing paradigm to the risk paradigm was on the rise, which somehow connected to the theory of reflexive modernization. At this time around 80 people worked in a Munich-based research center (SFB 536) on the empirical groundings and foundations of the theory. While Ulrich was focusing on issues of globalization and risks, John and the fast-growing community around him, including many of the scholars gathered here in this volume, emphasized and propelled the shaping power of "the diverse mobilities of peoples, objects, images, information and waste" for contemporary social lives, societies, and their economies. In many ways John's formulation from his 2000 book that the "development of various networks and flows undermines endogenous social structures" (Urry 2000: 1) could have been more or less in the same way a Beckian formulation. And maybe Ulrich was even (just) a (little) bit envious of the fact that it wasn't him who invented the mobilities turn and paradigm. As I wrote before a couple of times there is the paradoxical idea of a capitalist system which might be beaten by its own forces and victories which connects John's with Ulrich's way of thinking and which kept them against all differences in theoretical orientations and traditions in a somehow strained relationship to the very end of their working lives. Climate change, environmental degradation, increasing social inequalities, struggles over migration and between refugees and those who are citizens "by nature" or who have been lucky enough to be "already in," battles over who should pay for and carry the social, ecological, and economic consequences of a global production and trade regime which is based on exploitation and profit maximization, and so forth, all these were topics both theorists were deeply concerned with.

Around this time Ulrich started – for some of us in the research center it seemed overnight – the cosmopolitan turn, first within the research center by pushing it on the almost 20 research projects at the time. Later, his writing on cosmopolitanism and the cosmopolitanization of the modern world made quite an impact on the sociological community and beyond. I guess it has been this turn within his theoretical program which made his work even more influential than it was already at this time, in particular in terms of international reputation.

Finally, this was one of the reasons why it was possible to gather him and John with others such as Vincent Kaufmann (who I didn't know at this time), Weert Canzler, Norbert Schneider, Ruth Limmer, and others for a first mobilities workshop in Munich in 2003. We called it "Mobility and the Cosmopolitan Perspective." It gave its title to a book (Canzler et al. 2008) and also for the Cosmobilities Network (www.cosmobilities.net) which was founded the day after the workshop. In fact, it was John who figured out the name Cosmobilities together with the German journalist Bobby Langer who was in charge of the workshop documentation. They played around with the title of the workshop. Because John knew about my plans to start a website for mobilities scholars he said we should start the Cosmobilities Network right away, which is still alive and active.

Mobilities and proximity

Even if the constitution of the Cosmobilities Network seems to be the subject and product of some more or less coincidental encounters of a group of scientists in Munich it wasn't like this at all. Travel, proximity, meetings, and social networks always played a key role in John's work and in the mobilities paradigm in general. At the end of the day, Cosmobilities (and all the other networks, centers, and institutions John was part of organizing, creating, and initiating) benefited from this and became some sort of "applied research" for John and many others. On the one hand this comes from the fact that the mobilities turn has been strongly driven and shaped by the expertise and presence of sociologists, anthropologists, human geographers, and social scientists in general. This also generated a "unique selling point" that this approach has in contrast to many other networks in transportation research. It is the "bold" expertise in social aspects of mobility and transport which builds the knowledge base of the approach. On the other hand, the materialization and the manifestation of the new paradigm in scholars, research groups, institutions, workshops, conferences, and publications has been massively influenced and even carried for quite a while by John's capacity to bond and initiate networks. I recently learned that an invitation I received for a keynote was the result of one of John's (actually quite) famous recommendations to connect. Many of us suggest every now and then to connect with a scholar somewhere. But John was excellent in identifying who would match and where he could see the benefit for the people, for networks, and for scientific progress.

Against this background the high-growth speed the Cosmobilities Network experienced right after we launched the website in 2004 was also the result of many years and some thorough and meticulous work on social and professional relations within the rising community of mobilities scholars. If I say John then I mean more than just the person. He stands for a specific academic principle at work, a social technique of building scientific communities which is based on trust, the skills of maintaining social and at the same time professional relations, and, maybe the most important aspect, of steady collaboration instead of ongoing competition. John knew precisely who he was and that he was the owner of a huge social capital supporting and strengthening careers and reputations. But he was also able to transfer some of this social capital into "network capital" which was available, distributed, and shared. One example: John was a prolific writer and he published many books with others, co-edited volumes, but he also wrote and rewrote books with others. Apart from some rare cases he insisted on the alphabetic order of co-editors and co-authors. The message he was sending out with this was significant. He kept on doing this even if he knew that many scholars in academia could misunderstand this as if the first author was the one doing the most work. As I mentioned before, he knew who he was and that his name was well known and of the best reputation. But to those who had the chance of working with him he never became tired of saying that in the end it is important that co-editors and co-authors share work and responsibilities in the best possible and most equal way. The academic culture of freeriding on others' work and resources was not part of the principle he stood for.

I am not telling these stories to romanticize and idealize the person. It is about the fact that the culture of collaboration and mutual recognition within the professional mobilities networks and communities was highly efficient and functional. It enabled the members to make a strong contribution to the scientific agenda the mobilities turn had in social sciences and beyond. The "new mobilities paradigm" (Sheller and Urry 2006) belongs to the rare species of social theories which are rooted in sociology but inter and transdisciplinary by nature. Everybody who works in interdisciplinary contexts knows the most complicated issue is to find a common language and to deal with difference and tolerate a certain amount of lack of understanding which is characteristic for this important work.

Traveling networks, traveling social space(s), traveling theories

Therefore, persons are key to the dissemination of ideas and to what John Urry would have called the traveling of ideas. Even if he was an admirer of Kuhn's theory of paradigm shift he had a different understanding of how it happens. I remember a longer conversation on this where he talked about Randall Collins' seminal book *The Sociology of Philosophy* and his theory of intellectual change. John underlined with verve that the rise or fall of a scientific paradigm could never be reduced to a single person's oeuvre. It is always social networks through which ideas travel and which connect and constitute epistemic communities.

Coming back to the beginning of the text, my first ever flight, the one to Brazil, was some sort of premonition of what happened after. Now, while I am flying back to Europe from the US I realize that the airspace has not become a routinized "place" to me at all. But using airplanes has become an unwanted, disliked, and highly unsustainable element of my professional life. Like many of us I find myself from time to time in this treadmill of flying around the world because academic careers and the paradoxical attempt to build communities and coalitions for sustainable mobility needs global alliances and collaborative structures. John perfectly played the role of a "connector." His late work was seriously dedicated to fight against climate change and to work for a postfossil mobility system. But the ambivalence stays and stayed with him, too. If I hadn't once made the move to meet John and his colleagues in person at Lancaster University for a couple of months, my life, and not only the professional part of it, would have happened in a different way. By traveling there and staying for a while I somehow grounded and materialized even more what I have described in relation to the Brazil flight. I started building up network and social capital and using the different networks as infrastructures for my career. In this sense the answer to the question of "Why mobility?" might be: because it is a general principle of our modernity that mobilities can change lives and we need to change mobilities to keep our lives for the future.

References

Eribon, D. (2013) *Returning to Reims*. Cambridge, MA: MIT.

Kesselring, S. (2008) "The Mobile Risk Society." In W. Canzler, V. Kaufmann, and S. Kesselring (eds), *Tracing Mobilities: Towards a Cosmopolitan Perspective*. Farnham: Ashgate, 77–102.

Sheller, M. and J. Urry (2006) "The New Mobilities Paradigm." *Environment and Planning A* 38, no. 2: 207–226. doi:10.1068/a37268.

Urry, J. (2000) *Sociology beyond Societies: Mobilities of the Twenty-First Century*. London: Routledge.

Urry, J. (2007) *Mobilities*. Cambridge: Policy Press.

Urry, J. (2010) "Consuming the Planet to Excess." *Theory, Culture and Society* 27, no. 2–3: 191–212. doi:10.1177/0263276409355999.

Chapter 25

How one book and one meeting shaped my aeromobilities research

Claus Lassen

A winter's day in 2002

At the beginning of my PhD study, my supervisor, Ole B. Jensen, gave me the book *Sociology beyond Societies* by John Urry. This book focuses on the relationships amongst global work, knowledge organizations and increasing international air travel. I originally trained in transport and urban planning, and *Sociology beyond Societies* opened up a whole new world to me. The book was not only highly relevant for my thesis on global air travel, but it also gave me a new perspective on my own professional habitus as a transport planner. For many years, I had struggled to articulate my criticisms of conventional transport research and praxis but was unable to create a coherent platform or vocabulary for this criticism. John's ground-breaking book on societies in motion provided the lexicon I needed.

One day in February 2002, Ole and I heard a rumour that John Urry planned to visit the Department of Sociology at our university. This was a chance for me to meet the author face to face.

Ole and I immediately wrote to the Department of Sociology and asked if we, as employees of the neighbouring Department of Planning, might sneak into this internal sociology meeting with John. The Department of Sociology replied, 'Yes, you may come, but you need to leave again if there are not enough seats!'

The day came! Ole and I sat tensely in the meeting room and waited for John to arrive. We were the only ones in the room. We had become convinced that we were in the wrong location when the door suddenly opened and John and professor of sociology Jens Tonboe (the meeting organizer) stood in the doorway looking astonished that there were only two people sitting in the room, and we were not from the Department of Sociology.

Perhaps it was the intimate atmosphere created by this small crowd that made this first meeting with John so magical. That morning, we gained exclusive insight into John's profound ideas about a new agenda for mobilities research that he discusses in his book. At the meeting, John also invited me to come to Lancaster, a trip that later turned out to be vital for my career as a mobilities researcher.

From conventional transport research to the 'mobilities turn'

I arrived at Lancaster University in the autumn of 2003 as a visiting research fellow. During my stay, John and I had a number of supervisory meetings, and I also participated in John's course, 'The Tourist Gaze'. In addition, I participated at the inaugural workshop of the Centre for Mobilities Research (CeMoRe): 'Mobilities, Migrations and Identities'. This event strongly influenced me, and Ole and I later formed a similar Centre for Mobilities and Urban Studies (C-MUS) at Aalborg University.

At our first supervisory meeting, John introduced me to two of his articles: 'Mobility and Proximity' (2002) and 'Social Networks, Travel and Talk' (2003). These two articles became important for my professional transformation from transport researcher to mobilities researcher. For me, the most important contribution *Sociology beyond Societies* makes to the field is its aim to place mobility at the heart of the analysis of the 'social' and develop an understanding of how mobility forms and reforms social life. This not only opens up the classic sociological question – 'What makes the social possible?' – but also poses the question, 'What makes mobility possible?' Movement should not be understood only as mobility but rather as mobilities in the plural, including various forms of corporeal, physical objects and imaginative, virtual and communicative mobilities (Urry 2007: 47). Thus, we should focus on their interdependence instead of treating them as autonomous phenomena. In 'Mobility and Proximity' (Urry 2002), John criticizes some of the basic assumptions and approaches in conventional transport research:

> Transport researchers have taken the 'demand' for transport as a given, as a black box not needing further investigation, or as derived from the level of a society's income. Also transport researchers tend to examine simple categories of travel, such as commuting, leisure, or business. This though presumes that social activities can be divided up and then explained through such 'transport' derived categories. What is rare is to begin from the complex patterning of people's varied and changing social activities ... understanding such connections should not begin with the types and forms of transport. Transport is mostly a means to certain socially patterned activities and not the point of such activities. (Urry 2003: 156)

As John argues, 'black boxing' historically has been a widespread practice in transport research and praxis. The profession is founded on the basic assumption that physical transport should be seen exclusively as a derived effect of societal activities. From this perspective, the transport system itself is not seen as affecting the production and consumption of movements. The social embedment of transport has been ignored or overlooked. In this way, John sets a new agenda for transport research when he points out that 'the bases of travel are social' (2003: 171). His critique, however, is not limited to transport research; it also problematizes how social science traditionally has considered traffic a field only for transport researchers to investigate: 'Social science research has been "a-mobile", ignoring or trivializing the movement of people for work and family, leisure and pleasure' (Urry 2003: 156). A third and sometimes over-looked element in John's arguments is directed towards the critique of traffic in environmental studies:

> There is also a related 'environmental' critique of physical travel, arguing that the current hugely costly system of 'hypermobility' simply cannot continue indefinitely (Adams 1999). However, what this literature omits are the social bases of corporeal travel, and the present and future inter-sections and trade-offs possible between physical, imaginative and virtual travel. Indeed, the critique of 'hypermobility' needs to examine just how and why there is an apparent desire to travel physically, a desire stemming from the significance of intermittent corporeal co-presence within social life. (Urry 2002: 257)

John's commentary on a number of existing disciplines, including my own, and his formulation of a new mobility paradigm (Urry 2007) had a significant impact on me when I began to conduct my own transport research, especially as I started to explore long-haul international business travel. Through the new mobility paradigm, I found a home for my own concerns that transport research placed too little emphasis on the social motives for transport, focused too much on quantitative methodologies and mathematical language, and paid too little attention to interdisciplinarity.

Why do people travel in the global economy?

In conventional transport and tourism research, business travel has traditionally been seen as an output of work and business activities in the global economy (Lassen 2006). John's writings, particularly his analysis of the relationships amongst social networks, travel and talk, draw on work by Erving Goffmann, Deirdre Boden and Harvey Molotch (Urry 2003). His emphasis on the importance of various forms of co-presence in social networks opened my eyes to a central part of the social base of business travel:

> These moments of physical co-presence are crucial to patterns of social life that occur 'at-a-distance', whether for business, leisure, family life, politics, pleasure or friendship. So life is network but is also involves specific co-present encounters within certain times and places ... Meetingness, and thus different forms and modes of travel, are central to much social life, a life involving strange combinations of increasing distance and intermittent co-presence. (Urry 2003: 156)

John identifies three modes of co-presence: face to face, face the place and face the movement where physical proximity is obligatory, appropriate or desirable (Urry, 2002: 262; Urry 2003: 163). Co-presence consists of legal, economic and familial obligations as well as social obligations, time obligations, place obligations, live obligations and objects obligations (Urry 2002: 263). In relation to social obligations, John especially focuses on the importance of 'meetingness'. He asks: Why do we meet on the move? Then, he shows how motorway service stations, roadside cafes, pups, clubs, restaurants, airport lounges and hotel lobbies are full of meetings where colleagues or associates come together often to work on documents or engage in talk (Urry 2007: 251). At our first meeting during my stay in Lancaster, John drew my attention to several important works to help me understand the social base of air travel at global companies. These resources include Andreas Wittel on network sociality, Sean O Riain on global workplace and Berry Wellman on the internet and friendship. Likewise, John's class, 'The Tourist Gaze', inspired me to analyse some of the non-work obligations attached to business travel. Although business mobility has never been John's core focus, over the years he has played a strong supportive role to help this research field move forward, as he did with many other fields. For instance, in 2010, he took part in a workshop on international business travel at Ghent University. This workshop was organized by Jonathan V. Beaverstock, Ben Derudder, James R. Faulconbridge and Frank Witlox. John also served as co-organizer for the workshop 'Future of Business Mobilities' at Lancaster University with James Faulconbridge in 2011.

A life in corridors

Another area that John highlighted during my stay at Lancaster was the wider social importance of the 'aviation system', which materially and conceptually enables growing global air travel. Before my stay at Lancaster, I read the PhD thesis 'Sustainable Mobility' by Norwegian energy and transport planner Karl Georg Høyer (2002). Høyer introduced the term aeromobility but did not define it or reflect further on this new notion of flying. The first working paper I presented to John addressed this new notion. 'What a great word, this aeromobility, I love it … you should be the guy that knows everything about aeromobility', John said to me after he read the paper. Therefore, it was John who first made me aware of the opportunities to work in aeromobility as an independent field of research within the mobilities turn.

John had an admirable academic lucidity when it came to extracting the essence of other people's work and advising colleagues and students to clarify and further develop their main findings. At our last meeting during my stay in Lancaster, he suggested that my concept of 'a life in corridors' should play a stronger role in my thesis, 'The Mobilized Knowledge Worker' (2005). His inclination towards short headlines emerged and he suggested that I revise the title of my paper for the first 'Alternative Mobility Futures' (held in January

2004) from 'Rethinking Work and Travel in the Age of Aeromobility' to 'Aeromobility and Work' (Lassen 2006). 'This is a much better title,' he said. I followed his recommendation, and 'Aeromobility and Work' became the title of my article, which was published in the special issue. Afterwards, John edited this article together with Mimi Sheller. Similarly, John was excellent at connecting people with common fields of research interest, a talent I personally experienced during my stay in Lancaster, when John put me in contact with Sven Kesselring. This meeting also influenced my work.

Putting the social into aviation: 'towards aeromobilities'

In September 2006, John Urry and Sven Kesselring took the initiative to the conference titled 'Air-Times-Spaces: New Methods for Researching Mobilities', which was hosted at Lancaster University. The CeMoRe and the Cosmobilities Network became the very first to develop an international and interdisciplinary conference on airports and air travel grounded in the new paradigm of mobilities. The works of a number of international experts who presented at the conference were published in the first book on aeromobilities (see Cwerner et al. 2009). The introductory chapter of the anthology states:

> It is almost meaningless to analyse the dynamics and trends of work, business, family and personal relationships, higher educations, professional sports and recreation, popular cultures, tourism, diplomacy, and virtually all significant areas of contemporary social life, without taking into account the particular and distinctive time/spaces created by aeromobilities. (Cwerner 2009: 5)

In his contribution to the book, John emphasizes that 'air flights are central to performing the global order' (Urry in Cwerner et al. 2009: 26), and he invites us to think about how difficult it is to imagine global societies without aeromobilities. This book has had a decisive influence on the development of my research field. Moreover, it also influenced the establishment of aeromobilities as an independent field of research at Aalborg University.

Although air travel is a critical component of global competition amongst companies, cities and nations, only a limited number of social science research projects on aviation and airports had been carried out before the book was published. Historically, the conventional approach to air transport research into aviation and airports was rooted in a 'predict and provide' mind-set (Cwerner et al. 2009). Under this approach, the aviation system (airlines, airports and air travellers) has mainly been considered a closed system that does not include the societal and cultural embedment and importance of aviation (see Jensen 2013). It is thus an important theoretical rethinking of air transport research. Today, what aeromobilities research represents is newly socially aware and interdisciplinary; it encompasses aeronautical research and aims to incorporate knowledge of transport planning, sociology, ethnography, geography, architecture, design and economics studies to develop a greater understanding of the societal aspects of the production and consummation of air travel.

Futures of airport cities

Where will the legacy of John's work lead aeromobilities research in the future at C-MUS? Mobilities research at Aalborg contains a common thread with the creation of the new mobilities paradigm. Our latest research initiative – Airport Cities Futures (AirCiF) – is a project that will be supported by the Innovation Fund Denmark from 2017 to 2021. The AirCiF project, which Ole and I have developed together, builds on new society-oriented aeromobilities research and an in situ understanding of mobilities (see Jensen 2013):

> Airport City Futures (AirCiF) explores how Copenhagen Airport (CPH) can be maintained and developed as an international aeromobilities hub … This is done through an inquiry that, as the first of its kind, will analyse management, planning and design factors of aeromobilities, and combine this with analyses of the user perspective, how aeromobilities are experienced by the passengers. Thus AirCiF will be the first major Danish research project exploring air travel, airports and Airport Cities from the integrative and interdisciplinary socio-technical field of aeromobilities research. Giving special attention to the 'super users' of the airport, the business travellers, the AirCiF project focuses on a range of management, planning and design aspects, as well as social and individual behaviours, that influence travel experiences. (Lassen et al. 2017)

When the project was formulated in 2015, we planned that John should participate by guiding us to develop a variety of scenarios for the future of aviation in Denmark. In my last correspondence with John in April 2015, he wrote, 'I am happy for me to appear in the application BUT I do not promise to do much Actually just setting up NEW Inst for Social Futures which I might have mentioned and this will take most of my "spare" time John'. Unfortunately, we never got the chance to draw more on John's vast knowledge, but we received a grant in the fall of 2016!

My personal experience with the book *Sociology beyond Societies* and my first face-to-face meeting with John, which occurred by coincidence more than 15 years ago, became defining moments in my academic career. It has been a privilege to be a part of John's journey towards the mobilities paradigm. Therefore, it felt as if my journey as a researcher had come full circle because I returned to Lancaster University with my family for the spring and summer of 2017. We stayed for three months while my wife worked on her PhD in collaboration with James Faulconbridge, Monika Büscher and other people at CeMoRe. It was strange that John was no longer available for lunch, laughs and discussion on mobilities. However, there is no doubt that John's innovative work lives on at Lancaster, Aalborg and many other places. Every time I revisit one of John's remarkable books in the future, it will be like catching up with a good friend!

References

Cwerner, S., Kesselring, S. and Urry, J. (2009) *Aeromobilities*, London: Routledge.
Høyer, K.G. (2000) *Sustainable Mobility: The Concept and Its Implications*, PhD thesis, Department of Environment, Technology and Social Studies, Roskilde University.
Jensen, O.B. (2013) *Staging Mobilities*, London: Routledge.
Larsen, G., Lassen, C., Jensen, O. and Hyllested, K. (2017) Airport City Futures, http://vbn.aau.dk/en/projects/aircif–airport-city-futures(deffaaba-9f85-4177-87fd-fb08a573f140).html.
Lassen, C. (2006) Work and Aeromobilities, *Environment and Planning A*, 38(2): 301–312.
Urry, J. (2002) Mobility and Proximity, *Sociology* 36: 255–274.
Urry, J. (2003) Social Networks, Travel and Talk, *British Journal of Sociology* 54(2): 155–175.
Urry, J. (2007) *Mobilities*, Cambridge: Polity Press.

Chapter 26

Working materials

Mobile objects, ideas and people

Elisabeth Shove

Supervisors and students are both shaped by the process of making PhD theses and research projects and in my view co-supervision is a critical but often overlooked form of academic interaction. In this short contribution I reflect on experiences of co-supervising, shared with John and with Juliet Jain (2004), Nick Pearce (2006), James Tomasson (2010), Allison Hui (2011) and Owen Dowsett, and with Noel Cass who worked with us as a research associate in 2003.

Producing a PhD is a long and complicated undertaking during which all sorts of different ideas, methods and suggestions come into view. Many get ground down or simply fade. Some make it on to the pages of the thesis, some define future careers and some get lodged in the cracks. Over the decade or so that I co-supervised with John, intellectual preoccupations ebbed and flowed, but a handful of themes recurred. During the course of what must have added up to hundreds of hour-long co-supervision sessions we talked about the nature of mobility and access, and about objects in motion and at rest.

Doing mobility

In some loose sense the movement of people or things was a fairly consistent concern, reappearing in various disguises. This interest was sometimes quite tightly tied to issues conventionally understood to be about 'transport', including the process of learning to drive, the business of waiting for a train, the practicalities of studying car-parking or of doing research whilst on a moving bus. In so far as there was a common thread linking these studies, it was that of seeing 'transport' not as a means of getting from A to B, but as a much more situated, historical and contextualised endeavour and as a series of variable, distinctive yet linked social arrangements, none of which could be defined by travel, stripped out as a topic in its own right.

For example, the moment at which people acquire (or lose) a driving licence matters massively for the total number of drivers on the road and hence for the total kilometres travelled. Becoming a driver is also a key moment in the life of any one individual. That said, exactly how key or how critical this proves to be is not in any sense 'individual'. The significance of driving (or not) depends on the social and infrastructural world the would-be driver inhabits (Pearce 2006).

For young people, getting a licence can spell independence. Those who can drive and have use of a car have the freedom to come and go and to meet with friends as and when they want. But the detail is relevant. Exactly where are their friends located, are there (or are there not) other ways of getting around and how does driving fit into this wider ecology of social networking, and of infrastructural provision? At the time of these discussions John's father was alive and on the brink of giving up driving. These experiences fuelled our thinking about the very different, very situated meanings of becoming and being a driver, and of losing that status.

Moving, whether by car, plane, bus or train, also involves moments and sometimes extensive periods of immobility including parking, waiting, queuing and standing about. These periods of stasis rarely feature in academic discussions of life on the move, but they were critical for us. At its simplest, this reflected a basic sociological reflexivity, recognising that movement and stability are intertwined and that it makes no sense to think of one in the absence of the other. This is obvious once stated, but few have really explored the implications for how one might conceptualise systems of mobility in relation to stability. This is perhaps because such enquiries lead in seemingly 'boring' directions. Waiting and parking are not such glamorous topics, not for research students and not for research funders either. Looking back we did a good job of helping to pull these themes out into the open.

Amongst other notions, that of 'equipped waiting' situated travel not as a blank period devoid of activity but as a rather special, and in some sense protected period of time for those who had prepared to use it that way (Jain 2004). Simple things like luggage take on new significance when seen in these terms. As we discussed, mobile phones, wireless connection, laptops, power supplies and the potential to be 'always on' seep across other material arrangements, changing the very nature of being on the move, and placing new demands on intersecting and multiple infrastructure providers. Managing a rail network is no longer enough. Wireless connectivity is also increasingly important, not only in rail carriages but also in waiting rooms, stations and related facilities. Again, these ideas run counter to the still prevalent view that time spent travelling is time out of ordinary time, lost time, or time that should be economically discounted.

Matters of access: going where and going when?

John liked catchphrases such as 'equipped waiting' or 'the burden of mobility' (Shove 2002). This latter concept was invented to signal what seemed to be a societal escalation in the demand for movement. In brief, the argument was that effectively participating in society presented a 'burden' in the sense that it generated a set of obligations to travel in order to work, have fun and be part of family life. This rather speculative notion resonated with the experiences of a highly mobile academic existence but was useful in other ways as well. Involving John in a project on 'Changing infrastructures, measuring socio-spatial inclusion/exclusion' funded by what was then the Department for Transport, Local Government and the Regions provided a chance to think more about relationships between time, mobility infrastructures and various compulsions to proximity. The key idea was that discussions of social exclusion and inclusion needed to take account of all these considerations at once. This inspired a somewhat novel method of conceptualising 'access', opening the way for more subtle, more sociologically refined accounts of how 'needs' for mobility are simultaneously constructed and in various ways met. Parts of this work involved characterising public transport provision as that ebbed and flowed over the course of a day. Whilst access to certain locations was easy at certain hours, it was impossible at others. Whether this mattered or not was itself part of the story. A linked study of 'demand-responsive' transport provided further insight into the muddy territory of unknown, blocked and 'revealed' demand. John did not do any of the empirical work involved in these projects. Instead, his contribution was to help legitimise and develop this unusually broad way of conceptualising mobility. This most often occurred over lunch, during which Noel Cass, the research associate on the project, always had a huge plate of egg and chips. I suspect that the report we wrote (Cass et al. 2003) has sunk without trace in terms of national government, but some of those ideas have found their way into subsequent projects and research programmes and into our own and other people's writing (Cass et al. 2005).

Materials in motion

Not everyone has the chance to investigate the history of the Aga (a solid fuel cooker) in detail, or to consider the forms of nostalgia and the concepts of country living that might link Agas to solid wood flooring (Tomasson 2010). Nor do they often get to learn about the forms of mobility – of things, ideas and people – that constitute patchwork quilting, birdwatching, yoga and hiking (Hui 2011). These are just some of the fields into which the process of joint supervision led. Behind the scenes, these enquiries were oriented and guided by readings and suggestions, often as useful for the co-supervisors involved as for the students to whom they were ostensibly directed. The casual flow of references is never usually documented, but it constitutes a strong platform both for the building of common understandings and for appreciating the different forms of expertise that are brought to bear on the supervisory process. One of the items John suggested, and that I read and really liked, was Bruner's article on authenticity (1994). He suggested it to a student, not to me, but such suggestions form part of an unfolding stream of enquiry that links people together.

One of the good things about mobility studies is that it is such a broad field. It was therefore possible to move between ideas about the proximity of people, about how things and people come together, and about how such relations are constituted and how they change. For example, doing birdwatching depends on conjunctions of birds and observers: sometimes it is the former that move – flying through the birdwatcher's garden; sometimes it is the latter – as when enthusiasts travel to exotic locations to see particular species. So how is it that different variants of the practice of bird watching call for different forms of mobility?

For me, such lines of enquiry fed and were also shaped by my own work on social theories of practice. In co-supervisory meetings, various tracks and intellectual traditions get stirred together, not as part of a conscious strategy, but in the everyday process of engaging with a PhD project and a PhD student, and in jointly figuring out how research designs might proceed, how empirical materials might come together to form chapters and how chapters might come together to form the PhD as a whole. Again I think it is through these under-the-radar exchanges that academic debates (to put it rather grandly) routinely develop and evolve.

Craft skills in academic life

In between learning about the technical details of long-arm sewing machines, the history of field guides to bird watching and where the best places are to buy fabric for patchwork quilting we also learned to handle and cope with the struggles and traumas of people grappling with the process of producing a PhD. I don't think John and I had a formula for joint supervision – not at all – every student is different, but by the fourth or fifth time round we had a good sense of what role each of us might play and when: good cop, bad cop, sympathising, empathising, standing back, encouraging and sometimes chastising. Along the way we built up a library of what became familiar jokes, stock phrases and good, practical advice about writing, thinking and managing academic life. It is worth capturing some of that here.

'*What is the title?*' John always asked this, always knowing that if someone could clearly articulate the title of a piece of writing, a section, a paragraph, a chapter or a PhD they had figured out what it was they wanted to say. We spent lots of time helping new writers identify clear, meaningful and interesting titles, doing so as a means of both discovering and articulating the purpose of their text.

'*Writing is thinking.*' This was a phrase repeatedly deployed as a corrective to those who believed there was such a thing as 'doing' a PhD and then 'writing it up'.

'*Read things when you need to read them, not before, not after.*' This is excellent advice from John, but it is also advice that is almost impossible for most people to follow. Knowing which articles and books to read, and knowing how to read them is one thing. Knowing when to do so is another. This is the dilemma. Read something too early and you'll have forgotten the main ideas by the time you come to really work with them. Read the same text too late, after the direction of your writing is set, and it will be hard to slot missing ideas back in. Since writing is thinking (see above), the irony is that you cannot always know in advance what needs reading when. However, the real message is to think about what you are doing. Why are you reading this book now, why did you not leave it on the shelf for later, what function is this reading playing in your work?

'*Have a break, but recognise that this is what you are doing.*' We were probably quite demanding supervisors, both taking academic work to be central to what we do, and both expecting others to share this view. We also recognised the importance of play: John played tennis. I played floorball, occasionally with the PhD students we co-supervised. PhDs take a while to produce and no one can keep working flat out for a full three years. At the same time, the PhD process is remarkably unstructured, meaning that there is plenty of scope for prevarication. Partly because of this it is extremely easy to drift and to think that work is going on when it is not. So John's advice was to work in a highly concentrated way, and to then take equally concentrated guilt-free breaks.

'*Be encouraging.*' In my experience, supervising PhD students is one of the most rewarding and also one of the most frustrating and draining things I do. When times were hard, when work was not forthcoming, and when enthusiasm dipped to an all-time low John's response was to encourage. Encouragement and confidence build together and through this not-so-secret method he helped students wind their way back towards the doing of their PhD. I learned a lot from that as well.

Although I have written about them separately, it is not really possible to divorce the practicalities of talking, editing, thinking, criticising and making jokes from the process of animating currents of thought and of sparking, harbouring and nurturing ideas, some of which have taken off and some of which now have lives of their own. Nor is it possible to think of the many meetings we had without thinking about the low white Habitat table that John had in his office, or the pictures on the walls or the books on the shelves. These were all part of what made that elusive process of co-supervision special, not just for me but for everyone involved.

References

Bruner, E. M. (1994) 'Abraham Lincoln as Authentic Reproduction: A Critique of Postmodernism'. *American Anthropologist* 96(2): 397–415.

Cass, N., Shove, E. and Urry, J. (2003) *Changing infrastructures, measuring socio-spatial inclusion/exclusion*, Lancaster University.

Cass, N., Shove, E. and Urry, J. (2005) 'Social Exclusion, Mobility and Access'. *Sociological Review* 53(3): 539–555.

Hui, A. (2011) *Enthusiasts' travel: Mobilities and practices*, PhD thesis, Lancaster University.

Jain, J. (2004) *Networks of the future: Time, space and rail travel*, PhD thesis, Lancaster University.

Pearce, N. (2006) *Rights of the road: An analysis of how three groups make the transition from non-drivers to drivers, and the implications of this for road pricing policy*, PhD thesis, Lancaster University.

Shove, E. (2002) *Rushing around: Coordination, mobility and inequality*, draft paper for the Mobile Network meeting, October: www.lancaster.ac.uk/staff/shove/choreography/rushingaround.pdf.

Tomasson, J. (2010) *Aga cookers and wooden flooring: Case studies in consumption, routine and rural heritage*, PhD thesis, Lancaster University.

Part V

Complexity, risks and social futures

Chapter 27

Social futures

Monika Büscher

When social scientists are calling for 'affirmative critique', one might think that humanity's canaries have stopped singing. Environmental sociology, practice theory, the 'new catastrophism', and other future-oriented social science approaches have only begun to influence global policy with their diagnoses of humanity's failure to address the threat of a collapse of civilization around climate change, environmental degradation, anti-microbial resistance, and conflict. Yet, as political mechanisms like the Paris Climate Accord are choked by populism, some social scientists are promoting critique that 'affirms' survival.

Affirmative critique makes radical demands, including calls for post-human disloyalty to our own species (Braidotti 2016), drastic forms of population control (Haraway 2016), and life in the ruins of capitalism and modernity (Tsing 2015). It might sound like a swan song, but these forms of enquiry are creating unique momentum and hope for a revolution in 'worlding'. In his last book, John Urry put forward a powerfully simple call to action, observing that 'the future is now' (2016: 7; Figure 27.1).

He proposes 'social futures' thinking as a response to the world-shaping, future-forming nature of social life in the present, highlighting the inherent 'systemness' of the everyday. This recognizes that futures are social, firstly, because futures imagined and unfolding define people's lives here and now as well as intergenerational relations. Secondly, it starts from the understanding that futures in the Anthropocene are social because they are shaped by the accretions, excretions, and exhalations of the social. What is more, it appreciates that everyday social and material practices of mobility, energy use, consumption, and communication have complex multi-scalar systemic 'worlding' effects with resonances to Immanuel Wallerstein's world system theory and its echoes within critiques of global capitalism. Social futures are local, but also global, planetary, perhaps even interplanetary; they entangle inequalities, multiple pasts, presents, and futures, the material and the technological, the human and the non-human.

Most people 'are unaware of the systemness of their daily practices' (Urry 2016: 73). But 'the science is in', showing that what the 7.5 billion people on the planet do every day, especially those in the global North, aggregates to

Figure 27.1 A copy of a 1968 Paris graffiti
Source: OvO Reproduced under CC BY-NC-SA 2.0

reduce the earth's capacity to support human flourishing (Urry 2016: 38). Changing this systemic dynamic requires transdisciplinary science, but it is not a matter for science alone. John Urry's *What Is the Future?* sets out to 'mainstream the future', to engage diverse interests, knowledges, forms of expertise, creativity, and practice to envisage and contest what 'good' or 'better' futures might be, and to put into them now the things that might make them happen.

It is not surprising that John Urry was at the vanguard of this newly emerging 'social futures paradigm'. Like the 'new mobilities paradigm', 'social futures' thinking does not entail a complete departure from known theories and methods. Instead, it suggests a shift in analytical imagination, perspective, values, practices, and politics. As Wells argued in 1906: 'the creation of Utopias – and their exhaustive criticism – is the proper and distinctive method of sociology' (cited in Levitas 2013: xi). Using utopia as method not blueprint means that – like 'mobilities' – 'futures' constitute a diverse set of empirical phenomena and topics as well as an analytical orientation and methodology, and ethical and political commitments. This convergence of the empirical, analytical, creative, ethical, and political resonates deeply with other – posthuman, feminist, cosmopolitan, participatory, designerly, artistic, phronetic, utopian, and affirmative – approaches, creating much synergy, but also some confusion. Some might say, with Peter Adey, that if futures are everything, they are nothing. But in a complex world the very 'indiscipline' of social futures research could be empirically, theoretically, methodologically, ethically, and politically transformative of science and what it means for life on the planet.

Dark matter, hidden wealth, and social energy

If, with the new mobilities paradigm, Urry and Sheller captured Bergson's fact that 'reality is movement', *What Is the Future?* captures the ontological futurity of the social and the sociality of futures, with resonances to Heidegger, Adams, Prigogine, and many others. Complexity is an engine for this future-forming, 'affirmative' critique.

In my interpretation, complexity is key, because by acknowledging the multi-causal, non-linear dynamics of social change, a social futures approach turns the apparent oxymoron of affirmative critique into a catalyst for actionable research. Affirmative critique is not about agreeing with that which is being critiqued, but about acting on it with insight and – in Bruno Latour's words – radically careful and carefully radical creativity, coupled with a commitment to 'world' or co-create alternatives by 'staying with the trouble' (Haraway 2016). Critique becomes affirmative when the public role of social research to be responsible here and now is understood to go beyond policy recommendations. It requires social research to become response-able, to transpose or 'mobilize' conventional social research methods of listening and observing, alongside analysis of troubles, as well as an articulation of *responses to troubles* and public experiment with such response.

Collective experimentation with social futures calls for an 'infrastructuring' for discovery of unintended consequences, and contestation between divergent perspectives. It translates analytical negation into careful-radical imaginative reconstitution of society (Levitas 2013). By developing the role of public sociology through acting on insight in this sense, social futures methodologies enable human–non-human collectives to address the emergent and path-dependent entanglements of pasts, presents, and futures and their unknowability in more richly informed, more broad-based, democratic, and creative ways. They enact John Urry's earlier calls for a public sociological practice of 'creative marginality' where scholars cross borders and activate from within the social, alongside others, including activists.

These methodologies are not unique to the new social futures paradigm, but derive new energy from John Urry's careful observation of the 'dark matter, hidden wealth, and social energy' of lived social change, everyday creativity, and social innovation. In *What Is the Future?*, he argues that capitalism, progress, and technology may 'bend humans to their character', but that social 'structures of feeling' are a powerful source of resistance (Urry 2016: 12). They are 'dark matter' that can effect tectonic shifts in complex socio-economic orders (35). Wealth hidden away from the collective good through offshoring may have unhinged democracy and truth, but at the same time, people live de-growth alternatives in the cracks, leveraging a 'hidden wealth' of good social interactions, wellbeing, and low-carbon lives (179). And the way in which high-mobility sociability burns energy is counteracted by a 'social energy' that delivers communities from the fast lanes of high carbon into slow living, from land use into land stewardship and car-free city movements (181). Social futures thinking and co-creating of research around such alternatives amplifies the dark energy of the social stored in these hopeful prefigurative phenomena, and could tip humanity from hurtling towards collapse into a good life in the ruins of capitalism, modernity, and risk.

What could such futures look like? I will briefly sketch some contours of systemness, and new structures of feeling that begin to sense its precarity taking shape in disaster risk management, where a hidden wealth of social interactions and collective social energy give lived detail to these desire lines of hope.

Beyond control

People are unaware of the systemness of their daily practices, even if it has disastrous consequences. For example, '[n]o wars or terrorist attacks currently cause anything like' the 'toll of death, pain and injury' of road traffic with its 1.25 million deaths a year worldwide (Urry 2016: 131). Yet, locked in to automobility systems, most people do not reflect upon, let alone act, to change their role in the production of such systemic disasters. Since Immanuel Wallerstein's *World System Theory*, Charles Perrow's *Normal Accidents*, Ulrich Beck's *Risk Society*, and Sheila Jasanoff's *Learning from Disaster*, we know that geopolitical and socio-technical systems are risky beyond human control, for some more so than others. John Urry's work on complexity and mobilities has been pivotal to show how multiple forms of mobility and mobility systems are interconnected in this unequally risky runaway world. Many proliferate dangerous immaterial immobiles such as air- or water-borne micro-particles and plastics, climate-altering greenhouse gases, nuclear radiation, and anti-microbial resistant bacteria. And there are digital and cultural immaterial immobiles that cause trouble, too. Data have become Kafka-esquely noxious, erratically

splintering freedom, tolerance, equality, social solidarities, and values in surveillant assemblages, while cultural memes circulate, infiltrate, and shape cultural politics of (un)truth and emotion that inhibit understanding of systemness
and risks.

However, people are unaware of the disastrous systemness of their everyday
practices not just due to its immaterial immobile complexities, or their ignorance, apathy, or susceptibility to manipulation. Unawareness of systemness is
also actively produced by modern discourses of disaster risk 'management' and
'security' that are couched in metaphors of command and control. Even
though unknowability and uncertainty are widely recognized as intrinsic to
risk, difficulties in preventing or responding to disasters are regularly traced
back to a 'data gap'. Post-disaster reports routinely blame a lack of information,
inadequate organizational, legal, and technological interoperability, and social,
cultural, or political reluctance to share information for failures. A clamour for
more and more free-flowing data, better networks, visualization, and communication technologies drowns quieter calls to work with more humility and
respect for the incalculability of risk. For example, Rana Novack, founder of
the Refugee Admissions Network Alliance, wrote in *Wired* magazine in 2015:
'We should have seen this refugee crisis coming … we have the technology –
right here, right now – to create a new, agile, insightful model that will predict
mass migrations'. This is one of myriad calls for more data and data sharing that
sound hollow in view of the fact that, very often, 'we' already know. The
United Nations Office for the Coordination of Humanitarian Affairs and other
agencies routinely monitor the movement of people. United Nations High
Commissioner for Refugees figures readily available in 2015 showed that the
number of people displaced by conflict and persecution had increased dramatically, to 59.5 million (65.6 at the time of writing), with the total number of
people on the move across borders worldwide at 244 million.

Risks, such as conflict, drought, or famine, undermine human security and
underpin migration. Their systemness and connection to global everyday practices is extremely complex (see Figure 27.2). But it is not seen because there are
no data or analysis. The International Organization for Migration, for example,
has developed a contextual and strategic data-collection capacity on the nexus
of crisis and mobility, by continuously tracking the movement of people
through its Displacement Tracking Matrix. However, discourses of command
and control or security and calls for 'Big' data veil a social and political
unwillingness to acknowledge how the privileges of the few are on the same
map as the suffering of the many.

A new structure of feeling

But a new structure of feeling is emerging around people's experience of the
politics of command and control-based disaster risk-management reasoning.
The 'we' in Rana Novack's 'we have the technology' is no longer confined to

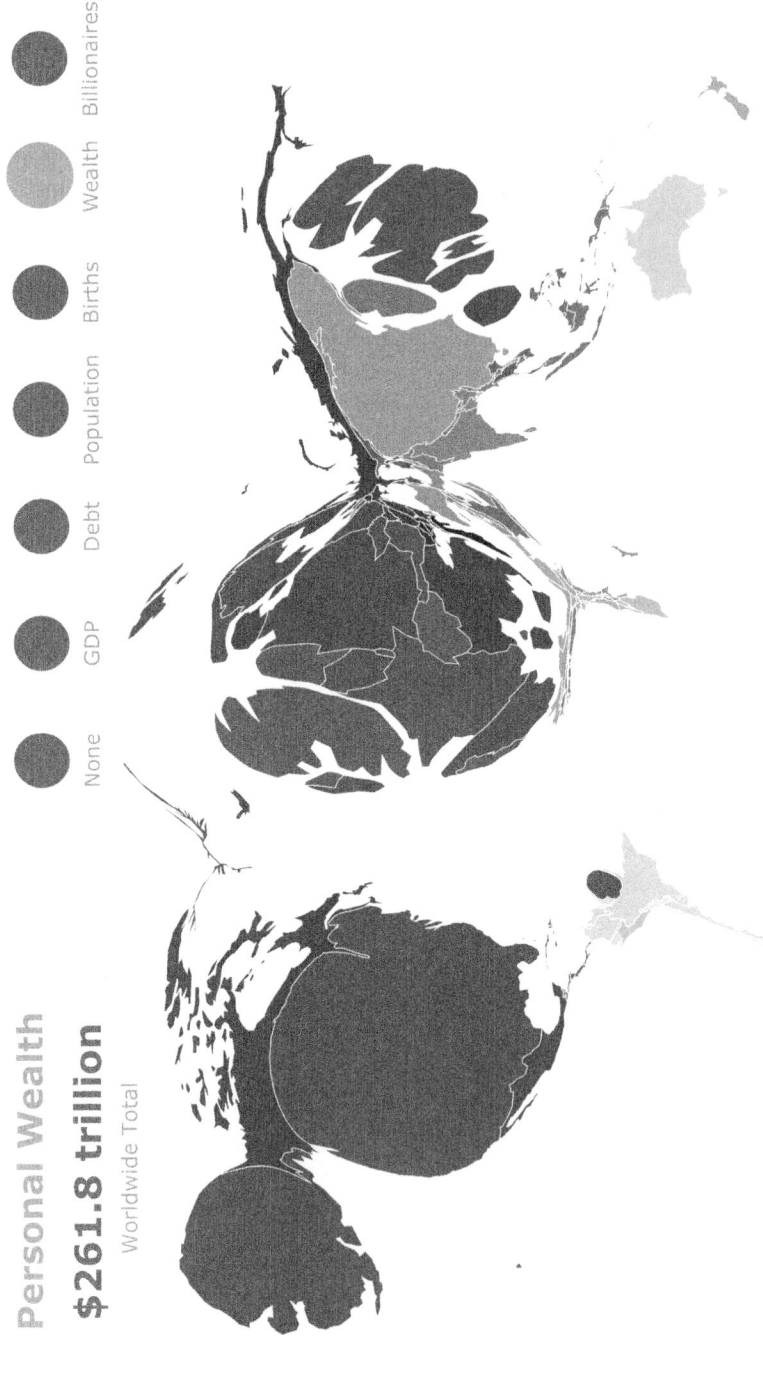

Figure 27.2a Visualization of global distribution of personal wealth and country-to-country net migration
Source: Max Galka, reproduced with permission, http://metrocosm.com/permissions/

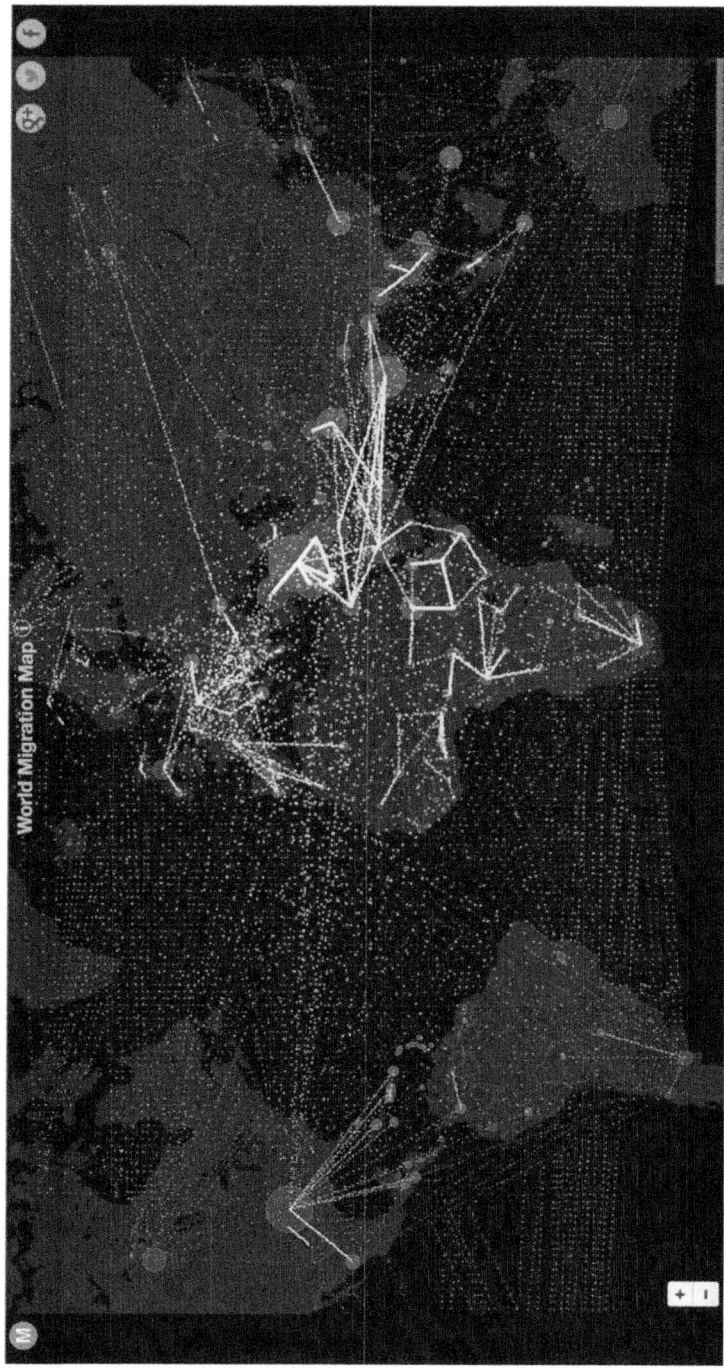

Figure 27.2b (Continued)

formal disaster risk-management agencies and expert analysts. People affected by risk have appropriated these technologies in quite different, less modern ways that open up new possibilities for new forms of system awareness.

Prompted by post-election violence in Kenya in 2007, the Kenyan Ory Okolloh set up the Ushahidi crowdsourcing platform, and designed it to allow Kenyans to report election violence and share information. In an environment where a government ban on live media reporting and self-censorship severely curtailed people's ability to know about the troubled election process, this was transformative beyond Kenya's borders. Ushahidi enabled people affected to report crises and needs with such ease that it prompted a group of people affected by the 2010 Haiti earthquake, in collaboration with 'digital humanitarians' gathering around Patrick Meier, a PhD student at Boston University, to set up the 'Ushahidi Haiti Project'. This allowed Haitians to submit situation reports and register their communities' needs in a way that was very direct and easy (provided one had access to a mobile phone), and it involved recruitment of a global 'task force' of supporters to translate, geo-reference, and parse the messages for visualization on a map. This passionate first mobilization of 'digital humanitarians' was by no means unambiguously positive, but it did provide information that was used by formal emergency response agencies to prioritize rescue missions. Since then, Ushahidi has reached over 25 million people in crisis in over 120,000 different deployments. Two of the most recent deployments brought it full circle, first (with some irony) to the 2016 American elections, and then back to Kenya in 2017, where over 1600 issues of election disturbances were reported. This latest deployment has also brought it into close contact with quite different, manipulative 'psychographic' uses of data by 'election-management agencies' like Cambridge Analytica.

Similarly conflicting intersections of crowdsourced and surveillant 'intelligence' are emerging in relation to refugee journeys. Websites, such as www.appsforrefugees.com, index a boom in the 'datafication' of refugee mobilities. This, too, is a highly contested field, with benefits for refugees who can access and share information more easily through these apps, but who also become more trackable and controllable through the way in which data are shared in surveillant assemblages of security and crisis-response agencies. At the same time, crowdsourcing and data visualization platforms like Max Galka's 'Metrocosm' or 'Our World in Data', supported by the Bill and Melinda Gates Foundation, are beginning to visualize the systemness of migration through socio-economic variables for 167 countries alongside analysis of country-to-country net migration (Figure 27.2) and by addressing the question 'Does Development Reduce Migration?' in the context of data about global inequality, extreme poverty, and environmental issues.

These are examples of how people are increasingly turning to social media platforms to document, debate, organize, and contest disaster risk management. A closer look at an example will allow us to trace some possibilities (and obstacles) for new forms of systemness awareness.

When, in the spring of 2011, the Japanese government failed to make measurements about radiation from the meltdown at the Fukushima Daichi nuclear power plant available, and even tried to raise the threshold for harmful radiation, some people self-organized grass-roots radiation-measuring communities such as *Safecast* (https://blog.safecast.org). They bought Geiger counters and, when they could not obtain them, shared knowledge online to learn how to build them; they measured radiation in their local environments and shared the data online, constructing maps of the effects of Fukushima's meltdown (Figure 27.3).

One day after Safecast published its maps, the Japanese government released its first maps, highlighting the political power of self-organized citizen sensing to force the hand of authorities. Moreover, the Safecast map differs starkly from these official maps, which showed areas of contamination risk as roughly concentric rings, where the risk diminished linearly the farther away from the nuclear plant one moved on the map. The crowd-sourced Safecast map, in contrast, shows complex micro-patterns of contamination along roads and shipping routes, in areas where people live and work, and children play, as well as areas of agricultural production. In a 2011 article entitled 'The Map Is the Debate', Jean Christophe Plantin describes how the communication and collaboration involved in producing the Safecast map constituted a public experiment, and a new way of sensing systemness and precarity. It did so by engaging people in experimenting with new ways of making (sense of) disaster risk. Quoting Noortje Marres, Plantin argues that 'the introduction of new techno-scientific objects to society involves much more than the addition of new knowledge and things to social life. It requires the reconfiguration of the wider social-material relations among which the new object is to be accommodated' (Marres 2009, quoted in Plantin 2011: 12). One such reconfiguration is a decrease of trust in governmental data and a growth of citizen sensing projects, not just in Japan. Over 1000 Safecast Geiger Counter kits have been bought in more than 90 countries and more than 65 million measurements have been submitted. Another reconfiguration is Germany's decision to decommission all its nuclear power stations after the Fukushima accident.

Positioned at different points of privilege, the people affected by the Fukushima disaster in Japan, the German population, politicians, and anti-nuclear campaigners, refugees, analysts, and visualizers of the systemness of forced displacement and migration seem to share a visceral awareness that 'precarity is the condition of our time', and they are asking 'What if the time is ripe for sensing precarity?' (Tsing 2015: 20). But they are also asking if it is time to sense precarity themselves and in its systemness. This is no smooth utopia of grassroots infrastructuring for human security. However, it changes how people inhabit risky worlds and understand systemness. It is beyond the scope of this short essay to specify the altered phenomenologies, ontologies, social practices,

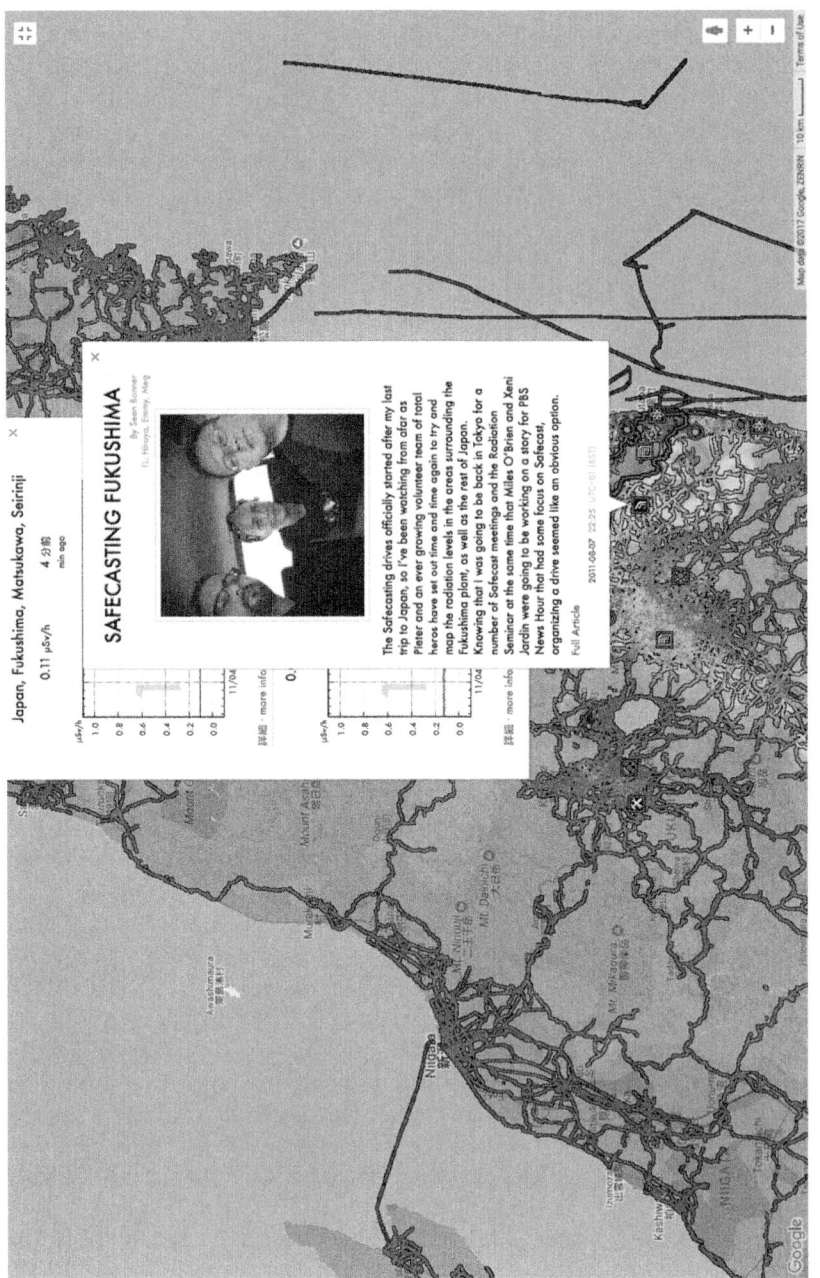

Figure 27.3 Safecast map with entries of measurements and observations

Source: http://safecast.org/tilemap/?y=37.92&x=140.38&z=7&l=0&m=0 (screenshot taken 24 June 2017). Reproduced under Creative Commons Attribution Share Alike License, https://blog.safecast.org/faq/licenses/

Figure 27.4 John Urry at the Institute for Social Futures, Lancaster University

ethics, and politics this generates, but perhaps enough of the 'hidden wealth' of good socio-material interactions has become visible to jog the sociological imagination for social futures research that intervenes with 'affirmative critique' in these dynamics.

To conclude

To conclude briefly, I would like to share a personal memory. At one of the first meetings of the team that set up the Institute for Social Futures at Lancaster University, one by one we went around the room. Each of us stepped up to a whiteboard and drew (with more or less skill) a picture of their motivation for, and contribution to, the new social futures paradigm. When it was his turn, John didn't know what to draw (he was not keen on creative methods). He laughed and, in the course of what I recall as a beautiful moment of intense intellectual sociability, he drew a frame around everything: a perfect capture of his most extraordinary skill as a map maker, charting troublesome socialities with such diagnostic vision and clarity, his great conceptual creativity, foresight, ethical, and political momentum (Figure 27.4). His public sociology of complexity, mobilities, and social futures is the best footing I know for affirmative critique, for putting the map to use to make a better future, in interdisciplinary and collectively engaging, experimental ways.

References

Braidotti, R. (2016) Posthuman Critical Theory. In D. Banerji and M. R. Paranjape (Eds), *Critical Posthumanism: Planetary Futures* (pp. 13–32). New Delhi: Springer India.

Haraway, D. J. (2016) *Staying with the Trouble: Making Kin in the Chthulucene*. Durham, NC: Duke University Press.

Levitas, R. (2013) *Utopia as Method: The Imaginary Reconstitution of Society*. Basingstoke: Palgrave Macmillan.

Plantin, J.-C. (2011) 'The Map Is the Debate': Radiation Webmapping and Public Involvement during the Fukushima Issue. In Proceedings of a Decade in Internet Time: OII Symposium on the Dynamics of the Internet and Society, 21–24 September, University of Southampton.

Tsing, A. L. (2015) *The Mushroom at the End of the World: On the Possibility of Life in Capitalist Ruins*. Princeton, NJ: Princeton University Press.

Urry, J. (2016) *What Is the Future?* London: Routledge.

Chapter 28

The future's never simple when it's complex

Social forecasting with John Urry

Kingsley Dennis

If the recent era of globalization has taught us anything it is that systems – natural, human, and artificial – have a habit of leading in one way or another into increasingly complex and interrelated relations. Life on planet Earth is embroiled in a veritable soup of entanglements, networks, and uncertain futures. And it was this realization that brought me into the sphere of influence of John Urry. After having spent a number of years at teaching institutions abroad I had come to the realization that the world was becoming a lot more fascinating; and a lot closer together as the internet and global technologies of communication were shredding the earlier binds of time and space connections. So I did a turnaround and returned to the UK to research this phenomenon after having indulged myself in the writings of Fritjof Capra and Ervin Laszlo concerning the webs of life and the evolution of systems philosophy, respectively. I arrived at John Urry's office in 2003 having read his book *Global Complexity* (Urry, 2002) and within the year we had established together the Lancaster Complexity Network with the aim to invite, gather, and give fortnightly talks on the broad, interdisciplinary research on complex systems. Whilst the majority of speakers were from within the Lancaster University community – management, geography, politics, and of course sociology, amongst others – we were also privileged to host a number of visiting speakers.

In our minds the complexity sciences were gaining credible traction within the social sciences, notably in the research areas of sociology that dealt with globalization, technologies, and networks. And at that time network theory was gaining great popularity as a way to frame emerging decentralized forms of engagement and interaction. And yet John and I felt that network theory lacked a sense of non-linear uncertainty – the unpredictable, the unforeseen, and the potentially catastrophic. Emerging forms of connection, communication, and collaboration also contained their own inherent instabilities. Or, put another way, they hovered dangerously close to potential tipping points. Such systems as we observed them were also assemblages of forces, energies, and patterns of natural, chemical, and human flows that were both unpredictable and vulnerable to external impacts. These systems ranged from the climate, energy production and use, technological assemblages, human mobility patterns, and increased digitization. I subsequently took on a role as research associate in Lancaster's Centre for Mobilities Research and it was a natural progression that John and I would take a complex systems perspective to our analysis of mobilities. Specifically, we decided on a project that examined the system of the automobile and how the incumbent fossil fuel-dependent car system had become locked in to an assemblage of unhealthy interests and knock-on systems.

Our project, which subsequently was published as the book *After the Car* (Dennis and Urry, 2009) attempted to argue that the days of the car are numbered due to a confluence of emerging powerful systems around the world that not only would undermine the current car system but also push into play new transport systems and regimes of mobility. In this respect we examined several major processes that could shape the future of how we travel, including: climate change; peaking of oil supplies; increased digitization of many aspects of economic and social life; massive global population shifts; and changing urban design and sustainable architectures. We envisioned that social, economic, policy, and technological systems were themselves open to fluctuations, bifurcations, and unprecedented and often unpredictable tipping points. And this uncertainty developed into another feature of the research between John and I – the nature of social forecasting and uncertain futures. Our collaboration produced a forecast of potentially bleak 'post-car' future scenarios. These we described as 'local sustainability', 'regional warlordism', and 'digital draconianism'. As John pointed out, in this and subsequent writings, the future is neither fully determined, nor empty and open.

The sciences of complexity are central to thinking on social futures, whether they frame the 'breakdown' mode of social collapse or the 'breakthrough' path of renewal through new emerging systems coming into play. Complexity shows how social practices are shaped by ways in which people use, innovate, and combine different technologies. There is no linear continuation in that doing one thing will produce a clear set of anticipated outcomes. Complexity shows us that life is now far too complex and interdependent for that. Part of our research dynamic was the understanding that futures are uncertain and unpredictable precisely because their component parts – systems, assemblages, technologies, human behaviour, and so on – are constantly 'in process' creating new connections, collaborations, and system patterns. That is, their mutable natures exert unintended consequences. The future then is always 'in play' and cannot be fully pre-determined; it can only be framed within parameters of the possible – the less or more possible, and the more or less, lesser, or least desirable.

The research that John Urry and I made into 'automobile assemblages' foresaw an emerging *digital nexus* that would come to see the individual car being adapted into upcoming technological systems and their applications. Although not naming Uber (the online transportation network) by name, we had laid the theoretical groundwork to its potential and almost inevitable emergence. We understood that technologies in the hands of individuals would give rise to increased car sharing as well as access to information that would enable transport-sharing schemes. In an act of serendipity, Uber was founded the very same year as *After the Car* was eventually published (2009). The future, it seems, is always catching up with us.

Another aspect of our collaborative research which has spiralled out beyond our forecasting is the new interventions of 'disruptive innovations'. Within complex systems there is open opportunity for great change to occur from the periphery, which then subsequently impacts the centre, forcing change in often unpredictable ways. Decentralized systems allow for emerging innovation that is seen as 'disruptive' as it comes not from the institutional 'big players' but from quarters, and often individuals or small groupings, that are not suspected at the time. What has subsequently occurred in the automobile industry is the intervention of non-traditional players, such as Tesla, Google, and Apple. Both John and I suspected that technological improvements in fuel systems (such as the battery); urban design toward greater restraint in car use; increased charges for city car use (congestion charges); and car sharing would alter the traditional landscape of car production and use. Yet what we hadn't foreseen were the technological giants of information and informational products – such as Google and Apple – expanding their domain into the car industry. Furthermore, we were amongst the majority when considering that driverless cars were still a far-off future potential. Yet again, it seems that the future is always catching up with us. With now driverless trucks joining the foray of driverless vehicles, the mobility system has just got a whole lot more interesting, as well as potentially both dangerous and dystopian, as we shall soon see when I come to talk about drones.

The 'carbon web' that John was so focused upon has, as he correctly anticipated, grown its complex tentacles through many intertwined practices, assemblages, and political agendas. Car manufacturers are now rebranding themselves as mobility organizations rather than just producers of the 'one product' model as they expand and team up with technology companies. Ford has announced that it is teaming up with Google to assist each other in developing what they refer to as autonomous vehicles. And at the recent Consumer Electronics Show in January 2017 Ford also publicly announced that it was teaming up with Amazon to turn its vehicles into super smart devices by connecting them to Amazon's Alexa service. Similarly, both Volvo and Daimler have teamed up with Uber to develop autonomous vehicles. The question that John usually brings up at this point would be whether – or how – these collaborations and alliances would create new system dependencies. Often it was a matter of when and not if. And it is only when disruptive events or the sudden exposure of obscure 'dark networks' arise that people realize the scale and depth of the system dependence. As John's thinking later came to focus on the murky mobilities of the offshore world, the social sciences gained insight into the darker aspects of global flows and the power that resides in places on the periphery.

Dark mobilities

John's later research after complex systems, automobile assemblages, and carbon webs led him into a world that fed itself through the economy of secrecy. Whilst John's previous focus had largely been on the increase in visible movement, he later came to see that in actual fact a great amount of mobility is often out of sight and involving ever more elaborate forms of secrecy. In a world of ever increasing and accelerating movement, especially across borders of various kinds, this inevitably also fosters a world of secrets and lies. And one of these shadowy mobilities was the economy and economic practices, which John recognized as generating its own ever increasing levels of secrecy. Similar to the thinking of sociologist Georg Simmel, John understood that modern societies both permit and require high degrees of secrecy. And the development of ever more sophisticated digital technology allowed for many components of national and local economies to be pushed out to what were once the periphery – and with great precision and efficiency. John's insightful research on offshoring (Urry, 2014) examined how peripheral and marginal places had been transformed into central nodes for the internationalizing global economy.

Whilst my own research was examining further how the new era of decentralized networks were facilitating the three Cs of connection, communication, and collaboration, with positive results, John was examining how such networks had produced a global offshore class that moved in exclusive and secretive networks. John's offshoring research was delving into the darker, more obscure domains, seeking out the murky world of offshore finances that had succeeded in creating a powerful world which is located nowhere and where, as John put it, money flows through secrecy space rather than known locations. John had moved on from his earlier examination of the end of organized capitalism and into a world where capital now flowed not to where it would be more productive but to where it is most secret and least regulated. And he was onto something, for in the last few years the issue of tax evasion has become more public, more spectacular, and without a doubt more 'celebrity news'. The year following the publication of John's *Offshoring* book, the Panama Papers scandal broke.

The Panama Papers were leaked in 2015 by an anonymous source, and listed 11.5 million documents that detailed financial and attorney–client information for more than 214,488 offshore entities. The documents belonged to the Panamanian law firm Mossack Fonseca, which had been operating for decades in establishing offshore accounts and offshore shell companies for wealthy customers. Or, as they often prefer to be called – high net-worth individuals. This massive leaking of documents led to political and celebrity scandals across the world, forcing many politicians to resign from their coveted positions. John's research on this issue had taken the social sciences into a world unused to prying examination and in doing so John had made the discipline of sociology more relevant than ever. There was the future, again, catching up with us.

Although my own research on informational flows had primarily examined the positive and constructive consequences, I soon came to appreciate that the 21st century had now become an era of secrecy and security. Big data was now being deployed more for security than for finance. And one aspect of the rise in security was the emergence and rapid proliferation in the use of drones.

John stated at the outset of his offshoring research that risks fuel the imagination for further powerful risks. And whether real or imagined, such risks legitimate new systems of security to monitor and regulate them. Hence the rise of drones that emerged as a way to offshore the human consequences of killing. The distasteful and dirty work of surveillance and assassination could now be performed at a distance. Drone warfare, created as a response to non-conventional risks, may itself pose a new security threat as it adds to the developing 'militarization' of our everyday lives. As if to corroborate this, on Monday, 12 December 2016 two researchers from John's own Centre for Mobilities Research at Lancaster had their article published in the *Guardian* newspaper with the provocative headline, 'Attack on the drones: the creeping privatisation of our urban airspace'. In this article, researchers Bradley Garrett and Adam Fish wrote how urban airspace is being radically reshaped by the proliferation of urban drones. And there is a race on for corporations to 'own the air' around their own urban locations. They are slicing the air into private strips, Garrett and Fish inform us. This constitutes a future where the 'new commons' is the very thing which flows around us constantly and invisibly, and which each human has the right to its access and use – air. The elite are once again establishing their firewalls to protect their secrecy flows in a world that has just become even more complex. And not only more complex but also more ethereal, less tangible, and trickier to track, trace, and transcribe. The solid is yet again melting away into air, yet this time in more technically efficient ways. As John said in his final monograph, the future has most definitely arrived, yet it remains perhaps the greatest of mysteries.

Complex futures

Futures are now everywhere, declared John in his book *What Is the Future?* (Urry, 2016). Another reminder to all us social scientists that thinking and anticipating the future is now essential for all societies. John was adamant that social futures should be reclaimed for the social sciences. Social futures are unpredictable, John noted, because technologies are constantly on the move. As such they continue to exert unintended consequences. Futures then are always 'in process', which makes the sciences of complexity central to the thinking on social futures. This merges my own interests between complexity thinking and futures thinking – both are made up of unstable, complex, and interdependent systems. By referring back to complexity thinking John was able to provide a framework in which to examine the memes in our popular culture that explored what he called the 'new catastrophism'. John observed that dystopian visions and explorations of social collapse were rampant in much of our current literature and film. We don't need to look far to see a barrage of zombie 'walking dead' films and television shows; the flood of dystopian teen fiction and their cinematic translations; the many apocalyptic visions of life on Earth after global collapse; and countless other variations on the theme of catastrophe, whether climatic, man-made, biological, other worldly, or pure bad luck. Our entertainment juggernaut is heavy loaded with catastrophism wrapped as bite-sized amusing distractions. Again, John was spot on in recognizing that a myriad of 'dark' flows and mobilities have engendered a 'new catastrophism' in social thinking.

John Urry's most recent work was at the forefront of marking out the uncertain terrain of future mobilities. He knew that not all mobile flows were visible, that not all decentralized networks were equitable, and that futures are anything but predictable. John has helped me to understand that as networks, systems, and connections develop they inevitably produce their darker components, such as the internet having the deep dark web. It is as if the social world out there is mirroring the darker aspects of our own psyche, leading to uncertain and unpredictable futures that herald great opportunity but that also display their inherent instabilities. John believed strongly that the responsibility of the social sciences was to reclaim their role in examining, discussing, and contributing to our social futures. And in this respect, amongst many others, the work of John Urry was at the forefront of sociology. Or, we should rather say, at the tipping point of all social futures.

References

Dennis, K. and Urry, J. (2009) *After the Car*, Cambridge: Polity Press.

Garrett, B. L. and Fish, A. (2016) 'Attack on the drones: The creeping privatisation of our urban airspace', *Guardian*, 12 December: www.theguardian.com/cities/2016/dec/12/attack-drones-privatisation-urban-airspace?CMP=share_btn_fb.

Urry, J. (2002) *Global Complexity*, Cambridge: Polity Press.

Urry, J. (2014) *Offshoring*, Cambridge: Polity Press.

Urry, J. (2016) *What Is the Future?*, Cambridge: Polity Press.

Chapter 29

From mobilities to mobile lives and beyond

The world according to John Urry

Anthony Elliott

Tennis, fish and chips, beer, mountain walking and sociology (but not necessarily in that order): this was the world I encountered when I first befriended the late John Urry. The year was late 2008. I was working at Flinders University in Australia, having just been seconded to chancellery to work in the vice-chancellor's office on a new research assessment exercise being undertaken across Australia. Drowning in administration, I was worried at the time that I was losing connection with the discipline of sociology given the new job in administration. But, luckily, I had kept a foot in the door, with a residual research Friday back in the department. Even better, I had invited John Urry – who I had vaguely got to know when I worked in the UK in the early 2000s – to come to Adelaide to deliver a public lecture and some masterclasses. To my surprise, John had instantly agreed. As if effortlessly, he jumped on a flight, arrived quietly into Adelaide and then set to work, dazzling students and colleagues as he presented an intellectual tour de force through the sociological fields of travel, transport and tourism. The good news for me was that I'd found the perfect escape from the dullness of research assessment planning, if only temporarily!

At the time, John was enjoying the fruits of his intellectual labors in developing the "mobilities paradigm" – his argument for a wholesale shift of thinking in the social sciences from a "static" to a "movement-based" conception of the relation between societies and individuals, machines and subjects, in the late modern age. "Mobilities," I would often say to John, is such an unlovely term. "Life on the move," we agreed, seemed simpler, more apt for everyday talk. It was to be our preferred descriptor for capturing how complex mobility systems restructure and reorganize the activities of everyday life – what we went on to call "mobile lives".

When we weren't talking sociology, we talked tennis (which we both had in common) and sometimes mountain walking (which he did, and I didn't). Throughout the weeks of his visit we talked and talked sociology, often as we drank beer, and I recall that he ate fish – on every occasion, at every meal. The night before he was due to fly back to the UK he said to me (as if presenting an afterthought): "we should write a book together". And we did. This was the beginning of what became our book *Mobile Lives*, and the commencement of my close working relationship with John Urry over the next eight years.

The emergence of new cultural forms of identity politics, individualism and do-it-yourself reflexive individualization reflects the imprint of the global digital economy. The impulse to reinvention – which I have previously argued lies at the core of the spread of the ethos of "new individualism" – arises from a dramatic speed-up in technology, along with widespread economic uncertainty and its associated impact upon both professional and personal life. There is, one might say, nothing necessarily individualist about new individualism. What matters in social and cultural life is a demonstration of the will to reinvent, which is arguably why, for example, the makeover industries and therapy cultures are big business today. Reinvention is a legitimate reason for social action per se; why one wants to change the self, or what one wants to change the self from and to, is perhaps of less pressing cultural concern. This is perhaps only further confirmation of the philosophical diagnosis offered by certain currents of modern European thought, namely post-structuralism and postmodernism: that is, that the ideology of individualism in our own time is now approaching exhaustion. New individualism is a cultural form in which the boundaries between self and society begin to considerably blur.

In all of these ways, the culture of new individualism also reflects the imprint of contemporary developments in worldwide mobilities, movement and migration. If a new individualist culture of reinvention based on instant change, speed and short-termism has come to the fore in the new economy of the early twenty-first century, this is partly because women and men are arguably traveling further, faster and more frequently than at any time in history. In this, a new individualist bent for reinvention sits hand in glove with life on the move – where travel, transport and tourism increasingly take center-stage. Consider some of the following worldwide mobility transformations:

- 2016 witnessed over 1 billion international flight arrivals. In addition, there were approximately 3 billion domestic and international passengers traveling worldwide.
- There are today approximately 650 million cars roaming the world's highways. That figure is set to skyrocket: a recent International Monetary Fund report predicts China's automobilities will rise from 23 million cars in 2005 to 573 million cars by 2050.
- The world's largest industry today is that of travel and tourism, which generates approximately $US7.5 trillion dollars.
- According to the 2015 United Nations High Commission for Refugees Global Trends report, the number of forcibly displaced people worldwide rose from 59.5 million to 65.3 million in 12 months. Of these 21.3 million were refugees and 3.2 million asylum seekers.

Such changes in mobilities carry major consequences not only for people's lives, but also organizations, nations, as well as multinational companies and transnational institutions. Yet there are other transformations – beyond physical mobilities – which are equally significant. In some ways, changes in communicative, virtual and imaginative mobilities rival those changes at the level of physical travel. We now live in a world, for example, where mobile devices outstrip landline telephones. Similarly, in this extraordinary age of the internet, the arrival of social networking sites, tablets (such as the iPad) and peer-to-peer instant video messaging (such as Skype) are transforming the entire landscape of virtual mobilities.

How might these extensive changes in mobility – physical, communicative, virtual and imaginative – affect the self? In what ways does a world of rapid mobilities, and the worldwide movement of people, goods, services and information, reshape the contours of selfhood? These questions are what John Urry and I set out to address in our study, *Mobile Lives*. The focus of this research, essentially, was to probe how complex mobility systems (automobilities, aeromobilities, cybermobilities) go all the way down into the fabric of lived experience and the textures of human subjectivity. The aim of the research, in other words, was to address head-on one of the major missing dimensions of the mobilities paradigm: identity, or the subjectivity of self. These are today questions which have been taken up by a growing field of academics and intellectuals concerned with analyzing the complex interconnections between mobilities and the self, or movement and identity. From automobilities to aeromobilities, life on the move significantly transforms many aspects of professional and personal life – especially the contours of the self. In a highly mobile world there are extensive and intricate connections between physical travel, new forms of communication and self-identity. Mobilities restructure the deepest links between the personal and the global, selfhood and society – discernible in everything from the rise of discount budget air travel or the wholesale spread of fly-in fly-out contract workers to the veritable explosion in enforced migration arising from political conflicts in various hot-spots across the globe today. In all of this, mobilities generate not only new forms of self-experience and modes of self-identity, but also new kinds of social deprivation and exclusion.

This chapter began with a short personal reflection on how I met John Urry, and of how we came together to write *Mobile Lives*. In the remainder of this chapter, I shall outline and examine the central parameters of the theory of mobile lives, seeking to demonstrate how our focus on life on the move at the level of the self significantly developed and deepened the mobilities paradigm. But by splitting myself into two, I shall keep with presenting some short personal reflections on John Urry throughout the chapter. In doing so, the aim is to take seriously the theoretical and methodological presuppositions of the theory of mobile lives. That is to say, mobilities are not merely an "out-there" phenomenon, but touch on the most personal and affective dimensions of the lives of human subjects.

John had an uncanny ability to raise thorny questions at just the right political time – something he did most startlingly with the publication of *Offshoring* in 2014, anticipating the global significance of financial outsourcing and tax evasion, as captured most recently by the Panama Papers leak of 2016. It's surely interesting that his last books raise urgent political questions, with the titles *What Is the Future?* and (with his protégé Thomas Birtchnell) *A New Industrial Future?* John was a sociological thinker to his core, and his version of social critique (of the kind practiced from the Frankfurt School of the 1920s to Zygmunt Bauman in our own time) was one that he did in spades and to brilliant effect.

Urry's own brand of social theory really took off in the 1980s and 1990s through his collaborations with Scott Lash on labor and capitalism, and subsequently bloomed with full force in the early 2000s with his research on mobilities and globalization. John captured the complex, contradictory ways in which the advent of the global electronic economy is intricately intertwined with movement, fluidity and the wholesale transformation of transport, travel and tourism.

Urry's "mobilities paradigm" had an enormous impact in the UK especially, and in various parts of Europe and Australasia, too. Understanding the breadth and depth of "life on the move" for institutions, organizations, regions, nation-states and indeed global governance was at the core of John's intellectual project. But so too was the impact of mobilities on professional and personal life, and in *Mobile Lives* there is a tracing of how complex, contested mobility systems reach down into the very fabric of human experience and reconstitute identities, socialities, friendship, family, intimacy, sexuality and the body.

Whilst less interested in the self–society nexus than me, John was profoundly alert to the various ways in which new technologies reorganize social relations and everyday life. John had, for example, critically interrogated the motorcar in his edited collection *Automobilities*, co-edited with Nigel Thrift and Mike Featherstone. He likewise looked at the rise of smartphones in *Mobile Technologies of the City*, co-edited with Mimi Sheller. Most recently, the 3D printer was something that provoked his critical attention. In *A New Industrial Future?*, he worked with Thomas Birtchnell to assess the systemic implications of alternative ways of organizing, disorganizing and reorganizing world systems of trade, and outlined novel sociological ideas in developments in the area of 3D printers.

Mobilities have been, among other things, a way of thinking afresh about changes at the level of the self. In *Mobile Lives* (2010), Urry and I examined what it means to live a "mobile life" at the start of the 21st century. Our book can be seen as part of a growing field of study – its leading theorists include, in addition to Urry, Barry Wellman, Nigel Thrift, Sven Kesselring and Mimi Sheller – looking at what is unique about the contemporary social world through the prism of "mobilities." Whilst the "mobilities paradigm" has been concerned with issues of movement in general, the aim of *Mobile Lives* was to demonstrate that the development of various mobility systems has a bearing on the way in which the self is constituted and transformed. By conducting an analysis of mobilities at this more intimate and personal level, Urry and I sought to question the notion that mobility is merely an "out-there" phenomenon, far removed from the individual self.

In order to grasp how complex mobility processes profoundly structure – and are restructured by – people's ordinary lives, we developed eight inter-related propositions in *Mobile Lives*. The first is that an individual's engagement with hugely complex, contested mobility systems (from automobilities to aeromobilities) is not simply about the "use" of particular forms of move-ment. Rather, the rise of an intensively mobile society reshapes the self – its everyday activities, interpersonal relations with others, as well as connections with the wider world. In this age of advanced globalization, we witness *portable personhood*. Identity becomes not merely "bent" towards novel forms of transportation and travel but fundamentally recast in terms of *capacities for movement*. Put another way, the globalization of mobility extends into the core of the self. Mobility of the self is an increasingly prized asset in the global electronic economy. Immobility of self, by contrast, comes to represent a kind of symbolic death.

Second, the trend towards individualized mobility routinely implicates per-sonal life in a complex web of social, cultural and economic networks that can span the globe, or at least certain nodes across parts of the globe. We can find a starting point for this phenomenon in the familiar experience that people have of finding "connections" in common, either professionally or personally. This is the "small world thesis," the idea that people's networks do in fact overlap through a short chain of acquaintances. As many business analysts have pointed out, networking practices are central to organizational redefinitions of the self. In our own time of the internet, digital media and wireless communications, however, there has been a further "shrinkage" of the degrees of separation of the world's population. On this view, the self is continually redefined and reorganized through globally connected networks of information and communication.

Third, Urry and I contend that life "on the move" is the kind of life in which the capacity to be "elsewhere," at a different time from others, is central. Due to the transnational spread of various fast "mobility systems" (from the car system to air travel, from networked computers to mobile phones), people seem to define aspects of their self-identity, as well as schedules of self and life strategies, through reference to de-synchronized, post-traditional or "detradi-tionalized" social settings, where such schedules are rarely shared. Such mobile lives demand flexibility, adaptability, reflexivity – to be ready for the unex-pected, to embrace novelty, as even one's significant others are doing different things and at different times.

Fourth, it is proposed that the onset of new mobilities opens up enticing opportunities, as well as unsettling challenges. On the one hand, access to some mobile technologies and systems allows people to move from place to place, network to network, in ways not previously possible. But on the other hand, this movement may involve the uncertainties of delayed and unpredictable journeys and the regular separation from family and neighbors. There are of course various virtual mobilities (mobile telephony, email and so on) to repair the journeys or to keep in touch; but these are only so good as long as they work, which they quite often do not.

Fifth, Urry and I emphasize that mobile lives are marked by a certain amount of social division, as mobilities typically presuppose the immobilization of some lifestyles. For every jet-setting professional, for example, there are also baggage handlers, check-in clerks, aircraft and hotel room cleaners and transit security officers. The movement of some, in other words, is facilitated by the "immobilization" of others. Mobile lives are intricately interwoven with regimes of immobilization.

Sixth, the self is today increasingly implicated in and generated through the deployment of what we have termed *miniaturized mobilities* – mobile phones, laptop computers, wireless connections. The concept of *miniaturized mobilities* seeks to capture both essential elements of communications "on the move," and specifically how digital technologies are corporeally interwoven with self in the production of mobile lives. Miniaturized systems, often carried directly on the body and thus increasingly central to the organization of self, are software-based and serve to inform various aspects of the self's communication with itself, others and the wider world. Techno-systems such as electronic address books, hand-held iPhoto libraries, iTunes music collections and digital video libraries usher in worlds that are information-rich, of considerable sensory and auditory complexity and easily transportable.

Seventh, we present a picture of "miniaturized mobilities" that departs from the conventional view that people mainly use such information technologies to transmit information from sender to receiver – the communications model of "inputs" and "outputs." The social impact of these mobile technologies can only be fully grasped if we can recognize how the use of various miniaturized mobilities involves transformations in self-experience. When people use miniaturized mobile devices, communication is not only cognitive; communication also occurs on an emotional plane, and people store and retrieve affects, moods and dispositions in these very objects. This storage and retrieval of affects and emotions is what generates new modes of identity that are less tied to fixed localities, regular patterns or dwelt-in cultural traditions.

Eighth, it is argued that there are traces associated with living a life "on the move." These traces are often deposited in space and time when one traverses across a mobility system like the air system or the internet. These traces can, in principle, be retrieved for review or regulation or disciplining at a moment's notice, as there are a range of institutions that routinely gather and report information about the self in movement. Thus, for a life "on the move," privacy may be increasingly difficult to come by. The mobile self is thus bound up with various regimes of surveillance and securitization.

Urry was indeed a rare bird in sociology, not least of which because – unlike many social scientists – his ideas were of direct relevance to non-academics, ranging from environmentalists to policymakers. He contributed to the Inter-governmental Panel on Climate Change and its work on transportation. He was also appointed to the UK Government's Foresight program on transport and policy futures, which in turn led to his vital research on social futures, as well as his setting up an Institute for Social Futures during what would be the final years of his life at Lancaster University.

More than all of this, however, is the sheer novelty of John's take on the world, the angles with which he could make the ordinary appear extraordinary, with all sorts of social, cultural, political and environmental consequences which previously had rarely been addressed. The world according to Urry was one of extensive and intensive mobilities – of people, objects, communications, information, data, protocols, algorithms. But, as John emphasized time and again, if the freely chosen movement of women and men was on the rise throughout the rich North, the underbelly of all this was also a world of enforced migrations, of refugees and asylum seekers. Mobilities and immobi-lities were flip-sides of the same coin for Urry. And as noted, he had the rare knack of being able to address both scholarly and lay audiences.

Above all, he was a gentle and generous man. It is with great sadness for my friend and colleague that I recall our time together, a wonderful time of fleshing out sociological ideas and investigating social-theoretical concepts; but heartening too that his influence is (and should remain) so extensive and profound, with an outpouring of books in his final years which are wholly testament to a mind untrammeled by the conventions of academic fashion.

Chapter 30

Liveable data

A low-carbon science fiction with John Urry

Laura Watts

His office walls were the colour of the sky, and the vertiginous mountain range that enclosed his desk was snow white paper. Through the window the sun flickered light and dark as we moved through or sideways through time, popped a cosmic string, and came to rest in some parallel, perhaps future world where John Urry leaned back listening. I spoke to him as Cassandra, earnest, perhaps unheard elsewhere, but John listened better than most. He said, and I quote,

> Much Greek mythology was based on the tragedy of those knowing the future but not being able to change it. Cassandra famously forewarned the Trojans not to accept the Greek gift of the Trojan horse but she was ignored, and Greek troops inside the wooden horse captured Troy. Although, Cassandra knew what was going to happen, she could not prevent these tragic events. (Urry 2016: 19)

The future I hoped to alter – my Trojan Horse – was another kind of container: a data centre, the 'box' or building that houses the servers and equipment that process internet data, the place where 'the cloud' lives and is made liveable. And, as ever with a Trojan Horse, what mattered was what was inside. I explained it to John:

'Despite the euphemism 'the cloud', data centres are sprawling buildings whose servers run hot as they process search requests, upload posts, transmit email, deliver videos, listen and tune advertising to every keystroke. Data companies from Apple to Facebook centralise – the label is on the box for 'data centres' – tens of thousands of square metres leading to acres of rural land being turned over to the digital world. But inside this Trojan Horse there are no people. They do not bring local jobs, they are not part of the local community. Perhaps only thirty or forty local technicians might be needed.'

John nods, smiling, perhaps hearing a sociology of data centres.

'What they do have inside is energy,' I say. 'Data centres require massive amounts of energy to compute, and even more energy to cool down the hot-running computers. What matters most to a data centre – to 'the cloud'– is energy. They are defined, not by computational power, but by their energy load and efficiency.[1] Estimates suggest that the data centre industry has a carbon footprint as large as the airline industry.' The combined mobilities and energy angle gets him, as I suspected it might, and he quotes the economist, E. F. Schumacher.

'There is no substitute for energy. The whole edifice of modern society is built on it ... it is not "just another commodity" but the precondition of all commodities, a basic factor equal with air, water, and earth.' Then he adds. 'This "basic factor" structures the social, temporal, and social organisation of societies and "life" itself (Urry 2016: 49).

'Exactly,' I agree. 'The big names – Google, Facebook, Apple – are all in the energy business, either generating or reducing energy use. And, more to the point, they are all in the renewable energy business. Large data centres are co-located with hydroelectric dams in Sweden, wind turbines in Denmark, solar farms in Nevada, geothermal energy in Iceland.'

He nods again, but his eyes wandered to the snow-capped mountains of his paper pile. This was not news to him. He was waiting for my point, for what else might be inside my Trojan Horse.

'But what happens if the energy inside the data centre is community-owned renewable energy? What does a data centre look like if you put people in – local people and their wind turbines living nearby, local communities who are living with the data centre? What happens if you put people inside the data centre, as a social and technical infrastructure?'

Unsure if my science studies approach grabs him, I try his language. 'You've talked about the smart "Digital City" versus the green "Liveable City". But what could "Liveable Data" look like, which combines both? Not just for a smart and liveable city, but for a smart and liveable community?'

He murmurs some curiosity, but he still needs more. He needs an answer. I shift forward in the old black, circa 1970s easy chair, one of several forming a square for seminars in his office. Around me, the friendly ghosts of colleagues and research assistants from decades past lean in alongside with their own energy and thoughts.

'I have an example, a proposal from my research fieldsite in the Orkney Islands, off the northeast coast of Scotland.' Then I take a breath, because I know I am about to rattle off with enthusiasm.

'Orkney is a test site for energy futures. The British wind industry came here to try their turbines in the 1980s, and the country's first electricity grid battery came here a few years ago. They've had various smart grids for over a decade.[2] They've got more micro wind turbines per person than anywhere else, and a host of community-owned large-scale wind turbines. They've got electric cars, and charging points in the public car parks. They've got community projects with hydrogen fuel cells.[3] They've got Tesla Powerwall batteries in their new affordable homes. And,' I have to pause for breath. 'They are the site of the European Marine Energy Centre, meaning they are the global hub for the wave and tide energy industry. Impressive for an archipelago of northern islands with only 22,000 souls, and probably rather more dead Vikings in the dirt – they were Norse a few hundred years ago.'

'My island colleagues and I have an idea for a locally owned data centre. Because if it happened, then all those energy futures already happening in the islands – the local wind turbines, electric cars, the community-driven hydrogen fuel cells, all of it – would travel through the electric cables into the data centre. The data centre is a Trojan Horse. It's a Trojan Horse because inside is not just data, but energy, and all the infrastructure and people which energy requires.'

I lean back, because now it's the fun part, telling John the story.

'It's easiest to tell as a scenario, a little science fiction,' I explain.

He nods in agreement, eyes to the ceiling as he recalls futurist, Brian Johnson,

> science fiction (SF) should be a method for futures work … SF is not just a resource to draw upon for possible imaginings of future worlds, but also a technique for generating scenarios through characters, plots and narrative stories: 'stories are not about technology, megatrends or predictions' – rather, the 'future is about people'. (Urry 2016: 113)

The data centre engineer is crouched down in a puddle of yellow patch cables, his face a monotone blue from the wash of coloured overhead lights. The vast more or less underground byre of processing equipment is not unlike, in principle, the cattle byres scattered through fields elsewhere in Orkney. Farming has always been a way of life in the islands, beginning with kye (cows), then wind, and now data. They all require land and professional expertise to manage their growth and flows, whether grain, beef, energy, or data. The vast metal-walled space around you is filled with the continuous roar of air-chewing cooling fans. Green and yellow-eyed computer cows are stacked and racked in dark stalls, lined up for eternal milking. The engineer beside one cabinet of equipment is wearing an archetypal farmer's boiler suit – perhaps he also has a small croft up the road.

As the heavy-set man reaches down to sort the cable at his feet, you see a distinctive pattern etched on his black t-shirt underneath the open boiler suit: three connected diamonds with a hashed pattern in the centre. Despite your stare, he doesn't look up from his work, just says, 'Aye, aye.'

Inga, the so-called data centre 'guardian', replies with something similar, and then calls you back to the guided tour.

She beams with warmth and genuine enthusiasm, a well-grounded young woman in navy fleece with a large pin-badge saying Orkney Gold Gigawatts.[4] She has that twinkle in her eye and a rich, thick voice that easily carries to the back of the group huddle, which makes you think she might double as a local storyteller in the evenings.

'Now, you might have noticed that some of the cabinets have names on them,' she says. Your eyes slide over to the dark metal cabinet of data curiosities beside her and, indeed, above all your heads, over the neat rows of cables and blinking lights, is white plaque on the top of the cabinet: Alice. Next door, a plaque says, Neil. Beyond, another says, Magnus.

'Folk sponsor a cabinet, and we put a wee plaque on it – like planting a tree. Sometimes to remember folk who've passed on, sometimes as a peedie birthday present.[5] We have one named after a school class, who've been studying it as a project. So, instead of walls of faceless cabinets they all have names of local folk. I mean, our lives are in here, and it's a big investment for us. There's one down that row named after my Nan.'

Inga waves you on down the narrow corridor, and you keep pace as she steps along, hands bundled to her heart.

You can smell the data in the air, that combination of fresh hot metal and new plastic.

At a juncture in the cabinet rows Inga gestures down to the right, and tells you her Nan's cabinet is down there.

'My Nan helped with one of the first island community trusts,' she tells you, as you wait for the stragglers to finish taking photos and selfies.

'It took them ten years to talk through getting their first wind turbine. They had to figure out what was right for them, talk about all their worries, make sure everyone had their say. It was a lot of cups of tea, as you might imagine. But the community wind turbines are so important, now. The money they generate goes straight back to supporting the islands.'[6]

You ask what the money is used for.

'New piers for boats, hydrogen-fuelled ferries, affordable housing, repairs to the community hall, insulation and warm housing, we have a business start-up fund, all sorts of things. We all get to vote on it,' she explains.

'Orkney Data Community Trust, which runs this place, is a similar approach. It was set up so that the data centre would benefit local folk, not just have the money go shooting off south.'

You ask what the data centre trust helps to fund.

Inga, one eye still on the lingering group behind, seems keen to explain.

'We're still working against fuel poverty. Just ridiculous with us having so much energy. But we're also working against data poverty, too. It's not right that folk can't watch TV, or get basic online services, or an education. We're so far from government, they're not interested. So we have to do it ourselves. Always how it's been.'[7]

'We have a community ISP, now, to access the high-speed fibre optic cable coming in from the Faroe Islands – that's the Danish islands north of us.[8] And we've set up a "last mile" fund to improve internet access, sort out the copper – the telephone cables. They're a real problem. We've got so many not-spots due to old cabling – people not able to download documents. We tried talking to the mobile operators, but they're national, all down in London, and don't really get us.'

You're surprised she is so knowledgeable. She laughs. 'Well, you've got to know. It's not like you can expect someone to drive up from south to fix things if there's rough weather and the boat's cancelled. I guess you can't take infrastructures for granted – if the lights go out or the internet goes down, we have to fix it. We're practical, experimental. We have to be.'

Before you can ask more, Inga turns away with a smile, continues walking down the corridor. She barrels along, taking the group with her, all the way to the blank silver wall that houses the data centre.

Running down the corrugated wall panels before you are a series of thick heavy pipes, tagged with colour-coded labels. The pipes turn and go under the floor. The data centre guardian steps up to the pipes and strokes one of them with absent attention.

'These pipes carry seawater around the building to cool the data centre,' she explains. 'You might think data centres are about, well, just data. But the data centre industry is a water industry. And here at the north of the country, we are not short of nice cold seawater.'

Her comment elicits a chuckle from some of those around you on the guided tour.

Inga looks down, and then back up with a slight smile, her rapport with you as a group established.

'As well as water, the other thing that comes in to the building is energy. Energy and efficiency is everything to us as a data centre.'

'We're lucky in that Orkney, on average, generates more than 100 per cent of its energy needs from renewable energy. Mostly wind, but we also have solar, biomass, as well as wave and tide energy – you might have seen the wave energy devices out in the water.' She gestures behind her, through the wall to the fierce ocean that lies beyond.[9]

'Now, as you probably know, the big issue with renewable energy is that you get it with the weather – when the wind is blowing – not necessarily when you want to put the kettle on. So storing energy is important. In Orkney, we have two solutions for that. Our electric cars, whose batteries hold a charge, and home batteries, which are very similar. Plus we have hydrogen fuel cells – in fact, our old oil terminal is now a hydrogen storage system.[10]

This means our data centre here can run on island energy, not just when the wind is blowing, but also when the data demand is high.

It's really important to us, because we want to process data when we get a good price for it – so we can generate revenue for the islands from what is, in essence, energy floating in the air.'

Someone behind calls out a question. You turn and see a tall man in pale clothes with a halo of white hair. He asks his question again,

> I noted … the emergence of 'low-carbon civil society' made up of a huge number of experiments and activists … The crucial question here is whether such a 'low-carbon civil society' can generate sufficient new practices,

habits and goods and services to power down societies on a global scale and so offset contending powerful forces especially those of carbon, financial and digital capital. (Urry 2016: 184)

Inga takes the question in her stride, her face thoughtful as she looks to the ceiling, and speaks slow and with great care for the details.

'So, those connections between carbon, finance and data are dead right. The data centre is part of a European-wide "green data network". And it is an experiment, yes. It's a test system – a big European project – to create a data market, like the energy market. Basically, data processing goes to where the renewable energy is. It's called a load-balancing network. The idea is that, rather than just big centralised data centres, who are limited by their immediate environment and its renewable energy, you spread the load to many places and to folk who can really benefit. The project we're part of is for communities and small organisations. It's about decentralised computing. We're a small green data farm.'

She grins, and looks back at you all, 'I had a woman last week who told me that we should use the word "cyber-crofting".'

People smile in response, although you wonder how many know the phrase from its heyday decades ago.

Inga turns away and leads you along the edge of the wall, towards the green illuminated exit sign. Through the door, you are pointed to a small antechamber, it might be a lunch room with tables and chairs, and a mural painted along one wall. The painting is in bright block print, with dramatic coastline and swirling connecting lines between buildings and abstract islands – you notice the data centre in the corner, connected to wind turbines and an unfamiliar silhouette in the sea. This room is where you began the tour, and where it ends.

Inga invites everyone to pick up their bags and coats, so you can head outside into the weather fray. She also points to a desk against one wall with some souvenirs laid out, and an honesty box with a handwritten note for e-payment. You take a look at the table: there are a few nice postcards of the hillside into which the data centre has been hidden, taken from the sea so you can see the beach in the foreground; some badges, like the one Inga wears, that say 'Orkney Gold Gigawatts'; and some tea towels with the same phrase and that distinctive pattern of three connected diamonds you saw on the engineer's t-shirt. You buy a tea towel (more use than a postcard – you can't remember the last time you saw one) and remind yourself to ask Inga what the pattern means.

You hit the outside like leaping from an aeroplane into cloud. A faint rain sticks to your jacket, and you pull your hat down lower. Inga walks out into the grass car park ahead, the plastic matting embedded between the blades making it tough enough for the minibus you arrived on. She seems unconcerned by the wet weather, elegant felt hat over yellow builder's wellies below.

You take a long breath so the salt air can reach the back of your throat, thick enough to taste sharp. Inga gives you all a moment to stop and take in the field falling down to the sandstone beach, and the shadow of dark cliffs rising up on the right. The clouds thin and for a moment you watch white spray blown from grey Atlantic waves as they crash and collide.

The wind gives a sudden hard gust, and people laugh, embarrassed, as they lose their footing. You all spread out, some attempting last-minute photos (it was sunny when you went in), others ambling towards the dry comfort of the minibus.

You look back at the unassuming entrance, a wide arc of metal that has cracked open the hill, with an inviting double door into its depths. There are other grass-roofed buildings set further back, which have more solid doors and bright yellow warning triangles, perhaps managing the power. Beyond the data centre, small farmhouses creep up the hillside until they disappear in the cloud. You can see little turbines spinning beside them.

As you take in the scene, you notice the diamond pattern once more, on a metal sign beside the entrance door. Three connected diamonds, outlined several times, a hatched pattern within.

You go over to Inga, and ask her about it.

She seems delighted by the question. 'It's Neolithic rock art from the Ness of Brodgar, one of our big archaeological sites – a prehistoric city they're still excavating. I recommend a visit.'

Your confusion about its presence at the data centre registers, and she explains.

'We had a school competition to pick a logo for the data centre, and this was the design that was chosen. The judging panel really liked how it emphasised that the data centre is a continuation of life and living in the islands. We've been farming here for, what, 6000 years. The data centre is another kind of farming. Part of what will keep us going for another 6000 years, maybe. They call it the *longue durée*. We endure. We change – we're not caught in amber – but we endure.'

When I finished telling my story, my future, I saw John's eyes wandering around the room, not in distraction but in thought.

'That's the Trojan Horse,' I say. 'The project that puts local people inside the data centre, with their own energy. Liveable Data is possible. It just takes a little commitment to *decentralised* low-carbon data. I don't think it's just about cities, I think it's also about communities and organisations who might be in cities, but who also might be on islands – even islands in cities. What do you think? Will the Trojan Horse be taken in to the centre, bring this energy future from the edge to the city?'

I feel like Cassandra, passionate but worried I am unheard, that the Trojan Horse of the data centre will remain empty rather than filled with the possibility for these social futures – a liveable data future – already happening in Orkney, and no doubt elsewhere.

John lifts his arms, and his long arms become fluid as he motions at the air like a magician incanting a spell. 'The futures world may be a murky world but it is one that we have to enter, interrogate and hopefully reshape. It should be a direction of travel for fateful analyses of social life within this new century' (Urry 2016: 192).

As I consider his words in the silence that follows, I focus on his sense of optimism, on the possibility for low-carbon science fiction and energy science fiction to create a direction of travel for future liveable worlds. I hear the energetic rumble of a Trojan Horse that is possible, whose promise forms the fateful dreams of 'big data' and 'the cloud' that we inhabit and, still, there are many liveable energy futures within.

Notes

1 Data centres are measured by the industry standard numeric, Power Usage Efficiency.
2 The islands had one of the UK's first registered power zones in 2006, and later an active network management system was added, which responds to load by switching generators on and off as needed. This is due to the islands' grid being at capacity – the islands are often generating more renewable energy than the grid can accept.
3 There are a series of hydrogen fuel projects in Orkney, including 'Orkney Surf n Turf' (surfnturf.org.uk), a project to store tide energy from the European Marine Energy Centre and wind energy from the Eday island community turbine and make the fuel later available to boats in the harbour; BIT-HIT (bighit.eu) is a European Union-funded project to build a hydrogen fuel network and territory in Orkney, as a European technology test bed.
4 'Orkney Islands Gold' was a high-quality brand of meat from the islands.
5 'Peedie' is an Orcadian dialect term for small or little.
6 For an overview of the development work and community energy generation in Orkney, see: Orkney Renewable Energy Forum (oref.co.uk), the Development Trusts Association Scotland, Northern Isles (dtascot.org.uk), and the latest Sustainable Energy Strategy from the Orkney Islands Council (orkney.gov.uk).
7 For more on local efforts to eradicate fuel poverty in the islands see the charity, THAW Orkney (thaworkney.co.uk).
8 The undersea fibre optic cable is SHEFA-2.
9 Orkney is the site of the European Marine Energy Centre, the world's longest running grid-connected test site for wave and tide energy devices (www.emec.org.uk).
10 This references the Flotta Oil Terminal, which is currently in operation, but ideas have been circulated in Orkney about its conversion to a hydrogen fuel storage system.

References

Urry, J. (2016) *What Is the Future?*, Cambridge: Polity Press.

Chapter 31

Mobility and simplicity

Peter Merriman

Mobility and movement have always lain at the heart of my research. Throughout much of that time, John Urry's writings have been an inspiration and important source of reference, but I have had some difficulty dating my first encounter with his work. I have a vague recollection of reading sections of *The Tourist Gaze* (1990) while completing a tourism essay at school in 1993.[1] But a far more influential set of encounters with the man and his work occurred between 1998 and 2001, in the latter phases of my doctoral research and writing. John's early writings on mobility, alongside those by Tim Cresswell, Doreen Massey and Nigel Thrift, led me to incorporate more conceptual approaches to mobility, subjectivity and sociality into what had, up to that point, been a fairly straightforward contextual history of England's M1 motorway. As these scholars have variously (and separately) argued, mobility does not simply occur in spaces or through places. Movements produce or co-produce socio-spatial configurations and distinctive geographies. John's bold manifesto-like statements (e.g. Urry 2000) appealed to me as an early career geographer trying to rethink mobility history and transport history through social and cultural theory. His synthetic sociologies demonstrated a broad and magisterial knowledge of their subjects, covering huge ground, and this was invaluable for me as a non-sociologist starting to think about the social dynamics of mobility and movement. I also recall John's encouragement and hospitality when I met him for the first time in May 2000, as I visited Lancaster to deliver a seminar in the Department of Sociology. During the following 16 years we crossed paths regularly in workshops, conferences, publications and thesis examinations, and I owe a considerable amount to John for his influence on, and support of, my work.

Throughout my career I have valued the theoretical ideas which John and others introduced to the field. His theoretical engagement with writings on process, embodiment, materiality, infrastructure, identity, gender, complexity, temporality, sociality, fluidity, networking, futures and inequalities brought both mainstream and new social theories to empirical research on mobility. Perhaps more importantly, John's position as an eminent, world-leading sociologist ensured that people listened to and engaged with his thinking on mobilities. As my own work developed I started to question some of the ways in which the emerging field of mobilities was positioned. For example, I have always been reluctant to affirm the event named the 'mobility turn' and the emergence of a 'new mobilities paradigm'. This is, in part, because these phrases rely upon theories of emergence which are rather grand and eruptive, suggesting a violent (perhaps colonial) revolution in ideas, rather than a slow emergence and more modest and partial influence. I have also felt that such phrasings tend to draw attention away from the much longer history of humanities and social science writings on mobility and movement. As John himself argued, his emerging concern with movement and mobility can most usefully be considered as part of broader concerns with process and relationality that became evident with the emergence and increasing purchase of post-structuralist, post-humanist, post-colonial and feminist thinking during the 1980s, 1990s and 2000s.

John was also instrumental in encouraging mobility scholars to reflect upon and diversify the methods they use to apprehend mobilities of various kinds. Mobile methods were promoted for their ability to enable researchers to move, see, be or experience *with* mobile subjects, and this call paralleled similar calls by human geographers for non-representational methods and methodologies that were capable of grasping the fleeting and dynamic nature of embodied practices and performances. As a historically oriented scholar writing across the humanities/social sciences divide, I felt some unease about a few of the stronger calls for (and engagements with) mobile methods, in part because of suggestions that more traditional social science and humanities methods had failed and should be abandoned. For me, the rush to incorporate new tracking and recording technologies resulted in a fetishism of co-presence and witnessing as ways of gathering accurate data, as well as a rather pessimistic abandonment of long-established yet evolving social science methods (Merriman 2014). What is important is that while encouraging experiments with mobile methods, John did not favour the abandonment of traditional methods, and in his own work he usually undertook textual and discourse analyses, often rooted in historical readings of situations.

My approach to mobility infrastructures owes a lot to John's writings on the complex infrastructures enabling mobile life – in which he emphasised the importance of moorings, topographic grounds and resources for enabling or entraining mobility practices. Here lie the key components of his later work (mobility ↔ complexity ↔ resources ↔ futures), and his thinking on infra-structures and moorings usefully parallels work on mobility systems by science and technology studies and actor network theory scholars, historians of trans-port and technology and theorists of materiality. What this focus on material moorings facilitates is a sensitivity to the entangled relations between mobile agents and fixed things, mobile practices and infrastructural moorings, and processes of speeding up and slowing down. As scholars such as Tim Cresswell have also shown, the regulation and governance of mobilities – and the broader politics of mobility – reveals practices and experiences of containment, slowing down, stilling and friction, as well as speeding up and smoothness. What's more, efforts to speed up the movements of elite travellers, perishable and high-value goods, capital and information are inseparable from the actual or relative stilling or slowing down of other bodies and other things. The close alignment between capitalism, state governments and attempts to control movement has ensured that a great deal of effort has and is put into smoothing or speeding up the mobility of certain bodies and things, and John's work on mobility and complexity has emphasised the significant levels of effort required to smooth these flows (Urry 2003). What results is experiences of seamlessness, smoothness, speed and simplicity resulting from a black-boxing of systems, delegation of actions and forgetting of distributed or collective effort. But does our push to highlight complexity and hidden processes detract attention away from the coherence and simplicity of embodied sensations, experiences and practices of mobility; a simplicity which is central to many movement cultures?

Driving, walking, emailing, shopping, Skyping and dancing. These are embodied mobile practices which are remarkable for their unremarkable, ubiquitous and ordinary occurrence. These practices *do* have distinctive geographies and histories. They *are* entangled with complex economic, social, political and cultural practices, and they *are not* accessible to all. There *are* complex infrastructural geographies and regulatory practices which enable and constrain them. Nevertheless, for the confident, competent and experienced practitioner there is an unconscious automaticity to these embodied knowledges and practices which registers as an un-thought simplicity. While it is easy to dismiss this simplicity as an illusion – a result of black-boxing – and seek to highlight complexity, acknowledging the ontological effects of simplicity, coherence, oneness and autonomy is vital to understanding the social and cultural practices at work. In short, an academic appreciation of the autonomous and monadic ontologies associated with mobility practices is key to understanding the addictive and joyful sensations of moving and communicating in certain ways, as well as the forgetting, displacement or bracketing off of the environmental consequences of mobility practices (whether by producers, consumers or governmental authorities). This passion and drive for moving appears to be primordial to the development of animate beings, while modern technologies have not only enhanced our capacity to move but have transformed mobile ontologies, even if this is only a momentary relational reworking of our sense of being. This sensation or experience of simplicity, this oneness, seems to be grounded in embodied knowledges and what Heidegger might describe as the 'tool-ness' of things. Complexity, then, always seems to be caught in a tension with experiences and sensations of immediacy, autonomy and simplicity. These two tendencies work against one another – simplification and complexification – and I would suggest that this binary tension is a useful way of approaching mobility systems and practices, just as mobility/fixity or mobility/moorings might be.

My key point here is that in our desire to reveal the complex systems enabling mobility practices, we should not neglect the experiences of mobile subjects. One of the great strengths of John's work was that he recognised the multiple agencies, experiences, lives, sensations and performances of mobile actors, as well as the infrastructural work entailed in facilitating these movements. These experiences may include autonomy, simplicity, seamlessness and smoothness, which are often seen as illusory effects of complex systems, as experiences associated with privileged elites, or as utopian values aligned with mobility practices. They may also include experiences of friction, disconnection and complexity – qualities and experiences that are hidden behind the utopian rhetoric of vehicle manufacturers, transport companies and transport planners but which all too often erupt as we wait for a delayed train or sit in a traffic jam. Research on elite mobilities has revealed the labour which underlies the smooth and seamless movements of the super-rich; but feelings of autonomy, freedom, smoothness and simplicity are much more widespread and ubiquitous than some of these accounts perhaps suggest.

A final theme of John's work I want to highlight is the situatedness or locatedness of his sociologies. John's sociological writings exhibit a strong sensitivity not only to the different spaces, places, 'scapes' and environments that are embroiled with our social worlds, but also to how distinctive places have been shaped by social and economic processes. In doing this he was influenced by a wide range of thinking – from the spatially attuned sociologies of Giddens and others, to interdisciplinary debates in new journals such as *Society and Space* and *Theory, Culture and Society* – as well as through his active involvement with the Conference of Socialist Economists Regionalism Group and, closer to home, the Lancaster Regionalism Group. These involvements clearly shaped his thinking on both mobility and space exhibited in *The Tourist Gaze* (1990), but they also led to important engagements with human geographers such as Derek Gregory, Doreen Massey and Nigel Thrift. In 1985 John co-edited (with Cambridge geographer Derek Gregory) the highly influential text *Social Relations and Spatial Structures* which reads as a Who's Who of Anglo-American socio-spatial theory in the mid-1980s – featuring important chapters by Phil Cooke, Anthony Giddens, Derek Gregory, David Harvey, Doreen Massey, Ray Pahl, Allan Pred, Peter Saunders, Andrew Sayer, Ed Soja, Nigel Thrift, Richard Walker and Alan Warde, and an index compiled by Cambridge graduate student Chris Philo. Urry's own chapter on 'Social Relations, Space and Time' tackles what now seems like a vast field, and the book as a whole can be credited as one of a number of important publications which helped to bridge the gap between sociology and human geography, and act as a focus of debates between quite different philosophical approaches to structure, agency and space – including Marxism, critical realism and structuration theory. John continued to publish in *Society and Space* throughout much of his career, and I have no doubt that the extensive dialogues between human geographers and sociologists working on mobilities in the early 2000s owes a lot to the dialogues he initiated with these colleagues two or more decades earlier.

Across his career, John's diverse outputs on mobility, space, tourism, time, complexity, automobility, futures, organised capitalism, nature and much more addressed big and sometimes difficult themes in an accessible manner, bringing an ordered simplicity to his work which enabled his ideas to reach a diverse multi-disciplinary readership. In particular, he has had a significant influence on debates surrounding mobility and related topics in the social sciences – ranging from the large number of influential scholarly outputs he produced, to the research and networking infrastructures he helped to establish – and these are likely to have a profound influence on mobilities research for years to come. Of particular note, for me, are the scholarly networks and publishing infrastructures he built. The Centre for Mobilities Research (CeMoRe) at Lancaster University continues to act as an important hub for networking, publishing and information dissemination on mobilities, whether as the editorial home of the *Mobilities* journal, the hosting of the CeMoRe email list or in organising key international workshops and conferences. While it is difficult to predict where mobilities thinking will move next, John's final works on energy and mobility futures are providing an important catalyst for ongoing debates with scholars in transport studies and environmental studies, while his strong support of emerging work on mobility in the humanities is reflected in the increasing influence of his ideas in disciplines such as English literature, film studies, performance and archaeology.

Note

1   The essay – on the social, cultural and environmental impacts of tourism – was, I recall, written for my A-level in Geography, and I remember finding the book in the library of what is now Canterbury Christ Church University.

References

Gregory, D. and Urry, J. (eds) (1985) *Social Relations and Spatial Structures*. Basingstoke: Macmillan.

Merriman, P. (2014) 'Rethinking mobile methods', *Mobilities*, 9(2), 167–187.

Urry, J. (1990) *The Tourist Gaze*. London: SAGE.

Urry, J. (2000) 'Mobile sociology', *British Journal of Sociology*, 51, 185–203.

Urry, J. (2003) *Global Complexity*. Cambridge: Polity.

Chapter 32

A planetary turn for the social sciences?

Bronislaw Szerszynski

In the 1990s sociology, like many other social sciences, underwent a global turn, with an explosion of interest in social dynamics beyond the borders of nation states. This was partly driven by a wide sense, growing through the 1980s, that the social world was changing in ways that demanded new concepts and priorities. The surface of the globe was becoming more interconnected; if it had ever been possible to have a meaningful bounded study of a local or national society, this was becoming ever more implausible. With the steady growth of global travel and communications, the emergence of an integrated global economy based on regional specialisation, and the increased intermixing of cultures and staging of mediated mega-events, the proper object of sociology seemed to be becoming a global society. More haltingly, there was also growing awareness that what needed to be globalised was not only the object of sociology but also the set of intellectual ideas and concepts used to study it, which were still overwhelmingly dominated by intellectual and political perspectives developed in Europe and North America. John Urry was a key figure in this global turn: in his books with Scott Lash, *The End of Organised Capitalism* (1987) and *Economies of Signs and Space* (1994), and then more explicitly in *Sociology beyond Societies* (2000), John argued that the object of sociology was changing, no longer bound together into settled, national societies, and that sociology needed to change in response. The project on global citizenship, cosmopolitanism and the media that John and I carried out with Greg Myers and Mark Toogood in the 1990s on global citizenship illustrated well that direction.

But in John's work there were also hints of another potential transformation of the social sciences, one which I want to call the *planetary* turn. While sharing some themes with the global turn, this nascent turn is strikingly different in its approach and implications. Above all, whereas the global turn was mainly about saying that the social sciences needed to respond to the growing interconnectedness of social processes across the surface of the planet, the planetary turn involves the recognition that the bounding of the social was *always already* problematic, and on another, more comprehensive front: that between human society as a semiotic, meaningful phenomenon on the one hand and the physical processes of the Earth on the other. It thus involves the rejection of what had been a key assumption of sociology since its foundation, human exemptionalism, an assumption which had already been problematised in the 1970s by the subdiscipline of environmental sociology with which John became increasingly engaged (see *Contested Natures* with Phil Macnaghten (1998), *Climate Change and Society* (2011) and *Societies beyond Oil* (2013)). John thus added his voice to the growing call in sociology, anthropology and science and technology studies for more attention to be paid to the social significance of material things and processes. Most explicitly, he called in *Sociology beyond Societies* (2000) for 'new rules of sociological method' that abandoned the notion of an a priori difference between humans and the objects with which their social lives are entwined, and across many of his works showed how in this task the social sciences could productively draw on perspectives from the physical sciences, especially from thermodynamics, theoretical biology and complexity theory (see for example *Global Complexity* (2003), *Mobilities* (2007) and *Climate Change and Society* (2011)).

While John engaged with many planetary themes in his later work, and made many of the theoretical moves necessary for a sociology that takes our planetary condition seriously, he left it to others to put this all together as a fully fledged programme for the social sciences. It is largely amongst social science and humanities scholars engaged with the concept of the Anthropocene, Gaia and the Earth system that this kind of work is being done (e.g. Clark 2011; Connolly 2017; Hamilton 2017; Latour 2017; Tsing et al. 2017); however, this remains a very heterogeneous field. In the rest of this short article, I will try to spell out what I think are the key steps involved in what is still unfinished business for the social sciences – a planetary turn. In so doing I will try to tease out some of the origins of my own planetary thinking in John's work.

Firstly, the foundational task of any planetary turn must be the interdisciplinary task of investigating *the planet* as a category of being in its own right, and the ways in which this conditions social existence in fundamental ways. This involves moving beyond the way that the figure of 'the planet' has figured in globalisation discourses, where the focus has been on a narrow range of characteristics of the Earth such as unity, boundedness, fragility and interconnectedness. Instead, we need a more complex account of 'planetary being' which is at once more general and more tightly specified. John's use of complexity, emergence and non-Newtonian time in books from *Sociology beyond Societies* (2000) onwards was a great starting point, but we need to draw in more detail from the Earth sciences.

For example, planets are made up of condensed, classical baryonic matter (i.e. 'normal' atoms), comprising a range of chemical elements and existing typically at a mid-range of temperatures between the cold of space and the huge temperatures of stars, and thus able to compose itself into complex entities with a deep compositional hierarchy (e.g. gases, molecules, atoms, subatomic particles) involving different properties and dynamics at each level. Planets are also gravitationally collapsed and differentiated, so that they form dense, approximately spherical bodies with their own gravitational fields (and hence a vertical dimension) organised internally into different strata and compartments; they also dominate an orbital region around their star and interact with each other to produce relatively stable orbits over long timescales. They are also (more or less) materially closed but energetically open, subjected to flows of energy over long timescales from their parent star and hot interior, which energy has to cascade through nested interacting subsystems before being discharged as long-wave radiation into space. These dynamic features, combined with the specific circumstances of their formation and development, means that planets become unique historical entities, capable of generating new kinds of phenomena that interact in complex ways on different timescales. A planetary social science would be aware of how these features of planets at once make possible and also condition human life. Such a 'planetary posthumanism' would situate what are taken to be the distinctive features of human social life – society, language, meaning, cognition, action, technology – within a more comprehensive picture of how new forms, powers and kinds of relation arise under planetary conditions.

Secondly, it follows that a planetary social science would be *volumetric*, concerned with relations not just on the surface of the Earth but also within and across all the different entangled volumes of the planet from its core out to its near space environment. As social scientists are increasingly arguing, we need to develop a 3D imaginary for the social sciences. John's work gave some pointers for how to do this, by going up into the atmosphere in his book with Cwerner and Kesselring on *Aeromobilities* (2009) and down into geological strata in *Societies beyond Oil*. But this volumetric approach needs to be developed more systematically, through a deeper engagement with the significance of the Earth's stratification into different layers and compartments – core, mantle, crust, biosphere, hydrosphere, atmosphere, magnetosphere – with different properties and stabilised on different timescales.

A planetary turn would also be concerned with the distinctive topological relations and thereby modes of existence and relatedness that are made possible by this stratification. Strata are often in asymmetrical relations of dependency with each other, and the surfaces and boundaries between different strata and compartments occasion radically different kinds of phenomena. The sub-aerial surface that was left largely reified and unproblematised in sociology's global turn starts to look different and far more interesting when we first zoom out to investigate the diverse forms of complex order that can be generated in and between other zones of the extended body of the Earth, and only then zoom back in to the 'critical zone' or 'boundary layer' of mixing between earth and sky that we ourselves inhabit.

Thirdly, a planetary social science would also have to engage with the *interplanetary*. One aspect of this concerns interplanetary mobilities – the study of the multiple ways in which the stories of individual planets can become intertwined through the exchange of entities and materials of different kinds. Here the critical social sciences can help avoid the unreflective projection of 'globalisation' narratives of imperialism and neoliberalism onto an extra-terrestrial canvas. But another aspect of the interplanetary, at least as important, is the comparative. The deepening understanding of our own solar system and the continuing discovery of diverse exoplanets orbiting other stars can help us to construct a far more expansive theoretical 'phase space' for planetary development, one that can accommodate diverse possible developmental trajectories of planets. For the social sciences this is an opportunity to counter the dominant geocentric 'observer bias' that takes the specific story of the Earth to be the template for any planet that might develop complex organised matter. Drawing on empirical astronomy, but also the more speculative practices of astrobiology and science fiction, a planetary social science can explore how the complex forms of matter, meaning and motion that we associate with society might have emerged through very different developmental processes and take profoundly different forms.

However, this comparative move is also one that should make us look at our *own* planet differently, as itself 'alien'. The Earth, and indeed any other planet, becomes what it is through becoming other to itself, on a number of timescales. As geologist Jan Zalasiewicz puts it, on the longest timescale, 'the Earth seems to be less one planet, rather a number of different Earths that have succeeded each other in time, each with very different chemical, physical and biological states'. But planets such as the Earth are also *constantly involved in the internal generation of otherness*; especially within the fluid elemental media of planets, alterity is immanent (internal to the region), gradual (manifests as gradients) and generative (constantly producing form and new gradients). Zones on apparently very different planets can also have more in common with each other than with zones on the same planet. Thus relations of difference between and amongst our planets are not merely external but internal; and relations of difference and alterity do not just divide planets from each other, but can also divide planets from themselves – and conjoin them with each other. To adapt the language of Sarah Whatmore and Marisol de la Cadena, to think *about* and *through* the Earth is therefore always already to think of it as 'more than' Earth, as the Earth 'but not only'.

Fourthly, a planetary social science would also be temporally extended into the *deep time* of the Earth, concerned with the geological and astronomical timescales of what John called 'glacial time'. Fernand Braudel's *longue durée* needs extending further into planetary history – not in order to diminish the importance of contemporary environmental changes but to recontextualise them. Planets as open systems maintained far from equilibrium and driven by thermodynamic imperatives pass through a number of irreversible 'bifurcations', 'major transitions' or moments of symmetry-breaking, which involves them arranging themselves in new ways and developing according to new logics. Attending to the geohistorical details of these transitions can reveal many social processes and dynamics to be examples of long-standing patterns in material differentiation and association in the history of the Earth. Furthermore, just as John taught us that glacial and instantaneous time can coexist in the same social formation, alternative possible metastable states of the Earth can neither be divided unproblematically into those that are actualised and those that are never actualised, and the former simply arranged in a non-overlapping sequence; instead, all possible states of the Earth, even if 'real but not actualised', are in some sense active and confronting each other at all times in a planet that teems with potential – with 'the virtual'.

But as well as situating the present of the Earth against its deep past, and finding its deep past (and alternative presents) within its present, we also need to develop ways of thinking about our planet's deep future. In *What Is the Future?* (2016), John rejected two common approaches to the future: one that focuses on individual rationality and agency, and another that sees the future as more or less determined by fixed structures. Instead, he insisted on the need to regard social futures as the product of self-organising complex adaptive systems, which pass through phase transitions and thereby behave in non-linear ways. This insight applies *a fortiori* to planetary futures. The Earth regarded in the way I have sketched above – as planet, as volumetric, as differential and as geohistorical – is one whose future cannot be known in advance. However, at the same time, these dimensions of the planetary turn can help us to discern the possibilities latent within our own time, and perhaps better steer towards more desirable futures for our own, precious home planet.

John Urry remained committed to the discipline of sociology to the very end, but showed us a way of doing sociology that was not afraid of embracing very different forms of knowledge and ways of knowing. He also showed a wider readership how sociology could perform an important role in providing an overall framework for highly interdisciplinary analyses of major contemporary issues, in a way that combined scholarly depth and range with passion and urgency. In so doing he developed an inspiring vision of a sociology that was both more capacious and more engaged. In order to continue and further develop that legacy, and in order to fully and responsibly inhabit the Earth, we still need to develop the planetary turn. John has left us with that task.

References

Clark, N. (2011) *Inhuman Nature: Sociable Life on a Dynamic Planet*, London: SAGE.
Connolly, W. E. (2017) *Facing the Planetary: Entangled Humanism and the Politics of Swarming*, Durham, NC: Duke University Press.
Hamilton, C. (2017) *Defiant Earth: The Fate of Humans in the Anthropocene*, 1st edition, Cambridge: Polity.
Latour, B. (2017) *Facing Gaia: Eight Lectures on the New Climatic Regime*, Cambridge: Polity.
Tsing, A. L., A. S. Heather, E. Gan and N. Bubandt (eds) (2017) *Arts of Living on a Damaged Planet: Ghosts and Monsters of the Anthropocene*, Minneapolis, MN: University of Minnesota Press.

Afterword

Lynne Pearce

As someone situated on the margins of John Urry's life and work until I underwent my own '(auto)mobilities turn' in the early 2000s, I was deeply honoured – and, at first, somewhat surprised and overawed – by the invitation to contribute an Afterword to this landmark book. However, when the editors reminded me that I'd known John for the 26 years I've been employed by Lancaster University and was – as someone based in English – well positioned to reflect upon the impressive interdisciplinary reach of his work, I accepted, and am very glad I did so. Taken together, the 32 chapters which comprise this volume represent a beautifully rounded and heartfelt tribute to a towering figure in the academic world: not only do they capture the breadth of John's scholarship, but also his legendary support to multiple generations of postgraduates and early-career scholars, myself included. For, with one or two exceptions, the majority of the authors represented here have been encouraged and mentored by John Urry at some point in their careers – either as doctoral students or co-authors (or both) – and their subsequent development as academics clearly owes a huge amount to John's very distinctive brand of leadership. Regardless of the fact that he was such a distinguished academic, both within the social sciences and beyond, John engaged with absolutely everyone he came into contact with as an equal, and – with colleagues – was expert in drawing out what was original and significant in their work. Indeed, it was arguably his eye for seeds of originality in others' work that led him to collaborate with so many of them, also ensuring that there is now a vast library of 'Urry books' for us to remember him by.

The last time I saw John to talk to was at the Institute for Social Futures reading group (February 2016) which had met to discuss the draft of his new book, *What Is the Future?*. We shared a joke about the chapter, 'Past Futures', which I said had more 'literary criticism' in it than my own book, *Drivetime* (2016), which was in press at the same time. I also remember him telling me how pleased he was with the cover of his book which he pronounced 'the best I've ever had': a photograph of sculptor Anthony Gormley's 'iron men' gazing out to sea at Crosby Sands. This amazing installation of 100 cast iron figures (moulded from the artist's own body) was originally intended to be a temporary exhibit, but has since been retained by popular demand (see www.visit1..com/things-to-do/another-place-by-antony-gormley-p160981 for images and further information). Looking at the image again now it is, of course, hard not to identify the men – gazing out to sea and an unknown beyond – with John himself and his visions of the future; hard not to discover in their mutability and resilience (disappearing and reappearing with the tide twice a day) a metaphor for his own approach to knowledge as well as his extraordinary legacy. In this short Afterword, I reflect upon both the exemplary openness of John's approach to knowledge and the certainty of his legacy in response to the themes and memories evoked by the chapters. My discussion opens with some thoughts on the ground-breaking interdisciplinarity of John's work, moves to a consideration of the tension between 'systems' and 'humans' that has become a defining feature of so much of it, and concludes with a snapshot of his 'working method(s)' drawing upon the many delightful insights included in the chapters

It was, indeed, very striking, as first I browsed through these chapters, to see just how many authors commented upon the impact of John's work to disciplines other than sociology: in particular, geography (Birtchnell, Merriman, Sayer), but also economics, political science, architecture and design. Moreover, it is clear that this reach and applicability depended not only on the inherently trans-disciplinary interest of the topics John made his own – tourism, mobilities, futures, etc. – but also the way in which his own disciplinary expertise in politics and economics rapidly spread into new territories as the result of a number of key collaborations in the 1970s and 1980s. Although some of John's more recent followers may be unfamiliar with this early work, the chapters included here by Jørgen Ole Bærenholdt, Kingsley Dennis, Phil Macnaghten and Andrew Sayer trace its fascinating genealogy. Of particular note in this regard is John's (early 1980s) involvement in projects focused on locality and region such as 'Changing Urban and Regional Systems', which laid the foundations for his subsequent work on tourism, as well as the wide-ranging impact of the book collection *Social Relation and Spatial Structures* (1985), which was co-edited with the geographer Derek Gregory. As Peter Merriman observes, this volume – which included chapters by a number of rising stars such as Doreen Massey, Nigel Thrift, David Harvey and Andrew Sayer – 'helped to bridge the gap between Sociology and Human Geography' and thus pave the way for a radical new approach to space and place in the next decade. Andrew Sayer himself, meanwhile, provides an illuminating account of John's evolving political and methodological standpoint(s): from the critical realism of the 1970s (here he cites one of John's earliest book publications, *Social Theory as Science*, co-authored with Russell Keat, from 1975); through postmodernism (in particular, John's collaborations with Scott Lash in the 1990s); to his most recent work on oil, climate change, 'off-shoring' and futures in which Sayer discovers a return to his earlier realist principles.

What Sayer identifies as the postmodern turn in John's thinking in the 1990s coincides with a shift of focus vis-à-vis the object(s) of his research: from (relatively) fixed social and spatial categories (e.g. regions) to highly mobilised human ones (e.g. tourists, drivers), whose subjective and affective experience of the world clamours for attention alongside their construction by, and through, multiple discourses and sign systems. This, in turn, relates to the way in which the 'human' and 'non-human' are placed in tension with one another; not only in John's work but in all of us who follow in his footsteps. A simultaneous regard for the deeply personal, emotional and seemingly idiosyncratic experiences of mobile subjects and their entrapment by, and within, largely invisible systems (be these linguistic, political or economic) is the painful paradox that now subtends so much of our cultural analysis and has become part of its rhetoric. On the one hand, writing about mobilities breathes new life into our thoughts and sentences – we reach for verbs that signify the breaking of boundaries, adjectives expressive of freedom and liberation, and pronouns synonymous with agency; on the other, it is hard to get to the end of a paragraph with a mobilities theme without acknowledging that all that moves is, itself, *moved* – and often in a coercive and disturbing way.

On this point, it is also important to remind ourselves that John's extraordinary oeuvre – 40+ books and hundreds of chapters and articles – straddles the 'birth' of the digital revolution whose growing consequence is felt not only in his own publications but also those of his students and other followers. Indeed, in terms of its widespread uptake (the first mobile phones; the origins of social media through online chat rooms, etc.), digitisation more or less coincided with the establishment of the Centre for Mobilities Research (CeMoRe), established in 2003, and the epistemological sea change which ensued is recorded in the early volumes of the *Mobilities* journal, established in 2005. By the same token, several of John's 20th-century interests, such as tourism, have had to be reconceived as material worlds colliding with virtual ones. This is vividly illustrated here in the chapters by two of his former PhD students, Jennie Germann Molz and Juliet Jain, both of whom trace the journey they – and John – travelled as they explored the implications of digital technologies on the ways in which we apprehend space and time, proximity and distance; even the 'death' of tourism that John heralded in *Economies of Signs and Space* way back in 1994 has had to be reconfigured.

Among the many tributes posted on the university website in memory of John is one by his colleague, Imogen Tyler, which registers his 'love of technology' and (some) social media (Twitter, not Facebook). However, the ways in which such technologies have combined with the material (if often invisible) political and economic 'systems' that are the focus of John's most recent work was evidently of grim concern to him, as captured here in the chapters by Jørgen Ole Bærenholdt and Bülent Diken. The former observes how many of John's articles ended with invocations of 'war, terror and Orwell's Big Brother'. Such dystopian visions are, of course, confronted, head on, in *What Is the*

Future? (2016); in particular, in the chapters which deal with 'Past Futures' (featuring textual readings of 19th- and 20th-century science fiction) and 'New Catastrophic Futures'. The latter includes a jaw-dropping two-page list of books published since 2003 which predict world apocalypse on account of one 'tipping point' or another. I remember John invoking the titles of at least two of these in seminars (Martin Rees's *Our Final Century* (2004) and Naomi Klein's *This Changes Everything: Capitalism vs. the Climate* (2014)) and, notwithstanding the characteristic cheerfulness with which he debated even the bleakest of topics – and his explicit critique of 'catastrophic thinking' – I have no doubt that he took these predictions very seriously. It is certainly a concern shared by another of John's long-time colleagues, Bülent Diken, whose own chapter here is the most foreboding in the collection. Diken forecasts that the 'indistinctions' of the social media age, combined with the 'dark', and largely invisible, mobilities of which John has written, has the potential to convert 'mobile sociologies' into a terrifying 'mobile hell'.

For the majority of the contributors, however, it was seemingly John's ability to keep the human in view, even while confronting the dire consequences of complex inhuman systems and their 'path dependencies', that was his distinctive achievement. As Thomas Birtchnell, one of John's more recent collaborators, sums up: 'I propose[d] to advance that it is the humanism of John Urry's work that will be remembered most as time goes on. A recurring thread in his publications is the necessity to adhere to scientific consensus and measured reason without neglecting emotion, empathy, altruism and care for others.' This is certainly a view shared by Laura Watts whose superb science fiction fantasy on the possible future(s) of mass storage centres (aka, 'cloud storage'), based on energy-sustainable initiatives currently being trialled on the Orkney Islands, features John as the sage, quizzical, yet always open and encouraging sounding board to his excitable young protégé's utopian visions. In line with Birtchnell's proposal, it is very fitting that, in Watts's story, 'the human' is very literally put back into systems and technologies that threaten to outpace the fragile infrastructure of the organic world. It is, moreover, a story which inevitably conjures up memories of John's care and solicitude as a friend, colleague and mentor, and I turn now to some reflections on the way he went about his daily work as evidenced by the many wonderful stories and recollections contained in these chapters.

As someone tasked with the responsibility of helping my faculty's PhD students develop their writing skills, I found the insight these chapters provide into John's own compositional method riveting. The first quality that distinguishes both John's thinking and his writing is, undoubtedly, its expansiveness: an ability to bring together disparate concepts, debates, trends and methods from across the disciplines before synthesising them into a new and compelling whole. In so doing, he follows what Mary Hesse (1980) and others have identified as the 'metaphorical' route to meaning-production: i.e. the premise that all knowledge begins with a collision of concepts and systems that, in turn, give rise to new ideas. Further, by shifting the context or application of a concept like mobility just slightly (or, as Thomas Birtchnell reminds us, by *pluralising* it), John was able to set it spinning in a new orbit with a whole new set of implications. Peter Merriman reflects upon this quality in John's work vis-à-vis the way it brought the disciplines of sociology and human geography into productive dialogue, and observes how John's 'magisterial knowledge' and 'manifesto-like statements' were helpful, and inspiring, to an early career researcher trying to map out the converging field(s). Yet Merriman also pays tribute to the 'ordered simplicity' of John's writing which 'enabled his ideas to reach a diverse and multi-disciplinary audience'.

The testimonies of John's ex-PhD and postdoctoral students, meanwhile, reveal that John was full of excellent tips for converting data and speculations into theses and arguments. This included – as Monica Degen recalls (and then elegantly, re-enacts) – 'writing your thesis on a postcard'; or, according to Vincent Kaufmann, 'cutting back on the theory' in order that your own voice be heard. However, the most detailed insight into how John's 40+ books got written as quickly and efficiently as they did is to be found in Phil Macnaghten's evocative vignette of how 'on a typical afternoon' he and John would play 'competitive' tennis and then review their latest chapters of their book (*Contested Natures*, 1998) in a nearby pub. This story vividly captures the extent to which writing and book production was part of the rhythm of John's everyday life for so many years, with Macnaghten recalling that this particular manuscript – like, it seems, most of them – was composed 'in a matter of months'. In this regard, it seems, John benefitted from the typist's (as opposed to the computer user's) skill of producing 'near perfect drafts at the first attempt' in order to escape the need for rewriting. In terms of his 'research methods', meanwhile, John may be seen to be equally traditional (Merriman observes that he favoured 'textual and discourse analysis, often rooted in historical readings of situations'). Yet this is, perhaps, to underplay the enthusiasm with which he embraced the 'mobile methods' that have become such a distinctive feature of the research pursued at CeMoRe over the past decade (see Büscher et al. 2010); or, indeed, the way in which he used his own travels as an academic as a 'mobile method' of sorts. Several of the authors in this collection comment upon this, with Jørgen Ole Bærenholdt recalling John's early embrace of digital photography on a visit to Roskilde in 2003, and Soile Veijola, his intrepid 'ice-fishing' trip to Finland in 2004; similarly, his recent collaborations with Claus Lassen on 'aeromobilities' draw upon the many hours John spent on planes and in airports. The further point to be made here, then, concerns what is probably best thought of as the 'anthropological' cast of John's thought; much as he synthesised all that he read in books, many of John's most distinctive theories were very evidently underpinned by his simple observations of everyday life. Indeed, this is what I remember most clearly about my own conversations with him, possibly because it echoes the way most of my own projects tend to start.

Having had the very great pleasure of reading all the chapters that comprise this volume before they go to press, and less than 18 months since John died, it has had the effect of bringing him very close again. It has also confirmed, unequivocally, that his is a formidable intellectual legacy that will endure. As should be apparent from the preceding discussion, this is not simply on account of the traction of the theories or their widespread applicability, but the fact that so much of John's work was developed collaboratively with ever renewing generations of young scholars. Through the gregariousness of his working method, John has ensured that his ideas have taken root all over the world and are, even now, shaping new lines of enquiry across a dazzling array of problems and disciplines. Further, he has nurtured at least two generations of scholars (many featured in these pages) who are already distinguished thinkers in their own right and destined to play a leading role in, and across, their disciplines. This said, for me, the true test of John's legacy lies less in the endurance and regeneration of his ideas than in our ability to replicate (to quote Andrew Sayer) 'his way of being an academic'. As was the case with the tributes posted on the university website immediately following his death, all the chapters gathered here tell what is effectively the 'same' story about John: a story centred on his humility and equality, his generosity and support; a story which reminds us how his office door was always open, that he rarely turned down a request, that he would answer emails almost immediately – both day and night. In this way, as in so many others, John was everyone's proverbial 'rock', and living up to these values and practices will, I feel, present a greater challenge to future generations of academics (perhaps to The Future itself?) than his out-standing sociology which, like Gormley's iron men, will doubtless continue to welcome and withstand the ebb and flow of the tide.

References

Büscher, M., Urry, J. and Witchger, K. (2010) *Mobile Methods*, London: Routledge.

Gregory, D. and Urry, J. (eds) (1985) *Social Relations and Spatial Structures*, Basingstoke: Macmillan.

Hesse, M. (1980) *Revolutions and Reconstructions in the Philosophy of Science*, Brighton: Harvester Press.

Keat, R. and Urry, J. (1975) *Social Theory as Science*, London: Routledge (reprinted in Routledge Revivals in 2012). .

Klein, N. (2014) *This Changes Everything: Capitalism vs. the Climate*, London: Allen Lane.

Lash, S. and Urry, J. (1994) *Economies of Signs and Space*, London: SAGE.

Macnaghten, P. and Urry, J. (1998) *Contested Natures*, London: SAGE.

Pearce, L. (2016) *Drivetime: Literary Excursions in Automotive Consciousness*, Edinburgh: Edinburgh University Press.

Rees, M. (2004) *Our Final Century*, London: Arrow Books.

Urry, J. (2016) *What Is the Future?*, Cambridge: Polity.

Index

Entries in *italics* refer to images. Titles of works and periodicals are italicised.

Printed in Great Britain
by Amazon